P9-CCZ-633

"Ruhe! Achtung!"

Alma's harsh voice made us all jump, then look up. You could have heard a pin drop.

"A very important SS leader is coming to visit the camp," she said. "One of the most important men in Germany. He's very interested in the orchestra; the orchestra is known about even in Berlin. It must be faultless. I will not tolerate even the slightest mistake!"

The orchestra! Her orchestra! There was hatred in the sidelong looks we girls exchanged, exhausted as we were by this enforced music.

And who was this great man? We would find out . . .

"MOVING AND HAUNTING . . .
A TESTIMONY TO COURAGE!"
—*MADEMOISELLE*

FANIA FÉNELON
PLAYING FOR TIME

with
MARCELLE ROUTIER

Translated from the French by
JUDITH LANDRY

BERKLEY BOOKS, NEW YORK

Originally published in France under the title
Sursis pour l'Orchestre

This Berkley book contains the complete
text of the original hardcover edition.
It has been completely reset in a type face
designed for easy reading, and was printed
from new film.

PLAYING FOR TIME

A Berkley Book / published by arrangement with
Atheneum Publishers

PRINTING HISTORY
Atheneum edition / August 1977
1st Berkley edition / May 1979
Third Printing

All rights reserved.
Copyright © 1976 by Opera Mundi, Paris.
English translation copyright © 1977 by
Michael Joseph Ltd and Atheneum Publishers.
This book may not be reproduced in whole or in part,
by mimeograph or any other means, without permission.
For information address: Atheneum Publishers,
122 East 42nd Street, New York, New York 10017.

ISBN: 0-425-04199-9

A BERKLEY BOOK ® TM 757,375
Berkley Books are published by Berkley Publishing Corporation,
200 Madison Avenue, New York, New York 10016.
PRINTED IN THE UNITED STATES OF AMERICA

ML
429
.F436
A33
1979

*I dedicate this book to the survivors
of Birkenau extermination camp*

Preface

Rain is glistening on the gilded buildings of the Grand Place in Brussels this mild October evening. I can hear it streaming down the dark hotel windows behind me. In the cloistered semidarkness, three women are sitting around a polished oak table. They last saw one another thirty years ago when they were aged seventeen, nineteen, and twenty-five and had just come out of the concentration camp of Bergen-Belsen. Death had passed them by and they left in search of life.

All three of them are elegantly middle class, though in subtly different ways. Two of them, Anny and Irene, sip their drinks abstractedly; the third, Fania, drains her glass with the same passion she had put into remaining alive.

They move towards their shared memories with commonplace, cautious little sentences. Forgetfulness has helped them in various ways; the dimming of memory has enabled them to survive and, like night birds, they feel painfully nervous of the glare of day. They have come to this gathering enthusiastic at heart but with some trepidation; it is impossible for each to guess which part of life in the camp the others might have decided to forget. Furthermore, one of them is Fania, a central figure in the music block, a catalyst, a person of

vii

merciless recall; the other two know that she has forgotten almost nothing, and yet they have willingly responded to her invitation.

Fania Fénelon is the smallest of the three women, less than five feet, with strikingly blue eyes and a vitality that her friends acknowledge gratefully.

"You pulled us through; if it hadn't been for you . . ."

Their sentences trail off; so much can be left unsaid.

"You made us laugh . . ."

They turn to me, an outsider, and confess solemnly: "We did laugh, like mad things."

Anny narrows down the observation: "Yes, we could still laugh—in the orchestra!"

This life-saving laughter now provokes some thought: today they wonder whether it was justified. Irene appeals to me: "We laughed, and we played music. An orchestra in a concentration camp—that must seem incredible to you?"

"I did know that they existed in several camps. The men's orchestra in Auschwitz was famous."

Fania corrects me sharply. "There weren't any in the women's camps, though. Ours was the only female orchestra."

Thoughtfully, Irene observes, "That orchestra saved our lives, didn't it?"

Their eyes see a world elsewhere; they have a knowledge of fate, of its whims and miracles, which is granted only to those who have been at its mercy. They talk of themselves warily, in small doses, their tentative approach to their past giving their recollections a distinctive tone. One can almost see Anny summoning up the image of the old Fania: "You know, if you hadn't been there, we would never have held out against the madness of those months. You were so sure we were going to get out all right, Fania. You were so alive that we had to follow you."

"You told us that you were going to write this book about our orchestra and we believed you; you were the only one who could.'' Irene moves back a little into the shadows before admitting, ''I've forgotten too much.''

She doesn't say ''fortunately,'' but the word hangs there, resonant in Anny's firm, definitive ''Me too.''

''Well, I haven't forgotten anything. Nothing.''

There is a note of provocation in Fania's assurance. The others look at her with a mixture of pity and admiration. ''Do you know when the book was begun? On April 15, thirty years to the day after our liberation.''

Knowing what that day meant to her, I asked her how she felt on its anniversary, and she answered without a moment's thought: ''Sometimes it all comes back so clearly that you really feel you're there.''

''Why do you say 'you'?''

''Because it's not me, it's us—I'm never alone in these memories.''

''Do you think about it often?''

''Apart from a day like today, it's not me who's doing the thinking, 'it' thinks *for* me.'' She went on vehemently, almost painfully: ''It's not that I want to. But particularly at night, I can't help it, I find myself back in the block at Birkenau, and *it* all happens, without any help from me. It never starts the same way: a woman shouts—Florette or Irene; someone is crying—Anny perhaps; there's a shower of insults, blows; there's Tchaikowska . . . I spend every night there—every night!''

''So in effect, you have never left?''

Stated so blankly this was almost too distressing; she joins her small, supple pianist's hands and repeats with unexpected resignation: ''I've never left the camp; I'm still there, I've spent every night of my life there, for thirty years.''

It is as though Anny is reading my mind, for she says thoughtfully, ''Yet you waited thirty years?''

Fania's answer is simple:

''First, like you, I've had to live, to have the youth we never had; we looked like old women and we were in our twenties. I needed to bask in other people's warmth, to eat, to make love, to love . . . to recover. I had to get over the camps. That took years. After thirty years of silence during which I tried to forget the unforgettable, I saw that it was impossible. What I had to do was exorcise the orchestra.''

Marcelle Routier

PLAYING FOR TIME

"Don't Die!"

"STIRB NICHT!" DON'T DIE.

The German voice made no sense; it had no power to pull me up out of the black gulf into which I was sinking more deeply every second. For days now, I had no longer possessed the strength to keep my eyes open. I wasn't sure whether it was my urine or the fever which alternately warmed and chilled me. Typhus was emptying me of life. I was going to die.

My head felt terrible. The girls' wailing and sobbing and groanings shattered it into needle-sharp fragments, little scraps of broken mirror which sank razorlike into my brain. I ordered my hand to pull them out, but my hand was a skeleton's claw that didn't obey. The bones must have broken through the skin. Or had the hand actually come off? Impossible. I must keep my hands to play the piano. Play the piano . . . those knucklebones at the end of my arm might just manage *Danse macabre*. The idea actually made me laugh.

I was horribly thirsty. The SS had cut off the water. It was days since we'd had anything to eat; but even longer since I'd been hungry. I had become weightless, I was floating on a cloud, I was devoured by quicksand . . . no, flying in cotton wool. Odd . . .

A trick I'd found to cool myself was to wash in my urine. Keeping myself clean was essential to me, and there is nothing unclean about urine. I could drink it if I was thirsty—and I had done so.

1

I didn't know the time but I did know the date—the girls kept track of that. It was April 15. What did that matter? It was just a day like any other. But where was I exactly? I wasn't at Birkenau anymore. There, there were forty-seven of us, the "orchestra girls." Here in this windowless shed, there were a thousand of us—burgeoning corpses. What a stench. Now I remembered: Bergen-Belsen. We had arrived here on November 3, 1944.

My head was in such chaos that I was no longer sure whether it was day or night. I gave up, it was too painful . . . I foundered.

Above me, over my face, I felt a breath of air, a vague smell, a delicious scent. A voice cut through the layers of fog, stilled the buzzing in my ears: *"Meine kleine Sängerin."*

"Little singer," that was what the SS called me.

"Stirb nicht."

That was an order, and a hard one to obey. Anyhow, I was past caring. I opened my eyes a fraction and saw Aufseherin Irma Grese, the SS warden known as *Engel,* the Angel, because of her looks. The glorious fair plaits which surrounded her head like a halo, her blue eyes and dazzling complexion were floating in a fog. She shook me.

"Stirb nicht! Deine englischen Freunde sind da!"

Could it possibly be? The Valkyrie had an amused glint in her eye as though the whole thing were a mild joke. I closed my eyes again; she was a wearying creature.

"What did she say?" asked Anny and Big Irene.

I repeated the German sentence. Irritated, they insisted: "Tell us in French, translate it."

"I forget . . ."

"But you just said it in German."

More exhausting people; I retired from the fray, defeated.

"Come on." They were pleading. "Don't die."

That triggered it off; I repeated automatically: "Don't die. Your friends the English are here."

They were disappointed.

"Is that all?" muttered Little Irene.

Florette joined in. "The usual rubbish! We've had that with the Russians, the English, and the Yanks. They fed us that dozens of times in Auschwitz."

I heard Big Irene's calm voice: "What if it's true?"

Anny spoke dreamily: "If only one could believe it and it could all end, now, just like that . . ."

I wafted off, and most of Florette's colourful rejoinder was lost on me. God, how hot I was. My tongue was a hunk of cardboard. I felt myself drifting. Then familiar voices reached me, as if from the end of a funnel: "Look, Irene, you can see there's no hope. She's stopped breathing, there's no mist on my bit of glass. This really works, they even do it in hospitals."

"Try again, you never know."

I wondered who was under discussion. Me? How infuriating they were. Admittedly, I had a pretty bad case of typhus, but I hadn't yet given up the ghost. I had to know the end of the story. I would bear witness.

There were bellowings and whistle blasts around the block; a sudden surge of panic swept through the shed. By way of a full-blooded background to the tramp of boots, the sound of machine guns cut steadily through the silence of the firing range. Their rattle ate into our brains, day and night. Some of these gunners were mere children of fifteen or so.

"They surely can't be going to have us picked off by those kids?"

"They're not noted for their delicacy of feeling," sneered Florette.

"But they're just children!"

All morning the rumour had been going around that they were going to do away with us. But unlike the rumour about the liberation of the camp, this one rang true. Lunatic laughter burst from all over the shed, from the various tiers of the *cojas,* the name the Polish girls gave our cagelike bunks. A crazed voice asked, "What time is it? I want to know the time."

"What the hell does it matter?"

"Because they're going to shoot us at three o'clock," the voice informed us confidentially.

Outside, superficially, all seemed normal; but if one concentrated closely, one could hear new sounds: running and calling. I was completely baffled. My head was swelling until it seemed to fill the whole barracks, to hold all the din within it like a reservoir. I had no more thoughts, I was sinking into the noise, it absorbed me and digested me. I was an echo chamber, I dreamed of silence.

No, I wasn't dreaming; the silence was real. The machine guns had stopped. It was like a great calm lake, and I let myself drift upon its waters.

I must have fallen asleep again; suddenly, behind me, I heard the familiar sound of the door opening. From the remotest distance a man was speaking; what was he saying? No one was answering him. That was odd. What was going on? Strange words reached my ears—it was a language I knew. It was *English!*

Tumult all around, women clambering down from the *cojas.* It couldn't be true, I must be delirious.

The girls, those girls of whom I'd grown so fond, threw themselves at me, shaking me.

"Fania, wake up! Do you hear, the English are here. You must speak to them."

An arm was slipped under my shoulders and lifted me up: "Say something."

I was only too eager, but how could I with that leather spatula in my mouth? I opened my eyes and saw dim figures through a fog. Then suddenly one came into focus: he was wearing a funny little flat cap on his head, he was kneeling down and thumping his fist on his chest, rocking to and fro repeating: "My God, my God!" He was like a Jew at the Wailing Wall. He had

blue eyes, but it wasn't a German blue. He took off his
cap, revealing enchanting red hair. His face was dusted
with freckles and big childlike tears rolled down his
cheeks. It was both awful and funny. "Can you hear
me?"

I murmured, "Yes."

The girls shrieked, "It's all right! She heard, she answered!"

Madness was unleashed around me. They were dancing, lifting their thin legs as high as they could. Some
threw themselves down and kissed the ground, rolling in
the filth, laughing and crying. Some were vomiting; the
scene was incredible, a mixture of heaven and hell.

There was a flurry of questions: "Where have they
come from?" "How did they get this far, to this
hellhole?" "Did they know we were here? Ask him."

"We found you quite by luck," he answered. "We
didn't know there was a concentration camp here.
Coming out of Hanover, we chased the Germans
through these woods and we saw some SS coming
towards us with a white flag."

"Did you slaughter them?" someone chipped in.

He looked uncomprehending. I translated.

"I don't know, I'm just one of the soldiers."

Around us, the girls were clamouring. "You must kill
them, you must kill them all. All."

I was upset by this outburst of hatred, deeply though
I felt it; I too wanted to shout, and tried to sit up, but
flopped back, too weak. For the first time now I felt
myself slipping. Everything became a haze. Yet I
smiled, or at least I think I did. I would have been
liberated after all. I let myself drift.

Irene noticed, and shouted: "No, no, not her, it's too
unfair."

The "unfair" struck me as wonderfully comical.

"Sing, Fania, sing!" someone shrieked. The order
galvanized me; I opened my mouth desperately. The
soldier thought I was at my last gasp; he lifted me out of

my filth, took me in his arms, showing no sign of disgust. How comfortable it was, how light I must feel (I weighed sixty-two pounds). Held firmly, head against his chest, drawing my strength from his, I started on the first verse of the *Marseillaise*. My voice had not died; I was alive.

The fellow was staggered. Carrying me in his arms, he rushed outside towards an officer, shouting, "She's singing, she's singing."

The air hit me like a slap. I choked and was reborn. The girls ran out behind us. Technically no doubt I still had typhus, but the moment I found the strength to sing, I felt I'd recovered. The mists cleared; once more I could look around me and see what was happening. And it was well worth observing: Soldiers were arresting the SS and lining them up against the walls. We had savoured the thought of this moment so often and with such passion, and now it was a reality. Deportees were emerging from every shed. The men from whom we'd been separated for so long were coming towards us, desperately seeking out relatives and acquaintances.

Then I was in clean surroundings, in the SS block. I was bathing in a marvellous sea of khaki, and it smelled so good; their very sweat smelled sweet.

We had been liberated by the infantry, and now the motorized units were arriving. Through the window I saw the first jeep enter the camp. An officer jumped out, a Dutchman. He looked around dazedly and then began to run like a madman, arms outstretched, calling, "Margrett, Margrett!" A woman staggered towards him, her striped tatters floating like rags tied to a pole—his wife, three-quarters dead, in a frightening state of filth and decay; and he hugged her, hugged to him the smiling, living wraith.

Someone handed me a microphone.

It was strange. The process of breathing exhausted me, my heart was positively economizing on its beats, life had become a remote possibility, yet I straightened up, galvanized by joy, and I sang the *Marseillaise* again. This time it emerged with a violence and a strength I had never had before and which I shall probably never have again.

Clearly moved, a Belgian officer sank his hand into his pocket and handed me the most marvellous present: an old lipstick. I couldn't imagine anything lovelier, three-quarters used as it was and despite its uncertain pedigree.

The microphone holder insisted: "Please, miss, it's for the BBC."

I sang "God Save the King," and tears filled the British soldiers' eyes.

I sang the *Internationale* and the Russian deportees joined in.

I sang, and in front of me, around me, from all corners of the camp, creeping along the sides of the shacks, dying shadows and skeletons stirred, rose up, grew taller. A great "Hurrah" burst forth and swept along like a breaker, carrying all before it. They had become men and women once again.

A few months later I learned that on that day, at that time, in London, my cousin heard me sing on the radio and fainted with shock: simultaneously she learned that I had been deported and that I'd just been liberated.

Madame Butterfly

"MADAME BUTTERFLY!"

Someone was calling Madame Butterfly—in Auschwitz, January 23, 1944, in the quarantine block. Impossible! I scanned the endless rows of gloomy, stinking, three-tiered *cojas*. On each tier, six or more women were packed head to tail like sardines, shaven and virtually naked, shivering with cold and hunger. I'd just been told that there were a thousand women in this barracks. Despite the *"Ruhe! Ruhe"*—Silence!— bellowed by the blockowa, our block supervisor, you had to shout to make yourself heard. So Madame Butterfly was somewhat incongruous.

I'd just had a beating in connection with a bucket of dirty water I'd emptied outside, which wasn't allowed. But what was? Tears of rage, mingled with blood, trailed down my grubby cheeks. I wiped the tears away with the back of my hand and huddled up against Clara, whose warmth afforded some comfort. I closed my eyes, and incredibly, it began again: in the midst of this babel a Polish woman was shrieking for Madame Butterfly.

"What is she saying?" I asked my neighbours.

"She's looking for musicians."

"What for?"

"For the orchestra."

An orchestra here? I must have misunderstood.

"*What* did you say?" I insisted.

"The orchestra. Now let it drop, what does it matter to you?"

"But I can play the piano," I protested, "and sing *Madame Butterfly*. I studied with Germaine Martinelli."

"Well, go and tell her."

I leant over, gesticulating; she had to see me. It was forbidden, but I decided to climb down.

Clare held me back. "They're getting at you, it's a joke. You'll get another thrashing."

"Too bad, I'm going anyway."

The girls helped me down. In a fog, aching all over, I hobbled in the direction of the mammoth creature standing in front of the door. A veritable mountain. She stared at me suspiciously: I was so small, so dirty, spattered with mud and blood. She asked loudly, in harsh, bad German: "You, Madame Butterfly?"

"Yes! Yes!"

It seemed that I didn't correspond to this leviathan's idea of a singer, if indeed she had any such Platonic image. She barked something incomprehensible at me. I was steeling myself for another beating, when a girl's voice translated from a lower tier of a *coja*: "She says follow her. One of the French girls in the orchestra recognized you and the *kapo* told her to come and get you."

The impossible was happening. As I followed close on the heels of this mound of flesh I thought in amazement that this could not logically be the outcome of the horror sequences I'd just lived through . . .

At Drancy prison in Paris, the crossed-off days on my calendar formed a little ladder ending at January 20, 1944; I'd been there nine months. Now I was to be taken to Germany in a convoy of deportees.

Six o'clock. From the third storey, our group began its descent of the exit stairway. At each landing hands stretched out offering chocolate, a pot of jam, a pair of woollen gloves. On the last landing there was a sudden scuffle and a jeering voice called, "Don't push, there's no hurry. No danger of getting left behind!"

It was Leon's voice. What was he doing here? Suddenly I felt a firm grip on my elbow, and heard the same voice, wheedling now, close to my ear: "I wouldn't have liked to let you go alone."

It was indeed Leon, brash as ever: a handsome little fellow whose exact line of business was unclear to me—brown-haired, perky, with a roving eye at present fixed on me.

"You see, I said to myself, 'That little girl is going to need a man to carry her things and put a little romance into her evenings when she's down.' I'm rather taken with you, and I don't want someone else stealing my place. So I came back, pronto."

"But hadn't you escaped? You surely didn't come back of your own free will?"

He laughed, like a child who has played a good joke. "Something along those lines. The toughest bit was to get myself put in the same group as you. It was hard to get them to swallow that one, because it's not the kind of trip people normally clamour for. But as you see, I've done it."

His words amused me and touched me, yet annoyed me. I preferred to choose the men in my life rather than the reverse. Still, it was certainly a declaration. Poor Leon; we were immediately separated. A security man thrust him into one of the first trucks.

I was surrounded by people I didn't know. My neighbours were a young woman of about thirty, very beautiful, with her two smartly dressed little daughters, and a girl of about twenty with a ravishing head set upon an enormous, deformed body. There was an immediate rapport between us; her name was Clara.

Early-morning Paris was a sinister place. It was very cold, and stalactites hung from the cracked and frozen gutters. The blue winking of the civil defence lights made the gloom seem colder still. Our truck was covered with tarpaulin and open at the back. The few chilly early-morning passers-by hardly bothered to cast a glance in our direction. And yet our convoy must have been rather unusual, with women wearing fur coats, men of all ages, old people, and children.

Awaiting us at the marshalling yard was a very old train which had seen action in World War I and a wheezing engine which certainly didn't deserve its insolently large, immaculate white V, Churchill's victory sign that had been expropriated by the Germans after Stalingrad.

We staggered beneath the weight of our luggage. Everyone had brought everything he'd managed to get together: clothing, food, drink, cigarettes, jewelry, money. There were a hundred of us, from all walks of life, all ages and races, crowded into the pitch black interior of a carriage meant for cattle. There was clean straw on the floor. The quick thinkers—and the strongest—did what they could to stake claims to their own corners: they dug in, flapping, shuffling their bottoms into the straw like chickens, acting as though they were going to be there for an eternity.

The enchanting young mother was quietly advocating various subtle points of etiquette to her children: "Don't make too much noise, there are other people here." Already there were quarrels of the "I was here before you" type. Laughable. People started telling stories, jokes, groaning, complaining, making conclusive but unfounded statements:

"We're going to a work camp in Bavaria, with little German bungalows, quite clean and decent, and comfortable, with little gardens for those with children."

"He's crazy!"

"I'll say. That camp is the worst of all, I know that for a fact."

Me, I . . . I, me . . . One opinion followed another.

The smell of the improvised lavatory soon became un-

bearable. At every jolt, there was a worrying ploshing
noise. The straw around it was already filthy. A child
sitting on the floor in the middle of the carriage kept
repeating in a piercing little voice, "I can see things
moving everywhere."

A woman called out, "Make that filthy brat shut
up."

"It's obvious you've got no children," shrieked the
mother.

"You're wrong—I've got six."

"Where are they then?"

"I'm not saying."

"Are you afraid I'll expose you?"

It was outrageous, but no one laughed. Quite the contrary—the two women leapt at one another. The tension
was exhausting.

The time came to eat: it seemed like a picnic without
the bonhomie. The whole crowd chewed; it wasn't an
elevating moment, but it was restful.

Clara looked worried. "Have you brought something
to eat?"

"Of course."

I offered her some of my treasures: sardines, real ones
in oil, sausage, pâté de campagne, a Camembert, some
jam. She gave me some foie gras and champagne.

"It's astonishing, it's like Christmas; and your Santa
Claus seems to shop on the black market!"

That broke the ice, and she laughed; in the darkness,
her small, regular teeth gleamed like the pearls in a
necklace. Devouring our luxury fare, quenching our
thirst with Roederer brut, we swore never to leave one
another, to share everything.

In the stinking atmosphere, heavy now with the smells
of food, people belched and dozed. Clare confided in
me that she had once been very thin. She'd begun to get
fat in prison. At Drancy it had been terrible: she had
swollen up as though someone had blown air into her
with bellows.

"Only my legs stayed slim. Look, I'm positively deformed. My boyfriend won't want anything to do with me."

Weeping now, she told me about her parents. Hers had been the life of a little rich girl, an illustration from a children's book, a protected, untroubled youth into which the reality of war had only just intruded. "You see, Jean-Pierre, my boyfriend, belonged to a network. I carried letters and arranged meetings, took telephone messages without understanding their importance. But I think they arrested me because I'm half-Jewish."

Here the young mother joined in. "My children are too. Since they couldn't arrest my husband, who's in the Resistance, they took us. They meant us to act as hostages, as a lure. Luckily it didn't work, my husband wasn't taken in. So they're deporting us. The main thing for me is that their father has escaped the Germans; he would have been in danger of his life, but for us it will be just a rather grim interlude."

"And what about you?" Clara asked me.

"Rather like you, really. I'm also half-Jewish, and I too did a favour for a friend in the Resistance, taking letters, arranging rendezvous; giving people beds for the nights when they needed them."

"But that was dangerous."

"Of course. Someone imformed on me and I was arrested. That night, a friend had slept at my place. I'd slept at a neighbour's. I was going back up to my room in my dressing gown, carrying my clothes. Imagine how I felt—there were three of them waiting at my door. They took me to the Quai de Gesvres. At first I wasn't too worried, my papers were fine, my ration cards absolutely authentic, made out by a police commissioner in the name Fania Fénelon, the name I use as a singer. I even had a night pass issued by the Commandant."

"Did you used to sing?"

"Yes, in nightclubs."

"I couldn't have heard you sing," said Clara rather

primly. "We'd stopped going out at night. We didn't mix with the Germans, and no one went to nightclubs except Germans and collaborators."

I fell silent, slightly ashamed; it had been very good business. How would Clara have judged the proprietress of Melody's, who looked like a madam—indeed, perhaps she was—but who protected us? How she would have despised those tarts who hung from the necks of German officers and gave us papers, photographs, and information.

"Did they find out your real name?"

"No. In the end I gave it to them. I was tired of being beaten—it's oddly monotonous. And they insisted that I was a Communist; it would have been difficult to prove, but they might have managed it. Then I could have been shot. If I was going to die, I preferred to die under my father's name, Goldstein. As soon as they knew I was Jewish, that settled everything. I was sent to Drancy, which seemed to me an acceptable way of staying alive."

Intrigued, Clara asked, "How did they beat you?"

"With an iron bar, on my back."

She clasped her chubby little hands. "Good Lord! And you didn't talk?"

"I hadn't much to say."

"I don't know what I'd have done in your position."

Despite her huge body, Clara seemed to me so weak, so vulnerable, that I was overcome by a wave of pity; she was like a child, to be taken under one's wing. She asked me a few more questions, which I evaded. I didn't want to relive the period that led up to the present. The little girls began to hum *Malbrough s'en-va-t-en guerre* and we joined in the chorus. Clara had a pretty voice, a light airy soprano. Other people joined in, euphoria reigned. But my rendering of "Lying in the Hay" spoiled everything; my sense of humour wasn't theirs.

"That'll do," they burst out.

"We're trying to sleep."

"You wouldn't sing if you knew what you were in for," one woman commented prophetically.

Another brightly volunteered a juicy piece of inside information: "I didn't want to mention it earlier, but I happen to know that we're going to be murdered in the train! They're going to machine gun us right here, all of us!"

"They're going to electrocute us."

I imagined our freight train with its sealed openings, doors bolted from the outside, crossing tracts of eastern France. At the level crossings, people would be saying: "There goes our food, off to Germany."

We'd been travelling for over fifty hours. The smell was frightful, the door hadn't been opened once. At first, under the supervision of the SS, the men in each carriage had taken out the buckets to empty them. Since then, our bucket had emptied itself by overturning.

We were desperately thirsty; all the bottles—water, coffee, wine, spirits—were empty. The stinking air was unbreathable, the ventilation nil; we were beginning to suffocate.

My watch was at twelve when the train stopped —midnight. Our door was opened. "Quick, fresh air," and everyone rushed for the door.

"Get out. Leave all luggage in the train." The orders were in French.

The younger ones jumped out, others managed as best they could. Searchlights lit the platforms, their blinding glare making the night seem darker still. There was a dizzying succession of images. Clara was beside me; there were cries and shrieks, and orders barked in a guttural German:

"Raus! Los! Los! Schneller!" Out! Out! Fast!

Shouts in the dark: "Mama, where are you?"

"Françoise, Jeannette, where are you?"

"Here," called a child's voice. "Mama, we're here."

"Where's here?"

SS soldiers climbed into the carriages and threw the

ill, the stiff, and the exhausted out onto the platform with kicks and rifle blows; last of all went a corpse.

Living skeletons in striped uniforms, their skulls shaven, moved among us like silent shadows, climbing onto the train; these strange "porters" took out our luggage, piled it onto trolleys, and took it away. The snow was thick and dirty, but Clara and I tried to melt some in our hands to drink.

There was a rumble of vehicles, military trucks, but with enormous red crosses set in white circles.

"The Red Cross is here," exclaimed Clara. "We're not in any danger."

The SS thrust the crowd towards the vehicles. Old people and children moving too slowly for the SS stumbled and picked themselves up, clung to one another and were hustled brutally.

Caught up in an eddy, I was about to climb up in my turn. A sergeant stopped me. "How old are you?"

I told him and he pushed me back. "You can walk."

The mother and little girls called to me from the back of the truck. I too could have climbed up there and joined them, under cover of darkness, but Clara stopped me.

"Don't get in there, we've been cooped up for days in that terrible atmosphere; it'll do us good to walk, even in the snow."

Two columns had formed, fifty men and fifty women; everyone else from the train had got into the trucks with the red crosses. The convoy moved off, skidding over the snow, sending up violent flurries of slush. From the back of the last truck the little girls waved good-bye to me; the older one fluttered her handkerchief. I smiled at them until they were out of sight.

At a barked command our column moved off, flanked by soldiers and guard dogs. We walked at a brisk rate, Clara and I arm in arm, almost cheerful. It was very cold and snowing heavily, but I had my fur coat and was comfortably shod in furlined boots.

"I wouldn't actually come here for a Christmas holiday, of course," I said jokingly. "The staff haven't quite been licked into shape yet; they're not what you'd call considerate."

Clara wasn't willing to follow in this vein; she was worried. "Those men at the station!"

"They must have been prisoners."

"Convicts, more like. Dead ones, at that."

"Don't worry, it's nothing to do with us," I said reassuringly. "You saw the red crosses on the trucks."

"It's odd, you can't see the sky; it's as if there weren't one. I feel that there's a sort of great screen of smoke between us and it. Look at the horizon. It's red—you can see the flames."

"There must be factories; that's where we'll be working."

A soldier was walking next to Clara. He had a totally unremarkable face, something between animal and mineral. Suddenly he addressed her in French, in a voice as devoid of expression as he was himself: "I'll get you some coffee if you'll let me make love to you."

Coffee? Either a woman wasn't worth much around here, or else coffee was priceless. She said nothing and he let it drop.

"Are we going to a work camp?"

He observed me at length with his small pale eyes. "Don't worry, you'll be all right."

I was hardly convinced.

After half an hour's walk, we arrived at the entrance to Birkenau, the extermination camp of the Auschwitz prison complex. A sort of porch let into a brick building, briefly lit by the searchlights on the watch-towers which burst through the darkness sporadically to scour the roadways of the camp. They caught on the barbed wire, scanning the night in a dreadful, disquieting dance. Above the main entrance was a sign: "Work Camp." It was almost reassuring.

We were driven towards a brick building marked "Reception Block." The burst of warm air filled us with pleasure. The light was dim but adequate. Sitting round a big table, comfortably dressed girls were chatting in Polish. They seemed well-pleased with their life of luxury.

I had the temerity to ask one of them: "Is it you who are going to give us back our things?"

The heftily built girl stared at me in bovine astonishment and replied by bellowing her worst obscenity in my face: "*Pja kref!*"

"I'm not *pja kref*, I'm French."

One of them must have understood my rejoinder, because she virtually wept with laughter. Irritated, the other continued to spit out a vengeful litany.

My *pja kref* grabbed my bag from me; I grasped the point and handed her my fur coat, feeling a dreadful pang at seeing that silky fur, the apple of my eye, pawed over by her stubby little fingers. My last contact with my past. Despoiled, naked like Clara and everyone else, I stood there with my clothes around me on the ground like the skin of a moulting snake. Meanwhile furtive shadows with shaven heads picked up these piles and took them away. On the table, handbags and jewels piled up.

SS women sauntered nonchalantly amid this extravagant jumble. Under their chilly, sneering glances I felt considerably less than human: a peculiar, grubby object upsetting the natural order.

Poor Clara! Pitiable with her enormous breasts flopping down on her fat stomach, she looked like an apple balanced on two matchsticks. We were taken in charge by a young Polish woman. Her ineffectual scissors hacked desperately at my magnificent hair, two thick jet-black plaits wound round my head. The girl persevered and at last they fell to the ground, lovely smooth shining snakes. The girl attacked my head, armpits, and pubic hair with a rusty, nicked blade and no soap or water; she clawed, scraped, rasped. It should have hurt dreadfully but I could scarecely feel a thing. My eyes were fixed on another brick-faced Pole who had picked up my plaits and was playing with them, whirling them through the air, taunting me and laughing hysterically. I felt a swell of anger rising within me, a violent desire to pursue, to destroy: "If I ever get out of here, I'll kill a Polish woman. And I'll see to it that all the rest die; that shall be my aim in life."

I always had to have an aim in life, and at Auschwitz that would be as good as any. But at the same time I loathed myself quite as much for having conceived of this ignoble plan.

Tattooing came next. Indifferently I watched the number 74862 appearing on my forearm. Apparently an SS had suggested tattooing us on the forehead, but Berlin hadn't approved. I still hadn't got round to laughing about that then.

The branding demoralized Clara. Dazed, still incredulous, she gazed at her round white arm: "Why are they treating us like this? They don't do that to their workers, do they?"

Innocent Clara, her soul as white as her skin. For me, everything was over, I'd understood. I'd asked an Alsatian girl to translate the various inscriptions on the walls: "The block is your home," "a flea means your death," "work is your freedom," "you're not in a rest home."

I took them full in the face like a slap. I was no longer anything, not even a slave. For me there was no longer either code or law; I was alone, abandoned, consigned to the executioner. We had arrived at the journey's end: hell.

I see us now, under the icy shower, arms pressed to our sides, then back in the room again, demoralized, shivering, tattooed, and hairless. It was odd, but that was the real humiliation: having no hair. Shadows swept up and spirited off the different kinds of hair like so many treasures.

After the shower we were thrown men's boots, a handkerchief for our shorn skulls, something approaching a slip and a dress. I got a flowered summer dress with a yellow triangle sewn on the front. I didn't need to ask what that meant; its colour spoke volumes. Yellow was the Jewish colour.

We were herded towards a sort of amphitheatre and settled in groups over its wooden steps. It was very cold. Next to me a girl, head lowered, hands round her knees, mumbled in Russian: "The monsters, the monsters, they'll pay . . . they'll all pay . . ."

"Where are you from?" I asked her, also in Russian.

She lifted her bumpy head, recently shorn, covered with crimson scratches. My head too must have looked like that. It wouldn't have been difficult to study my bumps, and it was devoutly to be hoped that I had the bump of luck. That was the only one that mattered now.

She muttered an answer: "Ukraine. Are you Russian?"

"No, French."

She stared at me in amazement, then continued with her monologue. I whispered, because we weren't allowed to talk, "Where are we going to work? When do we eat? I've not had even a glass of water for two days."

Presumably my questions weren't worthy of an answer, because she went on with her pious intonings, feeding her fantasies in a monotone. "They'll pay for this, every one of them . . ."

We stayed there, exhausted, for about two hours. Clara, squeezed against me, renewed her vow in a low voice: "We'll never leave one another. We'll share everything. For life."

The flat phrases echoed strangely in that icy amphitheatre. At regular intervals the searchlights on the watchtowers burst through the transoms, revealing snatches of the scene, wrenching details of hunched, shivering women from the shadows. From time to time, on the floor of the amphitheatre, the beam of a torch would range slowly, incomprehensibly, over the tiers. There was no sound from outside; inside, the occasional groan, a sob, a cry that was a prayer. "*Ruhe! Kein Wort mehr!*" barked an invisible woman guard and once again there was absolute, total silence, the silence of a graveyard, a graveyard peopled with the living.

If I wanted to stay that way, I would have to put up some kind of resistance, but how? I would learn that later, day by day.

A light went on. Below, on the floor, hefty creatures were coming in with a tub filled with soup, which was slopped out into our bowls. I had no spoon and felt sick as the thought of swallowing this viscous liquid in which nameless lumps were floating.

"Eat it, you must, it'll warm you up." The little Russian girl was firm.

Noisily, we lapped up this repellent stinking brew. Below, in the small yellow circle of light, the serving had finished and went unapplauded. The light went out again, the beam from the torch of one of our usherettes wandered over the tiers for a moment, then darkness and silence reigned. The show was over.

The winter day broke through, bleak and grimy. The waiting continued. At last the door opened and a volley of orders rained down. We were driven out with whistle blasts and blows, gasping in the icy air. My bare feet shrank in my odd men's shoes: one yellow, one black, one boot, one laceless oxford—size ten, and I took a size four. How could I march in line or keep in step with such things on my feet? A new terror seized me: to walk was to live; to fall behind, to fall down, was to die. I looked with loathing at the Auschwitz mud into which I was sinking, a clay soil which never dried out, even in the height of summer. Dark grey, deep red in places, it was like a flood of molten lava, it never stopped moving: rain, wind, and snow sent it sliding over its own base. It sucked me in treacherously. I was aware that my life depended on the length of this journey; luckily it was short. We stopped in front of an enormous light brick building, long and squat. "It's the quarantine block," the rumour ran. "You don't come out of here alive."

The Sign of the Cross

IT WAS A HUGE, dark, low shed. A thousand women were crammed into the three-tiered wooden shelving, with no more room than one's slot in the morgue. Indeed it was a sort of morgue; the smell of decay seized you by the throat.

Clara and I, who were among the last, stayed for a few moments by the door. For some reason I thought of the mother and her little girls. Might I meet them again? Foolishly, I questioned the blockowa: "Please, madame, where are the people who went off in the trucks with the red crosses?"

My temerity astounded her; she stared at me, weighing me up—was she going to clout me with her hefty club? Boldly, I repeated: "Where are the people who went off in the Red Cross trucks?"

She gave a sort of gurgle of a laugh and, seizing my arm in a viselike hold, forced me to pivot towards the open door: "Look . . ." She pointed to a low building about fifty yards away, above which rose a stubby chimney. "You see that smoke coming out of that chimney over there? That's your friends, cooking."

"All of them?"

"All of them."

They had not even been given whatever chance the quarantine block offered. The Red Cross trucks had been a lure.

The blockowa kept her grip on my arm; con-

23

fidentially she thrust her coarse fat face towards me.
"That's where you'll end up."

How could one doubt it?

"*Herunter!*" Down! yelled the blockowa.

"We're going to shit, and high time too," growled
Adele the redhead, leaping down from her bunk.

In line, paddling through the icy mud, shivering in
our cotton, we crossed a stretch of camp.

Who could have dreamed up such a place as the
latrine hut? It was an enormous hole dug out of the
earth, about forty feet deep, surrounded by an irregular
border of large stones, plank walls, and a roof. This
enormous, funnel-shaped sewer was ringed with
wooden bars. No sooner was the door open than,
breaking ranks, the girls rushed forward to sit on these
bars, buttocks exposed. Some, with dysentery, didn't
make it and relieved themselves where they stood, under
the blows and insults of the latrine blockowa.

I stared open-mouthed; I had to remember everything
of this stinking horror. Perched in this roost about fifty
girls were packed together like sick old hens, skeletal,
shivering, clinging to their dung-stained bars. Those
with long legs could touch the ground with the tips of
their toes, but the others, the smaller ones like me, their
legs dangling, had to grip the slippery round bar with
both hands with all their might. To fall into the pit must
have been a most terrible death.

The women from the opposite *coja* looked at Clara
and me coldly. We meant nothing to that row of skulls
in their various states of filth, coloured by varying
degrees of fuzz. Their bony hands, like birds' feet,
gripped the wooden frame of the *coja;* in their hollow
sockets, their eyes shone like candle flames lit inside
skulls for some diabolical sabbath. I stared back and
anguish rose within me: they became mirrors, they
reflected my image. How many days would it take for

me to become like them? I'd learned so many things in a
few hours, so many illusions had collapsed. Incredibly,
with an adroit flick of the wrist, someone would swipe
your soup, that vile concoction. Smaller prisoners like
myself were at the mercy of the larger; the strong preyed
on the weak; they pushed you towards death with utter
indifference. Work parties left and were not seen again,
the sick were sent to an infirmary known as Revier from
which they never returned, without anyone's being
remotely concerned about it. A dead person would
spend the night among the living without arousing the
slightest interest.

Once again I felt my fear of being swallowed up and
digested by this crowd. How could one escape it? Lying
on my stomach at the top of the *coja*, with Clara cutting
me off from the others, I wanted to close my eyes, bury
my face in my arms, and no longer see or hear. But it
was not possible. We had to keep our heads well away
from the soiled, stinking straw mattress which served as
common bedding.

Clara had begun to cry. Her sobs redoubled, which
was disastrous. I knew I had to talk to her, and I threw
out the first words that came into my head: "I'm going
to tell you a fairy story."

It was so bizarre, so unexpected, that Clara gazed at
me uncomprehendingly. Quickly I uttered the magic
words: "Once upon a time . . ."

It was a real jumble, and very long: jewels,
junketings, romance. The perfumes of Arabia burned at
the corners of luxurious divans; rose petals fell as thick
as snowflakes, spotless doves flew about in peerless
skies. The burning kisses of princes charming would
have awakened the mummies in the pyramids. Triumphantly, I concluded: "And they lived happily ever
after."

I looked around me and burst out laughing.

And now I was being taken off to sing Madame Butterfly. It was impossible, it couldn't be happening; and

yet I stumbled out after the monstrous Pole who strode ahead of me. The vicious cold bit at my ears. My feet shrank in my men's shoes and I sank into the icy snow where the mud sucked at my shoes and held them firm. The Polish woman wasn't cold, with her warm coat, boots, and head scarf. She was drawing farther away, she was proceeding without looking back. What if I lost track of her? I mislaid a shoe, lodged in the snow. Too bad, I threw off the other too and ran barefoot, a thousand needles of ice piercing my freezing feet. We went out of camp A and into B, where the "notables" lived.

The giant stopped in front of a barracks, turned round, and looked at me distrustfully, incredulously: what if I'd fooled her? Pressing her index finger against my chest so hard as almost to knock me over, she roared:

"You—Madame Butterfly?"

Seized with panic, I yelled back, "Yes—yes, me, Madame Butterfly!"

At the same time I fought back an insane desire to laugh.

A Band of Angels

THE POLISH WOMAN opened the door and I entered something closely resembling paradise. There was light, and a stove; indeed it was so warm that I could hardly breathe and stood rooted to the spot. Stands, music, a woman on a platform. In front of me pretty girls were sitting, well-dressed, with pleated skirts and jerseys, holding musical instruments: violins, mandolins, guitars, flutes, pipes . . . and a grand piano lording it over them all.

It couldn't be possible, it wasn't happening. I'd gone mad. No, I was dead, and these were the angels. It must have happened while I was crossing the camp, in the snow and mud. I was reassured: "Your journey is done, you have come to the paradise of music; that's only natural, since that's your main love. This is your first stopping place; you're in heaven and you're going to take your place among these marvellous girls."

A fair girl with a gentle face came towards me; with a sympathetic hand she wiped away the blood which had run from my mouth and nose, cleaned my face with a damp cloth. Angels are wonderful, I must say. Then she handed me a bit of bread; the bread and salt of the traditional welcome, a gesture which came to me from the mists of charity. I said "Thank you" and these words, already forgotten, filled me with delight. I felt as if I were walking on air as I smilingly proceeded towards the players.

No one spoke, no one moved, but all those charming young ladies were looking at me. It was an exceptional, divine moment. I was on a little cloud of pink cotton wool, I was floating . . . Then the picture became animated: the conductor, a tall dark-haired woman, dignified and straight-backed, addressed me in precise French with a German accent. "Do you play the piano?"

My "Yes, madame" was uttered with such fervour that it rang out like an alleluia in a cathedral.

"Well then, go to the piano and accompany yourself to *Madame Butterfly*."

Barefoot, I went over to the piano. It was a Bechstein, the dream of my life. I climbed onto the stool, put my toes on the pedals and my hands on the ivory of the keyboard, and they made me blush with shame. I wanted to clench my fists, to hide them. It was so long since I'd washed them. But it didn't matter; I was there.

A lump of gratitude formed in my throat; I who didn't believe in anything felt an obscure desire to thank God. Then the dream lurched into reality: I was there to prove myself. In a few moments I could be rejected, sent back where I came from. After all, these were not angels but women.

Lovingly, my hands made the familiar contact with the black and white keys, and I broke into *Un bel di*. Was Puccini going to save my life? Then I sang in German *Wenn es Frühling wird* ("When Spring Comes") by Peter Kreuder, its rhythm reminiscent of certain Gypsy dances.

My hands stopped moving but I kept them on the keyboard; as long as they were in contact with it, nothing could happen to me. I caressed the piano; it was my saviour, my love, my life. Against a background of pregnant silence the verdict fell in German:

"*Ja, gut!*"

Then a little more informatively, in French: "I'll have you in the orchestra."

A comforting warmth swept over me. I basked in its sweetness: I was in the orchestra. And Clara? I couldn't abandon her. I'd almost forgotten my promise. My exaltation made me incautious and I ventured, "Madame, madame, I've got a friend, Clara, who's got a marvellous voice. I must go and get her."

Faced with the cold, blank stare of those large dark eyes, I lost all sense of proportion. "I won't stay here without her. I'll leave, I'll go back over there . . ."

I simply didn't realize what I was saying or the extent of my foolhardiness. For me, a *Nein* would have meant the end of this world. More realistic, the girls looked flabbergasted; had I gone mad? No sign of emotion in the conductor's expression; she was a German all right. Then she made up her mind, called out: "Zocha." The female mountain came trotting up servilely. "Go and get Clara from the quarantine block and bring her here."

While I sat perched on my stool the girls surrounded me, asked me questions I had difficulty in understanding. My mind was on Clara: What if Zocha couldn't find her, if she'd been sent out on a working party, had fallen into the latrine pit? . . . Here in Birkenau fate struck suddenly, like lightning; in a few seconds everything could change, irreparable things could happen.

And I saw Clara enter, my Clara waddling like a duck, flabby and fat, so fat. Her physical appearance didn't concern the conductor, she barely seemed to notice it. What she wanted was a voice, and that Clara had: a positive nightingale, a light soprano, marvellous, rare. Accompanying her, I had no fears, and rightly.

"I'll have you. I want you both in the orchestra. I'll tell our chief of camp straight away and get you dressed."

At a pitch of excitement, the girls crowded around us and we all let out a barrage of questioning like the cheerful cackle of a henhouse. My ear selected names and in-

OUACHITA TECHNICAL COLLEGE

formation, my eyes grasped a face, an expression, the nuance of a look. Ewa, older than the others, was Polish and had gentle grey-blue eyes. I already had a memory connected with her—the touch of her pitying fingers on my face.

A hand pulled me forcefully towards its owner. "I'm Florette. I saw you in Paris."

She had magnificent green eyes, possessive, jealous and, at the moment, slightly agitated.

"It was you I saw singing at Melody's."

"Probably, I have sung there in my time."

"I thought so. We went there one night with my parents, a year ago. I was seventeen. As you see, I didn't forget you. But it was Little Irene who told the conductor."

Irene, who was even smaller than I was, must have been about twenty. She was amazingly pale-skinned, with eyes so dark one could hardly see the iris. Triumphantly, she murmured into my ear: "It was I who recognized you, you know! I'd heard you sing at Drancy; so yesterday, when I saw you in the quarantine block, I went to tell our *kapo*, Alma Rosé."

"There was a quartet with that name led by Rosé, first violinist in the Berlin Opera orchestra. I remember hearing them in Paris. He really was an excellent musician."

"Alma is his daughter."

"In that case, she must also be the niece of Gustav Mahler, the composer. I remember he was Rosé's brother-in-law."

"You're right," Ewa confirmed. "She's also a very fine violinist."

"And they've interned her?"

"Don't let that upset you," said Florette sarcastically, "her talent doesn't give her a warm heart. In fact you'll soon see that there's no shortage of bitches round here: our blockowa, Tchaikowska, is a pest, particularly with us Jews. As for Pani Founia, the head of the kitchen, another Polack, she's a real cow! Don't get the wrong idea—you're in Auschwitz, in the women's camp at Birkenau, and it's no picnic!''

This information disturbed Clara, for whom love of music wasn't enough; she pressed nervously for further details.

"This is the music block, we're the Birkenau women's orchestra. And you're from France?''

"Yes, from Paris.''

"How many arrived with you?''

"I counted twelve carriages on the train; there must have been about twelve hundred.''

"Fifty women came here, to Birkenau, and fifty men went over to the men's camp. The other eleven hundred have gone up in smoke. The figures are all too clear.''

"Well,'' I observed, "if Clara hadn't told me to walk, I'd have got into the truck with that woman who called to me. Clara saved my life.''

No one expended any emotion over this fact; things were pretty simple here.

A runner, eyes and nose red from the cold, burst in. From the door, she shouted: *"Achtung!* Mandel's on her way!''

Everyone froze to attention, and the result was no less impressive than the actual entry of Lagerführerin Mandel, the chief of camp. She was under thirty, very beautiful, tall, slender, and impeccable in her uniform. And then I was in front of her, arms dangling in my ridiculous flowered garden-party dress which hung so strangely, barefoot, my face dirty despite Ewa's hasty washing, with Clara beside me, equally pathetic. Irene murmured through her teeth that I should stand to attention. This was new ground to me, but I drew myself up stiffly. The Lagerführerin ordered us to stand at ease and feet shuffled, bodies softened. The girls relaxed but didn't disperse; they were waiting to see what would happen.

Alma, respectfully three steps behind Maria Mandel, introduced us: "Here are the two singers; the smaller one also plays the piano very well."

Mandel, hands elegantly on hips—long, white, delicate hands which stood out against the grey cloth of her uniform—stared at us, her hard china-blue eyes lingering searchingly on my face. This was the first time a representative of the German race had looked at me, had seemed to be aware of my presence. She took off her cap and her hair was a wonderful golden blond, done in thick plaits round her head—in my mind's eye I saw mine again, tossed by the Polish girl. I noted everything about her: her face, without a trace of makeup (forbidden by the SS), was luminous, her white teeth large but fine. She was perfect, too perfect. A splendid example of the master race: top-quality breeding material—so what was she doing here instead of reproducing?

She turned her head slightly towards Alma: "Which one sings *Madame Butterfly*?"

"The smaller one, Frau Lagerführerin."

"Tell them each to sing something," she ordered coolly.

I sat down at the piano and accompanied Clara, whose voice really did have something of the nightingale. Then, catching sight of Mandel's face, I sang *Un bel di*. I was aware that my life was at stake. If she didn't like my interpretation, didn't share my view of the piece, I'd be back where I came from.

Seated on a chair, her long legs sheathed in silk and prettily crossed, SS Mandel smiled faintly. "They must be dressed. Come."

I understood that we were accepted only when Alma said more explicitly: "Come on now, you're in."

The SS walked ahead with long flowing strides; she must have waltzed divinely. Deferential, Alma followed. Clara and I, mightily relieved, trotted behind them at a distance we deemed suitable. In their wake we went into a big hut, well-lighted and heated, another privileged place. There seemed to be no shortage of these in the camp. The entry of our SS woman galvanized those present. Mandel omitted to tell the assembled company to stand at ease, and the Polish women remained frozen at attention. It was an agreeable experience to see them locked in that respectful pose. Casually, after a pause, she released them and thus liberated they resumed their activities. Behind the counter tables they were sorting through piles of clothes, miscellaneous objects, some of them valuable, souvenirs, foodstuffs, the kinds of things a person would take when leaving home for the unknown. This was where our luggage ended up.

"Give them some clothes their size," ordered Mandel.

The girls bustled about, measured clothes on us. I half expected them to ask us our preferences, whether we'd prefer a pink slip with lace or a white satin one—it was like a high-class shop, a real pleasure to behold. I was given underpants, a slip, and some woollen stockings, all truly wonderful things to my newly opened eyes. A navy woollen dress and a warm soft coat completed my outfit. With big slapdash stitches and expressions of disgust, Polish or Slovak women sewed yellow stars on the two last items.

We were ordered to get dressed. Ideally, I would have liked to get washed first, but obviously one couldn't have everything; I obeyed.

Mandel approved Clara's outfit with a curt monosyllable. Then she examined me and looked down at my feet, which were swimming in shoes lent by Ewa, who wore size nine; she addressed the block *kapo* with a certain degree of courtesy: "Frau Schmidt, have you no shoes for my little singer?"

She clearly liked my size and my voice.

"Of course I have," twittered Frau Schmidt promptly. While a Polish woman picked through a pile of shoes, I stared at Frau Schmidt. She was magnificently dressed in a well-cut suit and blouse, and thin without being skinny. A formidable creature; her eyes had no colour and her mouth no lips.

I slipped on some black oxfords which must have been at least size eight. Fast losing such little patience as she had, Mandel said drily: "I meant, of her size!"

The request was apparently exorbitant. Since when had the right size to be taken into account for a yellow star, a *Jüdin?*

In an abusive tone, Frau Kapo enquired, "What size do you take?"

"Four."

That caused such a scandal that I felt at fault.

"We haven't got any. We don't have any such size, Frau Lagerführerin."

SS Mandel became livid; her words wrapped themselves around the offending parties like a whiplash. Then she strode furiously out of the clothing store. Too bad, I wouldn't have any shoes of the right size; I'd just have to stuff the oxfords with some paper. Under the venomous gaze of Frau Schmidt and her henchwomen, I followed Alma out, dragging my feet; irritated, she speeded up her pace, affording me the opportunity of losing my shoes in the snow.

Our hut no longer dazzled me, it no longer seemed a mirage I didn't dare take stock of for fear it might vanish; it was now a reality to be scrutinized. It was a wooden construction divided into two unequal parts: in the smaller, which served us as dormitory and dining room, bunk beds ran in rows facing one another along the white-painted walls.

"We've each got a bed of our own," Florette informed me, "with a sheet—why not two, I ask you—and a woollen cover! You put your stuff under the mattress too, the things you've been able to 'organize'; it's not very safe, but there's nothing better."

"What does 'organize' mean?"

"Doing a bit of wangling to get things you need from the girls in Canada."

Who were the girls in Canada? How and with what could one buy things? These were crucial questions but I put them off until later because the tour of inspection was still under way.

In the central passageway were three tables, one with kitchen utensils. On one wall were shelves with boxes on them.

"We put our 'treasures' in there," explained Irene. "It's two to a box, so you can 'box' with whomever you like. To store the stuff, of course, not to share it," she added hastily.

To share what? Our pathetic possessions? Anyhow, I didn't need to agonize, I'd "box" with Clara.

The other, larger part of the room, about twenty-six feet by twenty, was used as a music room. Along one wall was a large table covered with scores and papers. Around it sat the copyists, who transcribed the orchestral scores.

In the middle of the room was a small platform surrounded by music stands and the performers' chairs. The bedrooms of the conductor, Alma, and the blockowa, Tchaikowska, opened off this room. The floor was so well scoured that it was like satin, the walls were clean and white, and there was electricity throughout, an inestimable blessing.

"There are forty-seven of us living here. Do you realize what that means? Women from all over the place, cooped up in this small space and in these conditions—ten nationalities, the world in a sardine tin . . ."

Little Irene didn't finish the sentence. It was Ewa, in her sedate voice and in perfect French, who completed it: "In many cases they come from countries where deep-rooted and irrational hatreds have set them against one another; I'm referring in particular to my compatriots, the Poles. These women have different cultures and racial and ethnic origins, and conflicting religious and political ideas. So you'll understand that things don't run too smoothly here, particularly since there's a tremendous disparity in upbringing too."

I listened attentively, but it all seemed childish to me after what I'd been through a few hours before. The universe evoked by Ewa seemed both an oasis and a ghetto within the sprawling mass that was Auschwitz and its various dependencies. Later, I was to learn that it was also a sort of sandwich: a slice of music between two slices of wretchedness.

A runner was shouting: "Girls, to the showers!"

"Does she mean it?" stammered Clara.

"Every day, that's the ruling. Alma's very careful. The Krauts insist. All the women who might have to be anywhere near them in connection with their work have to be clean. We share our showers with the camp aristocrats—the girls from Canada, the black triangles, and everyone who has close dealings with the SS: runners, interpreters."

I had dreamt about this shower, and it had become a reality. Ewa even gave us a little piece of real soap, another marvel!

We were back just in time to hear the blockowa shouting the usual demands for silence and attention. She had just observed the entry of SS Mandel, who, in contempt of all accepted custom, had come in unannounced for the second time that day. Heels scraped the ground, bodies straightened and stiffened, except for the music copyists, who were allowed to remain seated.

The Lagerführerin was carrying an enormous box of shoes and looked surprisingly cheerful; she came towards me and let her motley assortment tumble pell-mell onto the floor: "Sit down."

I obeyed. She put one knee on the ground, like someone in a shoe shop, said: "Give me your foot," and tried shoes on me.

The other girls watched, wide-eyed. At their table, the

copyists were glazed, open-mouthed. At the door Alma, immobilized by this unprecedented sight, stared at the head of the camp kneeling at the feet of a deportee . . .

I savoured the spectacle.

A pair of fur-lined boots fitted me perfectly. Mandel straightened up, I rose, and she expressed her satisfaction: "My little Butterfly will have warm feet. It's vital for the throat."

Alma gestured to me and I attempted a position of attention: "*Dankeschön, Frau Lagerführerin!*"

Long May the Fun Last!

"STILL, AN ORCHESTRA in a camp like this," said Clara dazedly.

She had tied the little pointed scarf we'd both been given round her shaven head to hide it; the result was a slightly doll-like prettiness. Distrustfully, she insisted: "What does it do?"

"Gives us work through joy," said Florette ironically.

Clara was irritated: "I mean when does it play, and for whom?"

"For the deportees, of course."

"Are you making fun of me?"

"No," Irene intervened, "she isn't. It was started by Höss, the commandant of the camp at Auschwitz, as marching music for the work groups that leave Birkenau each morning to work outside and come back at night. Before that, only the men had an orchestra. Höss must have thought that it would make a good impression on the bosses when they visited."

"So we play outside twice a day?"

"Outside for the deportees, inside for the SS."

"We play for them too?"

"What did you think?" sniggered Florette.

And indeed, what did I think? After all, they were fond of flowers and moonlight, so why not music?

"At the beginning, when I arrived," Florette con-

tinued, "the orchestra was a joke, not even a circus fan-
fare. It was conducted by the filthy Tchaikowska. She'd
talked the Krauts into thinking she was a descendant of
the composer—what a descendant!—so they'd appointed her conductor. You've come here at a good
time, but I lived through quite a bit of that charade."
Leaning against a bedpost, she was well into her tale:

"I was in the quarantine block when a rumour came
through that there was an orchestra. That day, we were
almost happy; if there was an orchestra at Birkenau,
perhaps it wasn't as terrible as we feared. Perhaps the
worst moment was to move to the quarantine block, and
maybe after that it wasn't too bad. We were ready to
believe any nonsense. Anyhow, no need to draw you a
map, you've just been through it yourself. Only I wasn't
as lucky as you, I had a good forty days there, and it
seemed endless. The way I got out of the block was
rather like yours, Fania, the difference being that music
and I didn't get on all that well. I'd been forced to learn
the violin for seven years without really taking to it, and
it was three years since I'd touched a bow. Then one
morning a runner shouted to the company at large that
if there were any musicians among them, they were to
go forward. The girl I shared a mattress with told me to
go, said I'd nothing to lose. At the door I met two other
candidates, two Belgian girls from another part of the
camp whom I recognized: we'd been together in the
same transport. One was Big Irene, a violinist; we call
her that to distinguish her from the other little one.
That's Big Irene over there, rehearsing."

I looked: She was only seventeen or so, tall,
ravishing, a short fuzz of hair growing pleasingly over
her lovely round gilded skull.

"The other one," continued Florette, "was Anny, a
mandolin player, the big bony one by the piano. We all
arrived together; at the time the music hut was in camp
A, by the quarantine block and the Revier. Big Irene
grabbed her bow and played Bach's *Chaconne*

magnificently. You'd have needed to be deaf not to take her on. Anny, who scratches away quite prettily at the mandolin, was engaged too, though with rather less enthusiasm. When my turn came, utterly brash, I dared to attempt the *Méditation de Thaïs*. Massenet didn't have to put up with this sacrilege for long. Tchaikowska started an endless train of *pja kref*—that bag, she really was ideally placed to pass judgement. Watching her conduct was quite something. Marches were taken in three-time, waltzes in two and four. What a mess; she laid it on with the bass drum and cymbals—the idiot probably thought it gave the military touch! I don't know how the SS put up with that din, you'd think they had no ears. Then I was transferred to camp B, where we are now, and the day after I moved they asked for musicians again. As I'd learned that the orchestra had changed conductors, I tried again. It was Alma by then, and Tchaikowska had become blockowa. At first sight I thought the new conductor was wonderful, but I've changed my mind since. A real German. Anyhow, that day I asked permission to choose my piece and prudently chose something with a Gypsy flavour, the sort of thing that can best take mediocrity. I'd seen the music for it lying around. I trusted on my Hungarian blood to play the final czardas at a cracking rate. I can't honestly say that my performance was rapturously received, that would be going too far, but Alma did say unenthusiastically that she'd take me on a week's trial and that then she'd see."

"And you stayed?"

"That's another story; it's the only humane thing I've ever seen our *kapo* do. Instead of a heart she's got an empty violin case; it rings hollow. During my quarantine I'd been ill—in fact, I can't imagine how I survived; as I couldn't swallow anything, I'd set aside some bread rations with which I'd 'organized' a great pair of shoes with wooden soles. Wonderful, they were! It couldn't last, of course; four days later, someone had already pinched them. I was furious, desperate. But whom could I turn to? Here, you have to accept theft like everything else. As you know, the ground underfoot at Auschwitz is particularly disgusting. Two days later, when I went to the music block—at that time we weren't all housed together—I was barefoot. Alma takes everything very seriously, especially cleanliness; we had to be immaculate, and we didn't have anything to clean ourselves with. At the entrance. Tchaikowska had put a bucket of water and the girls cleaned their shoes in it on arrival. That bitch of a blockowa, seeing my bare feet coated in mud, forced me to dip them into that cold, greasy water. I burst out sobbing. Alma came out of her room, saw me shivering, my feet purple with cold dripping onto the concrete, and had a sudden pang of pity: 'Come on, I'll get you some shoes, you're part of the orchestra!' She put me in the third violin section, which was occupied by two Aryan Polish girls, Wisha and Pani Irena. Wisha was pretty feeble with the bow, nothing much came out. Pani Irena, who would purse her lips when Alma told her she was out of tune, had solved the problem by playing so softly that no one could hear her. I was put between these two to give the outfit a bit of body. The result was a bit of body and a few more wrong notes! Since then it's been more a question of raps on the knuckles than endearments, and I could draw up a dictionary of insults! Only music counts, for her. And you can imagine how she feels about working with us. Here you can count the real professional musicians on the fingers of one hand. But we're the material that inspired Alma to produce music. And I must say her arrival changed everything. Kramer, the camp commandant, and Mandel must have said to one another: "We'll have real concerts with this virtuoso.' To please the SS, Alma really goes to town on it all and gets us hopping mad. And furthermore, because of her claims, we're in danger of extinction from one day to the next."

"Why?"

It was Little Irene who answered. "Well, it's a bit complicated. As long as we played marches, the quality and variety didn't matter; I think people actually found our little circus quite funny. But now everything is different, we've become an orchestra. Kramer and Mandel know about music, and if they don't like our playing, they can disband our group. We were a product of caprice and we could vanish in the same way! We have to vary the repertoire, renew it, and how can we do that without new orchestrations?"

Big Irene had come to join us. Linking her long fingers, she explained in a quiet, careful voice with a slight Belgian accent: "Furthermore, they couldn't even send scores for us from Berlin; no composer in the world has written music for an orchestra with our combination of instruments!" Her gaze lingered on me. "You don't know how to orchestrate, by any chance?"

"I could."

Pandemonium broke out; amid the laughing and clapping, Irene said to Regina, Alma's orderly: "Go quickly and tell Alma we want to talk to her." Regina rushed off.

What had I said? It was true that I'd studied harmony and the art of fugue and counterpoint, that I knew how the instruments were placed in a score, but to say that I was an expert, that I knew how to orchestrate, would be rather too strong. Our *kapo* emerged from her bedroom, forgetting protocol; the girls flocked round her and told her the news.

Alma smiled. "You know how to orchestrate?"

"Yes."

"Come with me."

Jenny, a red-haired Parisienne with bright little mouse's eyes, observed that it wasn't overmuch for twenty-four hours.

Clara turned to me. "What have you done with your margarine? You haven't eaten it already?"

"No, I can't eat the stuff, it's like poison to me."

She became suspicious. "Have you put it in our box?"

The expression "our" box annoyed me and I asked: "Why do you have boxes for two? It's absolutely inconceivable. While there's anything at all, it's everyone's, everyone ought to be able to eat it, and when there's nothing, we all eat nothing."

They looked at me dumbfounded. Clearly, in their view, I was raving. Clara was the first to object, violently. "Oh no! I understand why perfectly. There's no reason to deprive oneself."

She fell silent, a little embarrassed, then continued: "I mean if I've got something, I'd certainly not be keen to distribute it—except in exceptional circumstances. With you it's different, because you're my friend. You share with people you get on with, after all."

I was staggered by her reaction, which the others seemed to find completely normal. For me, my father's was the example to follow. My mother used to tell the following story:

"When we were first married, we lived in one room, with a lavatory on the landing. We didn't have much, but still, your father did have two shirts. One evening, coming in, I somehow noticed that he had only one.

" 'Where's your other shirt gone?'

" 'I gave it away.'

" 'So you really are mad: you only have two shirts and you give one away.'

" 'That's true, but *he* didn't have one at all; now we've each got one.' "

I stared at them; they ate in silence, chewing slowly like people on the verge of famine. Their eyes were glued to their neighbours' portions, like mangy dogs surveying each other's rotten meat while devouring their own. They couldn't understand my story; all, to some degree, had acquired the camp mentality.

"Well, as far as I'm concerned," I stated rebelliously,

"I'll share everything I've got with everyone."

Anny, generous by nature, objected. "Surely not with the Polish girls; just look at them!"

Leaning on their elbows at the table set apart for Aryans, they were taking shifty looks at Ewa, who had come to sit beside me. Their bestiality had something stereotyped about it which made them particularly disturbing.

"Why should I make distinctions?" I persisted.

"Because they're monsters, pigs," Florette burst out, "and they're all anti-Semitic."

Here, in this camp where crematoria burned day and night, where these girls were daily present at our massacre, how could they still be against the Jews?

"Ewa, you're not anti-Semitic too?" I asked firmly.

"No, no, I'm not."

"I'll say not," Florette sniggered. "She, the grande dame of the camp, not an anti-Semite, my eye! She's like all anti-Semites, she's got 'her' pet Jew, but all the others are just about good enough for the gas ovens."

"No, that's not true, I'm not like that," Ewa protested gently. She pointed to her seated compatriots. "Unlike them, I didn't learn to like or dislike people according to their race or religion.

"But isn't the attitude of your compatriots justified by a total lack of communication?" I insisted. "They don't understand our language, and that cuts them off."

"Rubbish," interrupted Rachel, a Polish Jewess. "We talk their language and they keep to themselves, simply because we're Jewish."

"There's something else," Irene added. "They know that the non-Jews aren't gassed unless they're Communists, and of course these girls aren't—they're anti-Russian as well. So since they're in no great danger, they feel themselves superior. When the war is over, they know for certain they'll be going home. Add to that the fact that some of them have been shut in here for a long time and are seething with resentment: they've stored up hatred, it's their treasure. Lastly, whatever their age, they're always learned that if they're poor and oppressed, it's the Yids' fault. How can you expect them suddenly to admit that being anti-Semitic is ignorant and stupid? They don't know that, they haven't learned it!''

Incorrigible, I answered haughtily: "Then we must teach them!"

The general laughter shattered my eardrums but not my blind idealism. Ewa sighed. "There isn't even any point in trying; you'll never make yourself understood. All they understand is force."

Jenny, all angles, her pointed face covered with freckles, changed the subject. "That's enough of all this fancy stuff! Tell us about the old place—when did you leave the gay city? Are the Jerries still making everyone ill? Can you still get grub on the black market? What are the fashions like? Whereabouts are you from?"

Questions poured in from all sides: What were people saying in Paris? Did they think the war would end soon? Was it true that the Germans had cut up the Eiffel Tower because they needed the iron?

"No, no," I reassured them. "They've just melted down a few bronze statues instead."

Jenny was seized with momentary horror. "I'm no art lover, but they were part of history!"

In their passion for information, they mingled the important with the trivial: What was the makeup like? Had dresses gone up or down? And hairstyles? Did people still dance swing? And Laval and Pétain? Had I been to the Unoccupied Zone? Were there really places in the middle of nowhere where food was just like it used to be?

My answers were equally jumbled: shoulder bags, food supplies by bike, the Krauts as Sunday painters on the Place du Tertre, curls on the top of the head . . .

"Well"—Jenny sighed, stroking her shaven

head—"if that's still the fashion when we get back, we'd better think about getting this to grow!"

"Don't worry, it'll be us who'll be setting the trend. What are people wearing?"

"Last summer, very full skirts down to the knee, all kinds of colour and patterns. The girls looked like flowers; it was lovely on the Champs Elysées."

Dreamily they absorbed all this while I continued. "Since the Occupation, it's been forbidden to put up flags on July 14, so the women dressed in the French colours: a red top, a white skirt, a blue handkerchief. Individually it wasn't noticeable, but when they came together in groups, arm in arm from Concorde to Etoile, from République to the Bastille, Paris was tricoloured—it was beautiful!"

There were tears in their eyes.

"How did the Krauts take it?"

"They were green!"

Everyone laughed.

"Heels are this high . . . the girls look as if they're walking on stilts. Since there aren't any stockings, people paint their legs."

"Tell us the latest joke."

"It's about an SS man who buys his paper at the kiosk every morning and, every morning, the paperman says to him: 'Here you are, clot.' So one day the Kraut asks him: 'What *is* a clot?' 'It means "boss." ' Delighted, the German says: 'So, me little clot, Hitler, big one.' "

I was never to know another moment of glory like that one. They laughed so much they cried, and so did I.

I gave them all a feeling of the irreverence and banter of the Parisians. For them, France was a breath of fresh air, so strong that it went to their heads. They were moved; they laughed, cried, and sang, everyone slightly unhinged.

"And the latest songs?"

Clara and I gave a positive recital. They didn't want

us to stop. It was wild; no one thought of going to bed.
Even the Poles stayed up; Pani Founia and Marila her
slave sat quietly in their corner, even going as far as to
laugh when we did so as to seem to be joining in. They
probably thought that would raise them in our esteem.
We knew they couldn't know what *Compagnons, dormez-vous* meant to us. At the last line—*'Compagnons,
la France est devant vous!'*—the girls hugged one
another and cried. It was a unique moment. Welded to
one another by an exultant rush of fellow feeling, we
lived that exceptional night intensely. We forgot the
lights of the camp, the watchtowers, the electrified
barbed wire, the smoky sky. We didn't notice the dawn
approaching.

At seven o'clock a runner announced the arrival of
the SS wardens. Alma emerged from her room while
Tchaikowska bellowed: *Achtung! Zum Appell! Fünf zu
fünf!* It was roll call. We stood there at attention, in the
middle of our dormitory-dayroom, for what seemed like
hours. But however long it might seem I appreciated our
luck: At the same time in our camp, thousands of internees—men and women, half-naked and half-dead,
petrified into immobility—stood, sometimes for hours,
in the snow, rain, and ice.

The SS immediately noticed Clara and me. Rigid with
respect, Alma informed them of our status. Our
costume seemed to annoy them, and one commented
acidly: "And they're already dressed?"

"On Frau Lagerführerin Mandel's orders."

The roll call over, part of the orchestra prepared to go
out, wearing something approaching a uniform of navy
blue skirt, black woollen stockings, striped jacket, and a
triangle of white cloth on their heads reminiscent of the
headdress of German nurses. Thus dressed, they looked
more like a troupe of ill-nourished orphans than an orchestra, and now I noticed how thin they were. The
makeup of the band was as unusual as that of the or-

chestra: several violinists and guitarists, pipes, an ac-
cordion and, of course, the indispensable percussion.
The SS probably thought that the stirring power of
those booming drums, backed by the jangle of the cymbals, would have made the very dead march in time.
Meanwhile it was we, in rows of five by five, who would
walk in step: Alma first, me last beside Danka, the cym-
bal player—another whale of a creature. I had asked to
go with them; I wanted to see, to understand, if I could,
why we existed.

Our parody of a band went on parade, playing a
march of the cheeriest Tyrolean type, evocative of pic-
nics in the Black Forest washed down with cool beer.
Our barracks was about three hundred yards from the
place where we gave our strange concerts morning and
evening. The road was bordered with other barracks,
and in front of each of them the deportees awaited the
order of departure, which would not be given until we
were in our place. The double hedge of wretched
creatures between which our parade passed was the
reverse of reassuring. I couldn't see if these women were
looking at us—I didn't dare look at them—but I felt
their eyes boring into me like a thousand needles.

Our platform, at the intersection of camps A and B,
had four steps and lines of chairs: a bandstand! We
took our places. Alma turned her head towards her
audience as though sizing it up, turned back to her
players, raised her baton and, while officers and *kapos*
bellowed assorted *Achtungs* that echoed along the roads
of the camp, an *Arbeitsmarsch* burst out, martial,
exhilarating, almost joyful.

Eins, zwei, went Alma's baton; *eins, zwei, drei, fier* . . .
ordered the *kapos*, and the march past began. From
every roadway, every street, they passed before us. Now
I dared to look at them. I forced myself to, I had to
remember, because later I would bear witness. This resolution was to harden and give me strength until the end.

Haggard, tattered, paddling through mud and snow,

struggling not to stumble, sometimes supporting one another—one of the few rights left to them—the cohort of prisoners proceeded towards the exit. And I suffered them all, en masse and separately: a look of hatred or scorn was like a knife wound; an insult was like being spat on. "Quitters, bitches, traitors!" one of them shouted. Others shrugged the bony shoulders which protruded from their rags. Just as painful to me were those women who didn't even raise their heads, who passed by indifferently, detached from hatred and love, at the threshold of death. But perhaps those who smiled at me hurt most of all; their understanding was as painful as a complicity I had not earned.

It was only now that I began to grasp the insanity of the place I was in. In the quarantine block, shattered by the shower, the tattooing and the shaving, starving, dazed, beaten, I hadn't been aware of what was happening to me, to *me*. Here, in the icy air of this winter morning, in this geometrical landscape of squat, stumpy sheds with barbed wire above them, the watchtowers, without a single tree on the horizon, I became aware of the extermination camp of Birkenau, and of the farcical nature of this orchestra conducted by this elegant woman, these comfortably dressed girls sitting on chairs playing to these virtual skeletons, shadows showing us faces which were faces no longer.

In the early morning light so peculiarly sinister, the *Arbeits-kommandos* set off towards their regenerating work, work through joy! I couldn't begin to imagine that work. They were simply going to hasten their deaths. They, who had so much difficulty even in moving, were required to give their steps a military gait. And, painfully, I realized that we were there to hasten their martyrdom. One, two . . . one, two . . . Alma's baton set the pace for the endless march past. With the tip of his boot an SS beat time while the last woman, followed by the last soldier and last dog, went through the camp gate.

Our Bread, Our Hope,
Our Certainty

IT MUST HAVE been about five in the morning. I
couldn't sleep; something approaching anguish had
lodged in the centre of my chest. I wanted to escape, I
wanted all this never to have been. As quietly as possible
I climbed out of my upper bunk. The windows were set
high in the wall, and like a child I had access only to the
lowest pane. The searchlights cut through the night with
their gleam and it all looked rather like a marshalling
yard.

What had I come to look at through this window? To
look outside is to look at life, but here it was to look at
death. It was snowing, large lazy flakes which hovered
idly before touching down. Suddenly, at the end of our
roadway, a group of marching men appeared—soldiers
of the Red Army. Twenty men. Their tunics thrown
over their shoulders, they advanced in a solid block,
shoulder to shoulder, perfectly in step, barefoot in the
snow, eyes fixed on the middle distance, faces impassive. They seemed very big. They passed an SS man
and, with a single movement, without changing pace,
raised their shapkas to bare their shaven skulls. One of
them at the head of the group was singing; his voice was
beautiful, broad and deep, and the words reached me
clearly:

"A train is taking me far from Moscow
Day and night, the sound of wheels . . .
From the pocket of my tunic
I take out your photo.
Smoke will darken it . . .
That will make it all the dearer to my eyes . . .
I think of you, my dearest,
I know that we shall meet again."

In their tatters the Russians came forward along the roadway and I feasted my eyes on them. I already saw my liberators superimposed upon them. For me, they were the Red Army on the march!

Silent as a cat, Bronia, an Aryan Russian, joined me at the window. A ray of light fell on her high cheekbone, her blond plaits (non-Jews weren't shaved). She smiled at me, and her teeth were solid and white; one could imagine her on the plains of the Ukraine, sprawled on top of a haycart fork in hand or loading bales with her strong arms, a positive advertisement for the *kolkhoz*.

"Bronia, where do they come from, who are they?"

"I heard about those men when I arrived in the camp in April '43. In '41 the German army invaded my country and took soldiers prisoner. They were brought here, to Auschwitz. At that time it was just endless marsh with an occasional birch tree on the horizon. The SS decided that the Russian soldiers would build their own camp. But the Russians said: 'No, we are soldiers and we will not build our own cage.' The Germans replied that if they wanted to eat and sleep, they would have to work. The Russians refused. *'Arbeiten, arbeiten,'* insisted the Germans. More blank refusals from the Soviet soldiers. They wrapped themselves in their greatcoats and lay down then and there, in the mud of those swamps. The SS continued with their side of the exchange but the Russians stopped answering. They died of cold and hunger, one after the other. We don't

know what the Germans did with the corpses. Perhaps
they sank into the mud, this living Auschwitz mud—
perhaps they are here, right under our feet . . . Twenty
of them survived, still refusing to work. The SS knew
when they were beaten: they offered them clothes and
shoes, but the soldiers wouldn't take them because they
belonged to the deportees. The only job they agreed to
do was to distribute the bread, very early in the morning.''

Bronia was silent. It was impossible to disentangle
truth from legend in this tale.

"Look at those men, they are our bread passing by.''

Our bread, our hope, our certainty . . .

Seven thirty. The players were back now. I hadn't
gone with them.

"Oof! It's better in here than outdoors!''

It was Flora, the Dutch girl, expressing her satisfaction. It sounded so selfish, so cynical, that I felt quite
dismayed. Jenny's voice diverted me: "They're bringing
the coffee. Get cracking, we've got to be on the job in
twenty minutes.''

"We're coming.'' The girls were rummaging in their
boxes. Clara was crouched over ours, keeping a sharp
eye on the others. Her expression was savage and
distrustful; she might almost have been defending the
royal larder! As we had only just arrived, our reserves
were pathetic, a bit of bread and my margarine ration.
With the crafty air of a greedy peasant, Clara asked me:
"Since you're not eating it, will you give me your
margarine?''

Poor girl, her need to eat was so violently animal it
frightened me.

"Of course, take it!''

That earned me the warm, grateful look of a spoiled
cocker spaniel.

Gripping her steaming mug in both hands, Florette
growled: "It gets more disgusting every day—and what

do they make this bread with? Baked bones, to look at it! It's just incredible.''

What seemed incredible to me was to hear that phrase here of all places, but no one reacted. Flora smiled vaguely; perhaps she didn't even grasp the allusion. There was something utterly bovine about her that irritated me. Freckled Jenny tapped her piece of bread on the wooden table and joked: "Anyhow, no need for a hammer to resole your shoes. They mixed up the tradesman: it's not Fritz the baker who delivered the bread, but the ironmonger, Fritz the do-it-yourself man.''

I capped it. "You're right, it's even hard enough to smash Hitler's head in.''

Enormous laughter, out of all proportion to the sally. Only Germans and Poles looked disapproving; as they didn't understand, they always thought they were the butt of our jokes.

"That's some idea!'' Anny roared. "To kill Hitler with his own bread! It would be poetic justice, all right!''

There was a final chortle, then, one by one, we left the room.

Arbeit, Arbeit! The players tuned their instruments. Seated at the copyists' table, I took stock of my assistants. It wasn't a brilliant array—they were the rejects: Zocha, the enormous creature who had come to fetch me in the first place, a hefty country girl who was such an appalling violinist that Tchaikowska, her protector, had speedily relegated her to the copyists' table when Alma arrived. Danka, something of an athlete and probably the most dangerous because her hard expression showed intelligence; when she wasn't copying, she played the cymbals literally fit to deafen you, feeling no doubt that the violence of her clashing alone would stir the work detachments into action, that by her zeal she was satisfying the SS. Between these two assertive monsters was Marisha, aged twenty, so pale and self-effacing as to be virtually invisible; even her stupidity was of the washed-out variety. At the other end—here, too, Aryan oil and Jewish water weren't mixed—Hilde bent her obstinate, freshly shaven head over her paper. Intelligent, tyrannical, she immediately struck me as the führer of the German Jews of our block.

Pointing out my copyists to me, Alma had reminded me that she was the one in charge of them. What power could I wield over those Aryan Poles or over Hilde, who felt superior because she was German? I was a tamer without a whip, naked among vicious beasts. A charming prospect!

Alma appeared at the door of her room. Everyone stood up. I watched her come forward: she was not pretty, but she bore herself like someone making a stage entrance. I imagined the moment when she had put her beautiful hand on the door handle, prepared to open it, mustered up her public presence, consolidated it, breathed deeply, and pushed open the door to make her entry—the entry of a leader.

She passed impassively among the women, then stopped in front of me. "Can you orchestrate *Lustspiel*? The officers are very fond of Suppé's overtures. Some time ago they gave me the piano part. See what you can do. It would make a good start for you."

"Certainly, madame."

Enchanted, Alma smiled at me. At the table, the copyists observed me cautiously: if I was all I'd made myself out to be, I represented a guarantee of life for the orchestra. So it was not just my writing crew who had their eyes on me, but all the girls; even the thickest Pole had grasped my importance. It was up to me to show them what I could do. I asked Alma if I could have some paper.

"There's some on the table."

"I mean lined paper, manuscript paper."

Alma shook her head. "We haven't got any. They draw the staff with a ruler."

"Pen, ink?"

"Here, we have only pencils," Alma said curtly. "We must make do with what we have. There's a war on."

The phrase astounded me. It seemed that Alma was a German before all else. She was very tall: it was all too easy for her to look down on me, and she did.

"Is that all?"

Undaunted, I answered, "No, madame!"

All trace of a smile had disappeared; she was straight and thin as her baton. I knew that I had to assert myself immediately if I was to be respected.

"What do you need now?"

"I don't have enough copyists."

"*Gut.* You shall have more. There's no shortage of poor players."

That was true enough; indeed I was still wondering how we could possibly make music with such a range of instruments and attainment.

From her small platform, Alma gave her stand the traditional tap, then raised her arm. This gesture was the start to my day, which was to be as neatly divided as the manuscript paper I didn't have.

I found this Suppé, so highly thought of by the SS, not just mediocre, but unbearable. Detestable. However, I analysed the piano version with all the care and interest I would have devoted to a work by Prokofiev, and above all with the same anxiety: I had never done any orchestral scoring before.

As in all marches, the trumpets, trombones, and clarinets dominated, and I had at my disposal ten violins, a flute, reed pipes, two accordions, three guitars, five mandolins, drums, and some cymbals. No composer had ever envisaged such a combination!

I read the top part carefully, and everything fell into place: I would replace the high instruments—sax, clarinet, and so on—with my first violin and my flute. The guitar and mandolins would be the accompaniment. The accordions would bring the whole together and support it with their basic chords; the percussion would steady the beat.

I was delighted; I felt that I could do more than simply acquit myself honourably. Within me, with an ease in which I hardly dared believe, everything orchestrated itself. The instruments each led off in turn, became alive. It was intoxicating. In a way I was recomposing this march. I heard it—stirring, martial. I was conducting it, I was carried away . . . Then I saw the reality of the endless, wretched multitude before whom it would be played. I sat, pencil poised, unable to proceed, staring into space. To survive, I was not simply going to have to walk over my heart, as the Hungarians say, I was going to have to trample on it, annihilate it.

My three Poles stared at me, their thoughts written on their faces: I was hesitating, I was worried, perhaps I'd bluffed. Already they were crowing: this evening, the tigresses would be able to make mincemeat of the tamer. I smiled at their distrustful faces. I stretched my hand out towards the sheets that had been ruled, took them, counted them, and observed severely: "That's not enough, I need twenty-five sheets as soon as possible. Our conductor wants to start rehearsing this march right now."

There was a sullen silence. I lowered my head and began to work almost cheerfully. This new work absorbed me utterly, it was another way of making music, a wonderful form of escape! The notes formed rapidly under my pencil. I hadn't lost my touch, nor, unfortunately for me, my ear. Wrong notes burst forth at every moment, and I jumped at every one. Alma had trouble imposing the composer's tempo. There was good and bad in this orchestra: the good consisted of Big Irene, an excellent violinist who, by comparison, became our Menuhin. Halina and Ibi of the peachlike skin played quite adequately. At the lower end of the scale in a class of her own was Jenny, who had played professionally in motion picture theatres before the war. She maltreated her strings with great sawing strokes: scraping and grinding triumphantly, she played with a strength and conviction that drowned the other instruments. Apart from the violins, there were three valuable players, three professionals: Lili, an accordionist; Helga, the percussionist, and Frau Kröner, the flautist. My ears couldn't discern anything very distinctive among the mandolins and guitars, except for Anny, the Belgian, who played prettily. The disaster area was second and third violins, and the worst of a bad bunch was undoubtedly Florette.

Gloomily I contemplated the dusty cello and double bass cases standing up against the wall. I had resigned myself: Marta the cellist had gone into the infirmary just before my arrival. At a pinch I could do without her cello, but a double bass player really seemed indispensable. I had to have one; I would speak to Alma about it.

Alma, that impassioned musician, was suffering: her powerlessness to master her musicians technically exasperated her. She was conducting, as it were, a war of nerves in which she was the loser. Very soon I understood what was happening: Alma, a virtuoso violinist, couldn't conduct; she read her score as a player, not as a conductor. She got angry, burst out, bellowed insults, hit guilty fingers with her baton. She made the girls work over the same phrase tirelessly, came up against the same mistakes and produced new ones. The good players became exhausted, the poor ones sank into a near stupor, and I, amid this bedlam, had to write out a piece bearing no relation to what I was hearing. It was trying, but I managed it.

We did seventeen hours of music a day, without counting what Florette called nightwork. By this she meant the concerts which the SS came to, at times chosen by themselves, to relax after their "hard" work. It was these sessions that earned the orchestra its reprieve.

Soup break. Alma put down her baton, briefly summed up the quality of the rehearsal as *zum kotzen*—nauseating—and said sharply to me: "Wait here a minute."

Was she completely unthinking to make this request? Did she imagine someone would keep my portion of soup for me? Through the open door I surveyed the table with the cooking implements where the soup was given out and reassured myself: Marila hadn't yet come back from the kitchen with Pani Founia.

"Can you really do this orchestration?" asked Alma nervously.

My gaze elsewhere, I gave her a polite affirmative.

"Show me."

I showed her my scoring. She was reassured; now at last she was certain that I hadn't cheated her. Despite this easy beginning I was less at ease than she; it was important that too much shouldn't be asked of me. Yet that was just what Alma proceeded to do, somewhat dreamily. "Thanks to you, we'll be able to give real concerts."

I took advantage of her euphoria to ask for my double bass player.

"Yes, that would be good. I'll ask Mandel for a player from the men's orchestra to come and give lessons to—" She hesitated a moment, peered into the next room, and concluded, "Yvette. I think she'll learn fast."

Alma didn't share our mess and presumably she was rather less badly fed. She went back into her room, where Regina took her her tray, and I joined the others just in time to get splashed with the two ladlesful slopped into my mug.

"It doesn't stain," said Anny with feeling. "There's no fat."

What really was *zum kotzen* was the food, which was identical to that of the other blocks; no hope on that score. Clara, seated beside me, fixed the unlovely concoction with an air of disbelief, great tears trembling in her eyes.

"I'm so hungry, and it's always the same thing," she murmured.

Florette picked up that one. "What manner of luxury food did you expect?"

"I'm not that silly, but after all, we are the orchestra."

"Ah," sniggered Jenny. "One can see that you hung out in the better parts of Paris. You've still got a well-developed sense of privilege. Well, here you'll have to make do, it's shit for everyone. That's equality!"

Little Irene flared up, "I bet those wretched kitchen workers have stolen all the potatoes again!"

"Have you ever seen any?" exploded Florette. "I'll give you those bitches' recipes: anything, all the perishable remains from the suitcases and stolen parcels, everything that can't be put on the SS table or get sent to Berlin is for us—rotten bacon, musty raisins, mouldy jam, cake crumbs, treacle, sausage skin. In it all goes, and you stir it all about! It's nourishing and vomitatory!"

Suddenly my teeth came upon something slightly more solid, a couple of inches long; since I wasn't in high society, I proceeded to extract this unidentifiable something, which I contemplated with interest.

"Well, well," commented Jenny, "a bit of potato peeling. That proves that potatoes were on the menu. Eat it!"

"You're lucky, it's something to bite on."

No one smiled. Food wasn't a subject to be joked about. You could laugh about death, but not about what kept you alive.

We went back into the music room and, as on one of those clocks from which figures march out, Alma came out of her room the moment we were seated. She made her entry with such precision that it was almost as though she spied on our movements from behind her door. Indeed, why not?

The hours passed. The rehearsal was over. The orchestra prepared to leave; having "helped" the work detachments on their way, it would now "help" them to return. That was the end of the musicians' labour. All we had to do then was to undergo the second roll call, when again we were counted like cattle. Then came supper: a bit of bread and, this evening, a minuscule piece of cheese—a real feast; by some oversight it wasn't even mouldy.

This day etched itself into my mind as the typical day, the model of those to come, the first link in the chain. How many would there have to be before my account with fate was settled?

We were exhausted and famished, and escaped into oblivion.

The Girls in Canada

A CHAIN OF whistle blasts encircled the barracks with their web of sound. Around me no one woke, but the noise must have disturbed their sleep because some turned over and groaned. I looked at them and suddenly felt a rush of protective tenderness.

Outside, soldiers ran heavily; arms clicked, whistles blew, ordering incomprehensible movements. My heart beat furiously. Wasn't this colossal upheaval just the kind of thing that would precede the liberation of the camp? They would be running madly, beside themselves with panic, losing their heads and, pretty soon afterwards, their lives . . . I was impatient to know what was going on. Who could tell me?

Big Irene was sleeping like a baby, an impression reinforced by her protruding lower lip. Ewa, flat on her back, looked like a noble figure stretched out on a Polish tomb; Florette groaned in a voice woolly with sleep: "Shit! They make me sick!" Even in sleep her language was foul.

Little Irene sat up and looked questioningly at me. I didn't dare share my hopes, so I asked her what was happening.

"*Blocksperre,*" she said unilluminatingly.

"What does that mean?"

I caught a fleeting look of pity in her dark eyes, still dimmed by sleep.

"Of course, you don't know: Confined to quarters, no going out."

"Why?"

"Because they're going to make a selection."

There are some words that need no explanation. No sooner had I heard that one than I understood its meaning: the selection of those who were to die.

"Does it last long?"

"It depends on the size of the convoy—from two to six hours."

"Does it always happen at night?"

"No, but they prefer it that way. Things go better in the dark, it's all more efficient. People are half asleep, there's less shouting, less fuss . . ."

"So a *Blocksperre* also means the arrival of a convoy?"

"Usually, but it's not the only sort of selection during which we're confined to quarters."

I must have looked particularly uncomprehending, because Little Irene explained to me: "The camp of Birkenau mustn't have more than about a hundred thousand internees; to maintain this figure, they make selections, though of course this doesn't prevent the daily murder of individuals, which doesn't alter our lives at all. Five minutes don't go by without a sick person, a Jew, or a Moslem being put in Block Twenty-five."

"Why Moslems in particular?"

" 'Moslem' is the name given to those who are just walking corpses."

"Why?"

"No one knows. The person who first used it must have had his reasons, but it must have been a long time ago, and we'll never know."

I'd survived the selection of my arrival, but I didn't know what the criteria were, or how other selections took place. I wanted to ask, but kept a feeble silence. However, Irene talked on, perhaps wanting to unburden herself of the horror that was stifling her. One had to be new here to agree to listen to her.

"I think that the selections carried out on those who aren't new arrivals are the worst. You see, when you've just arrived you don't know anything. When you've spent some time here, you know, it's always the same saga: whistles blowing. They whistle at the slightest pretext: for supper, for coffee, to disperse the girls who go from block to block looking for something to trade or eat. In two minutes the camp is empty, a desert. The trucks arrive, stop in front of the blocks. Inside, a safe distance from the foul smell, the SS point out those selected: the thinnest, the shivering, the sick who try and hide, the girls who are disliked by the blockowa, the *kapo*, the kitchen girl . . . why not? And they're brought out with blows from rifle butts, clubbed, kicked, punched, butted. The blockowas, egged on by the SS, are the worst; they lash out most of all. Some women shriek and fight. I saw one throw herself at an SS man, nails clawing his face; he clubbed her down, and everyone was forced to walk over her body, still living, just one mass of red . . ."

I wished she'd stop, I didn't want to hear any more. But Irene continued, and I could only hope it was therapeutic:

"The scenes I saw in the quarantine block before coming here, Fania . . . Some climb in completely spinelessly, others sing, laugh. They climb into the trucks knowing quite well where they're going. I've seen the whole range of reactions imaginable before the most extravagant horror ever known. And the SS wander around amidst this, cool and casual as you please. When they've closed up the trucks they laugh and pat one another on the back as if they've just enjoyed a good lark. The ones who shut the doors of the extermination blocks where the Zyklon-B gas is react the same way. Afterwards they go back into their mess to have a quiet drink, play the piano, have a girl—never a Jew, that's not allowed—or they come here to listen to music: Viennese waltzes, Peter Kreuder. When it's over, after what they've done, they all want to do something else. And that's what I can't understand. Can you?''

"Perhaps they want to forget, not be alone with themselves? Or perhaps they get drunk to complete the pleasure of killing, to celebrate it. What do we know about them?''

"In the music block we're more isolated so we can stand up to it better, but once you've seen it, you can't forget it.''

A voice admitting of no nonsense called to us to be quiet, to go to sleep. I'd have dearly liked to. Already the crematoria chimneys were beginning to smoke; tomorrow, a sickening smell of charred flesh would impregnate our clothes, our skin . . . and I had to remain indifferent—indeed, to take no notice. To what kind of heaven should one turn to pray for this kind of insensitivity?

I must have fallen asleep again, because the entry of a runner startled me. She was out of breath.

"Achtung! Schneller, schneller! Mandel's on her way.''

Tchaikowska came out of her room like a jack-in-the-box; Regina, Alma's orderly, ran to knock at her door. Vigorously Irene shook Florette, whose aggressiveness was increased by this brutal awakening. Shouts and groans on all sides. The blockowa's bellowing rose above the hubbub; most of her random blows luckily fell on empty air. The pandemonium had a boarding-school feel to it. The headlong gallop had lasted only a couple of minutes. It was three o'clock when Mandel, cap on head, wrapped in her regulation cape, came into the music room, where we were awaiting her in an impeccable position of attention—even me—gazes fixed on the middle distance. A blink could land you in Block 25. What could she want at this hour?

I didn't know much about the camp, the activity of

the SS, but I knew enough to wonder where she'd come from and what her part was in a selection. Did she pick out the condemned, thrust children towards the crematoria? Did she stroll insouciantly, supremely contemptuous, among the shaven, tattooed women who were being prepared for their role as cattle?

In a manner bordering on the servile, Alma asked nervously what the camp chief would like to hear, trembling inwardly lest Mandel name a piece so old that the players would have forgotten it.

Maria Mandel was the perfect representative of the young German woman depicted in propaganda. She had a lovely Dietrich voice, guttural in the lower register. She pointed to me: "I'd like *meine kleine Sängerin* to sing me *Madame Butterfly* in German."

Alma translated the order. Catastrophe! That should put me in good voice. I didn't know it in German. Alma's expression became dangerously dark, she apologized lengthily; Mandel, irritated, cut her short with a gesture, and almost snappily Alma addressed me: "Sing it in French. I've said you'll learn it in German."

And in Russian, and in Moldavian, should the whim take her . . .

I felt my throat and lungs unresponsive with sleep. The incongruous thought of those singers who swallowed a raw egg to clear their throats nearly made me choke! I didn't even dare to cough. The orchestra moved off and I launched into Madame la Lagerführerin's favorite aria.

Mandel had removed her cape and sat down, looking dreamy. Could it be that she regarded herself as a sentimental geisha? I hated myself at the thought of giving her pleasure.

But was I? Her face wasn't smiling, or even relaxed. Later, I was to learn that it was the done thing for the SS to listen to us as if we were slot machines. Yet she must have been satisfied, because I had to sing it again. Apparently she nurtured a special love for that opera, and I was never to know why. It seemed an odd taste, but it was vital not to forget that it was because of Mandel's desire to hear her beloved *Butterfly* that Alma had sent for me in the first place.

The session was short, and the Lagerführerin left us, apparently satisfied. Little Irene commented as she went out, "It's a small convoy, the selection didn't last long."

"How do you know? We haven't heard any whistles."

"We will soon. The SS often come here just before the end of the *Blocksperres*. Work is over for them and they come here to relax with us."

How could Irene say that so calmly, with only a touch of irony? I was probably wrong to rebel, and soon, very soon, I would understand that that was how it had to be.

Florette said vituperatively, "To get woken up just to see her filthy Nazi mug . . ."

"Figuratively I agree, but in fact she's rather beautiful."

"Are you mad? Beautiful, that bitch?"

I stood my ground. "As an SS she's a bitch, but as a woman she's exceedingly beautiful."

The girls stared at me almost hatefully, noisily backing up Florette, and to my amazement I heard Clara's sedate voice: "Fania's flattered to have been chosen by her as a singer, so she makes allowances."

"Allowances? I call it arse-licking."

Their absurdity annoyed me; there would have been no point in answering that the SS didn't necessarily look like what they were, that one might find them good-looking without selling one's soul to them. I turned my back and climbed up to the top of my *coja*. I would close my eyes and forget about them and sleep.

This was the worst moment, the time when it was difficult not to give up. Despite all the wise lectures I gave myself, having entertained that SS woman after a selection filled me with the utmost disgust.

* * *

In the morning my mouth tasted bitter. Making my bed with the required absurd neatness, I remarked: "I don't know what I'd give for a toothbrush and some toothpaste."

"There are some girls who share one between five, they might take you on as a sixth!"

"The best thing for her would be to 'organize' one," Florette piped up.

"How does one go about it?"

"In our camp, there are two 'Canadas,' the small one near us and the big one, a bit farther away. In the small one you'll find toothbrushes, toothpaste, soap, scent, things like that; in the big one, nightdresses, slips, shoes, clothes, tins of jam . . . In fact, everything winds up there!"

What was she saying? Shops, here?

"What is this 'Canada,' and why is it called that?"

"No one knows. Perhaps because Canada is a rich country, a promised land. In fact, it's a general store." Florette continued, "To come here, we brought all our best things, the warmest and newest. The rich arrive with luggage containing fortunes: furs, jewels, diamonds, gold; groaning wallets, cases crammed with banknotes. Don't think I'm exaggerating. These thousands of cases arriving every week for years represent a fabulous fortune. Everything that isn't perishable is sorted, labelled, counted, packed up, and sent regularly back to Berlin. But what I find even more disgusting is that they filch our parcels."

I was stupefied. "Parcels—you get parcels? So our families know where we are? Do you mean to say that we can write?"

Florette laughed. Jenny positively hooted. "She's going to send her family coloured postcards wishing they were here!"

Ewa interrupted the flow of sarcasm: "It does sometimes happen that our families are informed of our presence in a work camp and that the sending of parcels is authorized. Of course, they never reach us; it's probably just another way of getting more for themselves."

"Yes, parcels arrive every day from every corner of Europe," Florette took over angrily. "Some Germans and Polacks get some of theirs, but we Jews never do. First, of course, you have to have a family left to send you any—they can't post them from the great beyond. And supposing parcels did arrive, the foodstuffs would be distributed at the SS canteen to privileged internees, black triangles, whores, thieves, criminals, the cream, in short! And the vilest thing of all is that the families are never informed of our disappearance, they go on depriving themselves so that the dead won't go short—a little butter bought on the black market, a small pot of jam made by grandmother with her sugar ration, a sausage, a rabbit paté (how pleased she'll be!), and some rusks so that little so and so can carry on her diet. The parents send and send . . . and the Germans are half sick with delight."

She shook with angry sobs. Little Irene put her hand on her shoulder. "Calm down or you'll be in trouble again."

Anny sought a diversion by telling us that on the evening we arrived she'd just received a parcel, the first since July '43. Even then it was an amazing stroke of luck that they'd left her anything, because they naturally helped themselves first.

"The whole thing doesn't proceed with the speed of light, though," Jenny snickered. "Don't imagine the postman gallops breathlessly across Europe to deliver you your parcel. So all the grub that isn't tinned has legs of its own by the time it reaches you."

"And when can one go to Canada?"

My question was a real wow, particularly with Jenny.

"You're a joker to the end! Do you think that Canada is some kind of luxury big store? It's not a question of 'being able' to go there, you idiot! It's *ver-*

boten. If Frau Schmidt saw you ambling about in her palace of wonders, she'd send you up in smoke. It's for the bigwigs, the big shots of the camp. Don't worry, we've got friends there, particularly Renate, Marta's sister—the cool type, but effective; no French girls, as far as I know. That cushy job is reserved for the Krauts, Czechs, Polacks, Slovaks, and so on. Someone'll be along shortly; they know you're here."

Still, I was worried. I could accept all privations except that of a toothbrush. At least, that was how I saw it at that moment.

"And if they didn't know, they wouldn't come? Anyhow, who told them?"

Ewa smiled. "Don't worry. In this camp everyone knows everything. The Canadas are also the main information centres. Every day the SS women visit Canada to choose what they want. The blockowas and *kapos* have access as well. People chat and news gets round. Also, we have the right to go out; even if we're just going to the lavatory, we meet people. The runners don't mind doing errands if they're not compromising. One way or another, you can be quite sure that someone will come; indeed it's actually odd that no one's been yet."

"And they bring what you ask them?"

"Goods delivered to any address, very high class!" chortled Jenny.

"And if they were caught?" I insisted.

Florette flapped a fatalistic hand. "When they catch one, if it's nothing very much, they shave her; for something slightly more serious, it's the work detachment; very serious—jewelry for instance—Block Twenty-five."

"What a risk!"

Jenny shrugged her shoulders. "Well? You're running the same risk, but they're guzzling sardines in real oil like royalty!"

"Can one get food?" asked Clara.

"It's not the easiest thing."

"How do you pay them?"

"With bread. That's the universal currency."

"But I haven't got any," moaned Clara, chagrined, her imagined goodies fading.

"You'll have to economize on your ration."

"That's impossible!" Clara's tone rose to the tragic. "I haven't got enough as it is."

"Well, do you think we've got all that much?" Florette had lost patience. "That's how it is, and even princesses like you have to go without."

"All you need to do is to find yourself a man; here sausage replaces flowers," Jenny advised her.

Clara's approach often bore the hallmark of childish simplicity: "How do you get taken on in Canada?"

"You need to appeal to Frau Schmidt, to have strings pulled for you, or to be a prisoner with special status, to be well built, to have survived the quarantine block. Or of course," Florette concluded pointedly, "you could always go and see whether there wasn't a 'wanted' notice on the door."

Clara was unaffected by this mockery and I could see the workings of her mind like a clock without a case. She worried me. It was clear that her obesity made her morbidly hungry, just the kind of complaint least suited to these parts.

We were getting ready for work when, like the messenger of classical times, a runner pushed open the door and trumpeted from the threshold: "A parcel for everyone to be collected in Canada from Frau Lagerführerin Mandel!"

Tumultuous joy; our shouts reached Alma, who was about to set us to work; when she was informed, her rather flat chest swelled with pleasure. "Frau Mandel must have liked our little entertainment last night."

Entertainment was a pretty word for it! Alma beamed her satisfaction towards me with a smile. I interpreted it as: "You sang well, Mandel was pleased, she'll come back. I shall be well thought of." Magnanimous, our *kapo* gave us permission to collect our generous presents from the nearby Canada. We rushed out.

"Not more than four of you!" thundered Tchaikowska.

To me that didn't seem many to carry so many parcels. Anny, Big Irene, and Jenny gestured to me to go with them, when Tchaikowska corrected herself: "Only three. Marila will go with you."

"Fania, you go instead of me," suggested Anny.

I followed them. This Canada was nothing like the larger one, which was a sort of general store reigned over by Frau Schmidt. Here it was rather informal, a sort of corner shop as opposed to a big store. If we, the orchestra girls, were some of the camp's aristocrats, the girls in Canada were its millionaires, with all the outward signs of wealth. They bustled about, sorting and shelving an amazing array of merchandise spread out over tables or in piles on the ground: used cakes of soap which I imagined having been patiently, jealously dried out on top of some cupboard, eau de Cologne, toilet water, and luxury perfumes stood side by side amid a pile of brassieres. A heap of handkerchiefs lay alongside a stack of slippers, which were half tumbling over brushes and combs and an assortment of toothbrushes. Oh to steal one, any one, even that little one with the sparse, splayed, yellowing bristles . . . couldn't the person who'd brought it have afforded a new one?

The person who'd brought it . . . To think of her was already to move towards that woman's anguish, towards the fear that had seized her, that morning or that night, at the moment of entering the gas chamber with its shower fittings symmetrically aligned along the ceiling; she was holding her towel and her soap in her hand, perhaps one of these pieces here . . . To let oneself slide towards such thoughts meant becoming vulnerable to everything, to others and oneself; it meant squandering the strength you needed to enable you to hang on, until the end—theirs, not yours!

The girls from Canada were splendid, confident creatures with long, shiny, well-brushed hair and makeup; they laughed and smoked. In Birkenau bread was currency, but cigarettes were bullion; with cigarettes, almost everything was possible.

Little Irene addressed the blockowa, a Slovak who was staring at us with little superfluous affability: "Pani Marie, we've come to get the parcels for the music block."

In a tone implying that we would do well to get our rubbish out of here, she ordered: "Take all this." "All this" was forty-seven packages the size of two large matchboxes wrapped in pieces of crumpled paper. Typically, I'd imagined us laden with armfuls, needing a wheelbarrow to cart the treasure away!

The treasure. That indeed was the effect our parcels produced when we put them down on the table; the girls ran up and surrounded us, pushing and shoving. Excitement was at its height.

"Put it all in your boxes, *schnell, schnell!*" Tchaikowska bellowed.

Regina, Alma's mild orderly, butted in: "Quick, quick! Frau Alma is just coming into the music room."

To let her enter an empty music room would be a crime that would be promptly punished. In a few seconds, hearts beating, our minds all on the contents of the parcels, we were in our places.

In the evening there was a mad stampede towards the priceless packages; some sniffed them before opening them.

"What a stench! More remains from the dustbin!" Florette commented.

"Would you believe it, there's some sugar!" exclaimed Anny gleefully.

"Hey, girls, some sausage, real sausage from France!

All we need is some Camembert and a litre of red wine!'' cooed Jenny, tears in her eyes.

Clara dipped a gourmet's finger into the minuscule portion of rancid butter which greased the "parcel's" paper. "It really is butter! On bread, it'll be . . ."

She couldn't find the right word, and her voice trailed off as she savoured her rapture in advance. Everyone made an inventory, aloud or silently, of her stock, cast a nervous eye over her neighbour's. Next to me, our Greek accordionist, cautious as a cat, licked delicately at the soupspoonful of jam which lay beside four lumps of sugar, the round of sweating sausage, the bit of rancid butter, the six biscuits, and the bit of bread. This bread was a positive fortune for me: it represented the toothbrush I previously hadn't been able to afford. Marvellous, wonderful parcels! We laughed rapturously. Life was magnificent, we were eating. In the middle of this riotous dissipation Renate came in, very beautiful, cold and distant. Some girls had already started buttering their bread and spreading the jam on top. To eat three things at the same time was a luxury, madness.

"I see you're not in need of anything from me," Renate commented.

"On the contrary, it so happens that the two new girls need you."

Her sombre, distant expression showed so little interest that I wondered if she even saw me. I mentioned a toothbrush; she suggested toothpaste and soap.

"How much would all that come to?" I wasn't sure I could take on such onerous commitments.

Renate took her time, calculating carefully. I certainly wouldn't have enough to pay for the lot. I was tempted to cut out the toothpaste—one could always brush one's teeth with soap.

"Look, as you're new I'll make you a special offer."

This dealer's language didn't surprise me; on the contrary, it made our transaction seem more normal. At last she produced her figure: "One ration of bread and two of margarine. What with the cold, I'm being asked for more fats."

Nothing could have pleased me more. Clara gave me a black look as she saw me delve into our box and extract my two pats of margarine. Renate proceeded to explain the fluctuations of the rates:

"One can't keep the rates steady, they change all the time. It depends on how the consignments come in, on their freshness, on their country of origin—things from France are much sought after. The SS value them particularly and take everything, which sends prices up. Demand also has some effect. Do you understand?"

Perfectly—it was just like the black market. Amazing: we were talking just like shopkeepers.

"Will there be anything else? In the transport that's arrived today there are marvellous scents."

"No, I'm absolutely broke," I answered gravely.

Already I had stopped reacting as I would have done a few days ago, for it took me a few minutes to grasp how outrageous our conversation had been.

As she left, Renate stopped to pick up several further orders.

The girls, elbows on the table, ate slowly to spin out their pleasure, take stock of their boxes, cut a shaving of sausage, suck an atom of mouldy jam from their fingers and laugh, laugh like lunatics. I laughed with them, though somewhere within me I acknowledged the illogic of this scene.

Yet our reactions were understandable: death, life, tears, laughter, everything was multiplied, disproportionate, beyond the limits of the credible. All was madness.

Auschwitz: A Very Peaceful Little Town

THIS MORNING, the SS warden came in with long angry strides, her heels resounding on the concrete of our floor as on a pavement; Tchaikowska was so rigidly at attention that her great wobbling chest trembled like blancmange. One sneeze and our blockowa would send us to Block 25. Here, everyone wielded the power of life and death over you.

Planted in the middle of our room the warden, chin high, yelled as though she were receiving instructions straight from the Führer: "Jews to the right, Aryans to the left!"

Mechanically, passively, I was about to obey, when Clara grabbed me firmly and dragged me into the middle, between the two groups which were forming. With our yellow stars on our chests, we must have looked suspect standing there stolidly, isolated and incongruous.

Tchaikowska's fist was clenched so that the knuckles showed white.

"What do you think you're doing there?" bawled the SS woman.

"We're half-Jews, Frau Aufseherin."

"Was is das?"

Alma, surprised, translated the astonishing statement: *"Mischlinge!"* I wondered how this farce—I couldn't regard it as anything else—was going to end.

Yet it would have been surprising if our case had not been anticipated. I was to learn later that half-Jews were more rarely deported, particularly if their mothers, as in our case, were Aryan.

The little mud-coloured eyes of the warden, as lively and gentle as a concrete wall, settled on us incredulously; then she seemed to be going over the small print in her mind, but apparently her superiors hadn't expressed themselves on this subject, because, hands on hips, legs apart, she said flatly: "I see, you're half-Jews. Well, well, we'll have to see. I'll have you taken to the Auschwitz office of central administration. I'll get some light thrown on this matter. We'll sort it out!"

She departed with the same vengeful step.

Apparently indifferent, shrugging her shoulders, Alma went back into her room; our gesture certainly didn't warrant breaking the pattern of old habits. The Aryan Poles sniggered, Tchaikowska and Pani Founia gesticulated in our direction. I laughed openly, to be berated by Clara: "For goodness' sake, shut up; you are maddening, you're making the whole thing look ridiculous."

I answered solemnly: "What if they were to give us half-rations as a result?"

"You're completely mad," said Clara, irritated. "You don't take anything seriously."

The grinding voice of Rachela, a swarthy, angular girl, protested something in a medley of Polish and Yiddish which Ewa roughly translated for us. "Rachela says that you're wrong, that you need only a Jewish great-great-grandfather to be considered Jewish, and that all you'll get out of this is to end up you-know-where a bit more quickly."

"I don't think so," said Little Irene. "After all, it's the truth. They'll find out whether it makes any difference."

"They'll go out, see the town—the shop windows perhaps!" Anny said dreamily.

"Rachela says you won't be given a chance to tell your story, that they won't take you to Auschwitz but straight to the gas chambers."

Florette on the other hand thought perhaps we'd be lucky enough to be half-gassed.

Ewa summed up by saying she thought we were right. "After all, they should have their noses rubbed in the absurdity of their racism. And it's just possible that they might deal with you according to Aryan regulations."

The discussion was cut short because a new topic of interest presented itself: a runner announced the arrival of a musician from the men's orchestra. This was an important event. When he entered, kept at a distance by the furious invective of Tchaikowska, who forbad us to approach him or talk to him, we devoured him with our eyes. He was tall, a cap covering his shaven skull, thin as a post but decently dressed in a clean striped uniform. He looked embarrassed and asked for Alma. Tchaikowska bore down on him and swept him into the music room. Through the open door we followed all his movements with a liberal commentary:

"Look, he's getting the double bass."

"He's definitely a musician."

"He's Yvette's teacher."

Alma sent for Yvette and forbad us to enter the music room. A man in our block—times were indeed changing. We were expressly forbidden to go near them, and in any case their appearance was rare in the extreme. Sometimes we came across an electrician, a plumber, or a carpenter doing repairs. Jenny pointed her ferretlike snout and observed: "It's a real private lesson, if I were you I'd keep an eye on her; her teacher might still have just enough strength in his trousers to deflower her."

Rolling her *r*s ferociously Lili responded: "In Greece, where I come from, women have a sense of honour."

"Let's not have any of that stuff. French women are no more whores than you are. My man enjoyed me. It may make you laugh but that's how it was!''

We laughed in the obvious hope that *he* might hear us, that *he* would look round and see us, that we should exist for him. His presence was enough for us to utter all manner of absurdities, chattering hen parrots preening their feathers for a chance male who'd happened upon the hen house. Poor fellow, I thought as I watched him give Yvette her lesson; she was dwarfed by the large instrument. He had the precise movements of a professional. Ewa thought she recognized him as an excellent Polish concert cellist. He was young and his hands were tender and caressing with his instrument, as they would have been with a woman. Under Alma's severe eye, he placed Yvette's fingers on the strings, held up her wrist weighed down by the heavy bow.

We fell silent. We contemplated that male hand, that shoulder—bowed as it was—level with Yvette's head, and we daydreamed.

The next morning a Wehrmacht soldier came into our block. He had come to fetch Clara and me. The girls told us that it was a good sign it was not an SS man. Young, barely seventeen, rifle slung across his shoulder, he beckoned to us to follow him. And what if despite everything he were taking us to the gas chambers? Tchaikowska ordered us to put a nameless striped garment, a sort of dustcoat, over our clothes. The girls from our little group, Ewa, the two Irenes, Anny, Florette, and Jenny, smiled at us, not daring to embrace us. The Poles clucked, and I wondered which of their distinctive qualities was the more grievous, their stupidity or their spite.

We set off on foot. Well-shod, warmly dressed, we emerged from the camp like smartly turned-out princesses, or so we thought. It was good to walk along a road. Under a stiff layer of snow, I saw a bit of yellowed grass: ''Look, Clara, grass! It still exists.''

I was about to stop, but the sight of our guard pre-

vented me. He was so young that he shouldn't have been
hardened yet, unless of course he was all the more
fanatical because of it, but his eyes, which had a fine
golden look to them, glinted coldly when they came to
rest on us, as empty as the gaze of the others, all the
others.

What was marvellous was that, as we moved away
from Birkenau, the frightful smell of burnt flesh which
always filled our nostrils faded, giving way to smells of
life. It was an easy two miles to Auschwitz, which
seemed to be a peaceful little town. Its Polish roofs,
rather flat and snow-covered, stood out clearly against
the cold, pale winter sky.

"Fania! Houses—chimneys with smoke."

It was true. This smoke was that of people who were
alive, warming themselves, preparing food; it was light,
blue and yellow, so different from that which, black as
soot and thick as tar, billowed from our crematoria.

People were going quietly about their business; the
shops had windows even if there was not much in them.
We passed a few people, women, little old ladies trotting
along, elderly men. Not a single young person of either
sex. Where were they? At the war? It was a silent town;
the snow we sank into muffled all noise. As we passed,
no one turned round, no one vouchsafed us a look.
There was neither curiosity nor hostility; we didn't exist.
When would we cease to be nothing?

These people, doing normal things, going in and out
of their houses, these women doing their shopping,
holding young children with apple-red cheeks, did they
know that they were happy? Did they know that it was
marvellous to see them, that for us they represented
life? Why did they begrudge us a look? They couldn't
fail to notice us, to know where we came from; our
striped garb, the scarfs hiding our shaven heads, our
thinness betrayed our origins. When they went out
walking, they were not forbidden to pass by the camp of
Birkenau, whose sinister appearance hardly concealed

its function. Did they think that those five chimneys, with their sickening smoke, were for the central heating? What exactly was I asking for? That that little town of five or six thousand inhabitants should revolt, that its Germanic population, resettled there since the German victory, should rise up and liberate the camp? Why should they have felt responsible for us? A sudden surge of violence sent the blood into my head: they were all responsible! All men were. The indifference of a single one was our death sentence.

I stared at them intensely. I didn't want to forget their ratlike faces. They didn't see us. How convenient! They didn't see our striped clothes any more than they saw the detachments of "moslems" who wandered haggard through their peaceful little town, surrounded by SS and dogs. I was sure that later, after the war, those people would say that they "didn't know," and they would be believed.

Clara took my arm. "You are looking glum. Take advantage of our walk, it's marvellous to be here. Our guard isn't bad; he's leaving us be. It's better than being cooped up in the block."

She was right. One had to savour the fleeting moment, get the maximum pleasure from it.

"Why didn't they question us at the camp?"

"I imagine our case doesn't concern them, it must be a matter of civil administration."

We stopped in front of a wooden hut, presumably an annex of the general administration building. We went up three steps and our soldier stood aside to let us pass. This politeness was unexpected. What wasn't, though, was to find ourselves face to face with an enormous portrait of Hitler.

The room was furnished as an office, and behind a big table was an SS man, big, fat and dirty. Beside him was a French prisoner of war, a big red *F* painted on his old uniform jacket. Our hearts beat faster. He was par-

ticularly nondescript, but to us he was a living wonder.
We were made to sit down, some way from the table,
and the interrogation began. The German did the
questioning and the Frenchman translated:

"Name of your mother?"

"Bernier, Marie."

"Nationality?"

"Aryan Frenchwoman."

"Religion?"

"Catholic."

"Father's name?"

"Goldstein, French Jew."

"Nein," grumbled the SS.

I had to answer one question at a time. We began
again.

"What was his job?"

"Engineer."

"Where?"

"He died some time ago."

He shook his head; it must have annoyed him to think
that nature was sometimes allowed to take its course.

"Have you any sisters?"

"No."

"Brothers?"

I had two brothers whom I adored; the elder was in
America, the younger in the Resistance. Brightly,
firmly, I lied:

"I'm an only child."

Now we began on the rest of my family, back into the
mists of time. Having negotiated the problem of my
parents, I could cope with that of grandparents with
ease and felt that previous generations could be dis-
pensed with. "I don't know anything about their
origins."

My breeziness astounded the Frenchman. He translated my answers slowly to the fat white worm of an SS
man, who, clutching his sputtering penholder, tran-

scribed them into German so painfully that I nudged Clara's elbow, wondering whether he really knew how to write.

Clara knew her family tree to perfection, though she gave a noticeable and understandable bias to the Catholic side, which left our interpreter and our laborious scribe quite indifferent. While the SS continued to scratch away and shuffle his papers, the Frenchman asked us why we had come here.

"So that you should know that we're half-Jews."

"What can it matter what you are, what good can it do you?"

"It might save us the trip to the 'little works.' "

"What?" he asked, alarmed.

"You know, the little factory that processes you into smoke."

He turned green. "That's enough. You know that you're not supposed to know anything about that. None of you must know. Don't even talk about it. It doesn't exist."

"The corpses from the crematoria died natural deaths, did they," I sniggered, "from hunger, for instance? No one is killed, are they? They must think we're blind and mad."

He paused and didn't dare raise his voice: "That's enough! I don't want any trouble!"

I didn't sympathize with his fear. "That imbecile beside you doesn't understand anything," I hissed.

"How do you know?"

"Look at him; if he has such trouble writing, I'd be very surprised if he knew French."

"You don't know them. There may be someone listening behind the door. The guard might speak our language. I've every intention of getting back to my wife and children, personally."

"And we've every intention of staying alive!"

With thick stubby fingers the SS man fingered the papers he'd just filled up, then raised heavy lids and spat out a few words to our interpreter, who translated:

"You're to take off part of your star, just keep the part that says *F.*"

Clara couldn't move fast enough to take advantage of this delightfully ironical authorization: the star of David thus dismantled, all we had left was a yellow triangle with an *F.* We really were half-Jews. The administration had arranged for everything!

His task over, without a look, the SS ordered us out.

Our return journey was somewhat slow and painful. We were out of practice for walking and due to three months of undernourishment we were exhausted by the time we got back to the block.

We had a bizarre reception. As we entered girls moved, groups formed, as in a play. Florette, Anny, the two Irenes, Ewa, Jenny, the little Greeks Yvette and Lili, curious and well-intentioned, questioned us. What was Auschwitz like? What about the people? Were there children in the streets, things in the shops? Where had we gone? What had they asked us?

"Well, well, you really are halves," exclaimed Jenny, pointing at our chests.

This gesture attracted the attention of the others. The Aryan Poles sniggered, Founia slapped her thighs. We were certainly providing some merriment. Tchaikowska, fingers of her right hand imitating scissors, cut her left index finger; then the imaginary scissors fell to the floor and the mime became obscene. Clustered around those two horrors, Irena opened a black mouth with yellow stubs, Kaja crushed the thin Marisha with her bulk, Wisha, holding Zocha by the shoulders and Marila by the waist, smiled foxily—a charming picture! Only Halina's face remained expressionless. The Poles weren't satisfied with laughter, they proceeded to vituperation. In execrable French Danda, waving huge fists that could have sent a healthy bullock to its knees, expressed the group opinion: "You filth, you ashamed of being Jews. But you will be Jews,

never you Aryan, you afraid, so you deny parents.
Judas!''

This last insult, oddly, seemed to be particularly
appreciated by the Polish Jews, Rachela and Masha,
and even by the only Czech, Margot, who was intelligent and well-educated.

"You've behaved like dirty goyim, that's what,''
Rachela lectured us. "You shouldn't have said you
weren't Jewish, you've dishonoured the Jews in your
families. They spit on you and curse you through us!''

So now Clara and I were caught between two groups,
the neutral and the others—two accused facing a
bawling mass. How could one blame them? All the
hatred of their masters accumulated month after
month, drawn from those days, hours, and minutes
during which they'd undergone the worst humiliations
in silence, now rose from within them and poured itself
over us; we had become a pretext, we had enabled them
to explode openly, virtuously. Craning their necks, vin-
dictive as a gaggle of geese, twelve German Jews rose up
against us: Helga, the brutal, vulgar percussion player;
Karla, the fat round little thing who played the pipes;
Sylvia, only fifteen and clay in the others' hands; Lotte,
the guitarist, who might have been less aggressive had
she been prettier; the other Lotte, whose stupidity was
her only excuse; Frau Kröner, the ultra-timorous; and
the acrimonious Ruth, perhaps the worst of all. Even
the meek, passive ones were in the ranks: Elsa, a
violinist who had been going into the leather trade;
Regina, Alma's "chambermaid''; Julie the silent. At
their head, leading the attack, were Rachela and Hilde,
the Zionist, scorn blazing from her lovely inspired black
eyes. "You've allowed the star of David to be cut in
two. It's not you who have denied us, but we who reject
you . . .''

She sought her words carefully, mingling French and
German; she rose to biblical heights, involving our

posterity down to the seventh generation. I couldn't take this diatribe seriously. It all seemed ridiculous, disproportionate, unimportant. It was like a child's theatre, with puppets gesticulating from the wings of a stage occupied by a tragedy. They bored me, I felt like turning my back on them and was just about to do so when I heard Clara's confident, piping voice:

"I didn't expect this sort of reaction. You're just jealous. There's no reason why we shouldn't have told the truth, I can't see what it matters to you . . . If we can avoid the gas chambers, we'd be wrong not to do so."

Her voice rose in a crescendo, the others answered back violently. Alone, as was their custom, the Russians remained outside the debate. The more moderate, like the Greek Jews, Julie and Lili, whom Yvette was bound to follow, called us "poor idiots." The others ended their lecture calling us "liars."

What had truth to do with it? Had we not the right to cut ourselves off as much as possible from the "chosen race" when faced with the other, the "master race"? It would be afterwards, if there were to be an afterwards, that we would have to fight, to vindicate our portion of Judaism. In the name of which virtues should we not have seized this opportunity if it existed?

I was silent but, as they say in Russian, I'd roll that round my little finger, I wouldn't forget.

There was an abrupt drop in pitch; alerted by our uproar, Alma had come in and was staring at us coldly.

"You're back?"

Did she think we wouldn't be?

"Are you satisfied?"

Her ironic gaze lingered over our unusual star. Without a word, she turned smartly and went back into her room. I felt I was blushing, and that struck me as the most absurd thing of all. Behind me, I heard the discussion being endlessly continued around our squat black stove:

"It's ridiculous to accuse us of betraying the Jews; since we're half and half, we're just as much betraying the Catholics," reasoned Clara.

"Typical half-caste dilemma," pontificated Little Irene.

I considered that the whole pathetic business was being paid too much attention. Personally I'd made my decision and I calmly sewed my second triangle back on.

"Why are you doing that?" asked Clara nervously.

"I don't know, but I am."

And indeed I didn't know; but something drove me to that gesture, the same something, in all probability, which also led me to tell the police my real identity, preferring to die under my father's name rather than under an assumed one.

A few moments later, grumbling: "Your absurd gesture is forcing me to do the same. I could hardly stick it out on my own!" Clara also reconstituted her star of David. A curious star, that one, whose "magic" virtues have earned it the name "David's shield."

The Day of Rest

THAT SATURDAY STARTED BADLY. It was very cold outside; the windows were frosted over despite our stove. Almost all of us had been troubled by nightmares or desperate insomnia. Since yesterday, the deportees had been at work finishing the railway which would enable the transports to come right into the camp about fifty yards from our block, between the men's camps and our own. The little station of Auschwitz would become an ordinary station once again. This would put an end to transport by truck, which used up too much fuel.

Florette slept on and I felt sorry for her; she had told me that her sleep was peopled with fairy-tale dreams and princes charming. What a marvellous escape. Each morning it was the same struggle: she clung grimly to her refuge. I shook her but she didn't even groan; she was totally oblivious.

"Wake her, or Tchaikowska will be down on her like a ton of bricks!" Ewa warned me.

Too late. Pani Tchaikowska, shouting *"Aufsteben!"*—Up!—fit to snap her vocal cords, made her morning entrance, accompanied by the inevitable Pani Founia. With head raised—Florette slept on the third tier—Pani Founia belted out her repertoire of Polish insults. To no effect. Florette slumbered on. She slept on her stomach, head prudently in her arms so that her ears were blocked. Pani Founia went off promising darkly that this matter would be taken care of by higher authorities. I had no chance to climb up and shake the dogged sleeper one last time.

"Achtung! Zum Appell! Fünf zu fünf!" Accompanied by angelic-faced Irma Grese, Frau Drexler, the chief inspector, entered, her gunner's gait particularly martial this morning. She first cast her eye upon the empty beds, with their impeccable hospital corners. She froze in front of Florette, the horizontal line of her mouth shrinking still further; with her leather-gloved hand, she flicked off the cover. Innocent, childlike, a bare foot appeared. She seized it: Florette's body seemed to become dislocated, like a floppy puppet's, her head seemed almost to shatter on the concrete. My heart beat in my throat. Florette lay stretched out on the floor, her nightdress raised to reveal thin thighs, pitiful little flabby buttocks. She stirred, sat up, then got up and stood there, in her nightdress (which was expressly forbidden), eyes wandering dazedly, immobilized in an approximate position of attention.

The look of lofty disdain which Drexler cast the poor girl teetering in front of her filled me with rage. Beside her, Grese of the corn-coloured plaits smiled vaguely. Her pure, innocent eyes settled curiously on Florette, her slim black riding whip tapping her leather boot imperceptibly. She couldn't have been more than twenty. Numerous stories were told about her, all demonstrating her unusually meticulous ferocity. The women had learned to dread the penalty of her attentions, the least of which meant a whiplash on the nipple. She was said to be sensitive to feminine charms, and Florette, something of a tomboy with astounding green eyes, was very beautiful. That would be the last straw. My imagination ran riot. The wardens didn't even honour the poor girl with an insult. They passed by hurriedly, other roll calls awaited them.

After their departure, Alma marched coldly up to Florette to deliver her stinging slaps on both cheeks. Her

gesture disgusted me, my constrained silence a measure
of my powerlessness. As a punishment, she was ordered
to wash out the music room. Hardly had Alma turned
her back than Florette broke into furious curses, and on
this occasion I approved. Then she sank down, collapsing at the foot of the bedpost, sobbing desperately:
"Papa, mama . . . mama . . ." I bent down and took her
in my arms.

"Come on, Florette, stop that. You know you've got
to get up. You put yourself in the wrong and those
bitches take advantage of it. Tomorrow I'll get you out
of bed, I'll make it for you . . ."

She wept furiously: "No, you won't and I won't
either. They make me sick!"

The calm but authoritative voice of Little Irene cut
short the crisis. "That's enough of that. Get dressed,
make your bed, you won't have time to drink your coffee. The room must be washed before the rehearsal. I
can't imagine what pleasure it gives you constantly to
create problems for yourself like this!"

Wonderfully calmed and crestfallen, Florette agreed.
"You're right, I won't let it happen again."

Little Irene was the only one who had this power over
her. Some minutes later, on her knees, cloth in hand,
Florette was rapidly washing the floor of the music
room and complaining, "Those cows, those filthy
cows!"

"You see," observed Little Irene to me, "she's incorrigible."

"It's true, she's unbearable. Her behaviour will land
us all in trouble," chipped in Clara acrimoniously.

The mild, doll-faced Clara who had huddled against
me in the quarantine block had changed beyond
recognition. These wolves were turning her into a
hyena.

"Fania!" She was looking at me, her eyes bright with
astonishment.

"What?"

"Fania, your hair . . ."

"What about it?"

"It's growing again, but it's white. All white."

Outside, the roll call had been interminable. I thought of the girls out there dying of cold. As the strings tended to snap and as the orchestra was prevented from playing by frozen fingers, we were temporarily exempted from parades, but the others, the work detachments, went out. Those poor creatures, haggard, fleshless, dirty, dragging the dogged remaining flicker of life within them around, those women transformed into frightened, breathless little animals, more dead than alive—for us they were the "others." An awful term. I thought of them constantly, their existence obsessed me, seemed to me to deprive me of the right to be warm, clean, and comfortably dressed. The only thing I had in common with them was hunger, and even then I hadn't seen any moslems in the music block; we definitely had a stronger grip on life than they did.

I'd hardly been here ten days; sometimes it felt like a year and sometimes an hour. My experience was not sufficient to answer the questions I perpetually asked myself. Our relationships with the "others" worried and disturbed me. Little Irene told me she'd tried to contact the camp Resistance and failed; men and women alike had wrong ideas about the "orchestra girls," they were suspicious of us. Contact between us was at best sporadic. However, one of these women did come to see us, briefly. To sit on a chair, to be beside a stove was to risk punishment, or indeed death. It was through her that we learned of their working life:

"The SS make us build houses, we have to pile stones one on top of the other; they're covered with ice, they burn our hands. When they don't like what we've built, we have to climb on our wall and throw down the blocks we've just built up with such difficulty. Other prisoners who bring the blocks to the wall are working below; as they're forbidden to move, we try to throw the stones as far as possible, but some of us can hardly lift them, and yesterday three were killed by stones falling on their heads. Our corporal laughed. He said: '*Ach,* these *Jüdinnen* are no good for manual labour, they're so clumsy they kill their own friends . . .' ''

She stretched her arms out towards us, mere bones wrapped in a loose covering of cracked, wrinkled skin.

No wonder they hated us.

The general atmosphere was even more gloomy since a *Blocksperre* had just been announced.

"Any news of Marta?"

It sounded an insignificant question; there was a pause, then Ewa said: "Alma probably knows."

I looked forward eagerly to the return of this Marta, our only cellist, whom I'd never seen. With her the music would improve, and thus it seemed to me that we would be more protected, less exposed to the whims of our masters. Had Alma concerned herself with the matter at all? And who would dare to ask Alma these questions? It was Florette who responded: "If we relied on her, we'd all croak!"

Her peevishness annoyed me. "You're wrong," I butted in. "I always have to do a cello part for every new arrangement, as though she knew that Marta would be back any minute."

"I don't believe it," Florette persisted. "Her sister Renate never comes to see us anymore, that's not a good sign; and the Revier isn't a holiday home, it's more of an anteroom to Block Twenty-five!"

"Well, you got out of it."

"I was lucky, but I couldn't have hung on another forty-eight hours. Survivors are very rare. When the doctor said that I had an infection and she'd keep me there, Tchaikowska, who'd brought me in, positively gurgled with glee and was already paying her last respects; she was sure she'd never see me again. I stayed there six weeks. It was so ghastly that I'd rather die than go back there: no medicines, no care of any sort, no food. The infirmary is a pool for selections, the SS draw on it every day. Death cures all ills, after all.''

"Still," said Jenny, "without Marta the orchestra does limp rather, and here limping's not healthy!''

"She's been away three weeks already,'' Ewa said, trying to calm the situation, "and our double bass player means we can afford to wait.''

"Double bass playing in five lessons! That's all Yvette's had,'' Jenny sneered, "and she's never touched a string before in her life. You can't run up a concert in a matter of hours.''

Jenny's street-corner banter often made us laugh, but now her spiteful pessimism was exasperating. At the word "double bass" Yvette's elder sister looked up: "Are you saying my sister doesn't play well?''

"Jenny's being unfair,'' I intervened. "It takes years to make a good double bass player. Yvette doesn't do too badly. All we expect from her is some simple accompaniment.''

"I can well do without your views,'' Jenny rounded on me cantankerously. "First, what do you know about it? If your Kraut mate Mandel doesn't like your so-called simple accompaniment, she'll send us all to take a death shower.''

Not to please—that was what we all feared. Faces turned towards Yvette. Lili planted herself protectively in front of her sister. Hands on hips that still had some semblance of a curve, she was trying desperately to adopt a dignified posture, an attempt annoyingly counteracted by her small figure and round, moonlike face. With *r*s like drum rolls, she burst out: "You can't put the blame on Yvette. I'll protect my little sister from your poisonous jealousy.''

"Cut that out,'' interrupted Jenny. "You're swelling that brat's head with your rubbish. Don't do this, don't do that—you make her sick and us too.''

Lili was almost speechless with indignation but clung to her right of *mater familiae*; she explained to us that she alone, as a former music teacher, was capable of judging her sister's potential, and that it would be a "*grrr*eat" disaster if Yvette (as a result of our collective stupidity) wound up in the gas chamber because, as she claimed, "our family would thus lose its finest light."

"Don't worry, with you it will keep its greatest blight," said Jenny.

In the face of her opprobrium we collapsed into laughter, schoolgirls giggling in the midst of death.

Four in the morning, one of the worst times to wake up—the mind a prey to nothing but destructive thoughts. Our stove, now cool and bursting with ashes, no longer had anything friendly about it. I was half asleep when a caterwauling, followed by a sort of heavy snore, cut across the stillness: Yvette, upset by Jenny's sarcasm and her sister's reproaches, was practising the double bass. I hadn't time to stop her before an "oooh" of horror rose from the music room. I leapt down to find Yvette in front of the double bass case, sobbing bitterly. "My God! Whose trick was this?"

The front of the case was disgorging an enormous quantity of used sanitary napkins. We were helpless with laughter at the absurdity of the thing; Pani Founia, looking more grotesque than ever, stared at us uncomprehendingly, and Tchaikowska belted out her usual insults. Alma emerged from her room scandalized that we should have dared to make such a noise. She was even more scandalized on seeing the unlovely cause of the uproar. "*Ach! Schwein, Schwein*, where does the rubbish come from?"

Furious, she expressed doubt as to our mental health, accused us of having no sense of honour; she was within inches of saying that we were unworthy of the camp that housed us!

"Throw it all away immediately," she flung out in the

direction of Tchaikowska, whose gaze was seeking a victim on whom the order could rebound. It was Yvette.

"You found it all, you can remove it."

This form of justice relieved her. Dignified, Alma withdrew, and Tchaikowska, followed by Founia, did the same.

"Those napkins must have been 'organized,' " observed Florette. "I can't believe any of us still has periods."

All eyes turned towards Lili, who, since she hated taking a shower, perpetually excused herself by saying, "I can't have a shower, I've got my per*rr*iod . . ." which made the Poles say: "Of course she's dirty, she's a Yid."

Little Irene shrugged her shoulders. It was beyond belief: not only would Lili never have played such an unpleasant trick on her sister, but it was quite clear that she was lying—she didn't have periods any more than we did. She just didn't like water.

So the centre of interest moved off, the search for the culprit had become unimportant: simply, everyone envied her. It could only be a Russian or a Pole, since some of them still did have their periods. Florette and Jenny claimed that they put something in our soup, but there was no need for that; the trauma we'd undergone and our physiological wretchedness were quite enough to bring it about. It was just as well, too, because at the beginning, for those who did have their periods, the situation was extremely awkward: nothing to wash themselves with, nothing to wear. The blood ran down their thighs and dripped from between their legs. Always sticklers for cleanliness, the blockowas struck them, forced them to wipe up the stains. And yet at this moment everyone envied the unclean unknown, and Margot, the Czech girl, summed up the general feeling: "I'd like to be in her place."

"It's upsetting not to go through those unclean

periods," Hilde reflected. "You begin to feel like an old woman."

Timidly, Big Irene asked: "And what if they never come back afterwards?"

At her words a ripple of horror swept over us. Those who didn't understand French asked to have the sentence translated. Catholics crossed themselves, others recited the Shema; everyone tried to exorcise this curse the Germans were holding over us: sterility.

How could one sleep after that? Our giggles turned to silence now that the untold privilege of a fruitful womb seemed threatened. Would those who ever got out of here have to pay for the misery of having been here at all by the hidden mutilation of no longer being a woman? None of us had sufficient medical knowledge to be able to say anything helpful about the matter. So we lay awake, this fear lodged within us.

The following day I got three new copyists: one of the German Jews, Elsa, a rather nice girl with red hair, a little freckled face, and dark eyes; and two of the Russians: Alla, aged twenty-two, who always averted her tawny gaze, though whether through shyness or distrust it wasn't clear; and Sonia, one of the special-status prisoners—not exactly a certificate of excellence. She was a Ukrainian, a solid well-covered girl, also not a point in her favour; but she was meek and unassuming and, much more important from my point of view, a good musician. Alla and Sonia were our pianists but now they had no instrument; some days after my arrival, soldiers had removed our magnificent Bechstein, probably originally taken from a Jewish household, to take it to the mess of the camp's valorous officers. I was very sad about that; I'd hardly had any time to profit from it! But on the few occasions I'd laid my hands on the keys, I'd thought of the person whose hands must have been there before mine: a concert pianist, child prodigy, rich man's son?

Alma came towards me smiling: "That's good, you'll be able to do us some new arrangements." Without waiting for my acquiescence, she turned back to her musicians: "Tomorrow there's a concert, and I want it to be im-pec-cable. I've put *Madame Butterfly* on the programme and we'll rehearse it now."

Wrong notes seared painfully through my skull. Alma swore: *Blöde Ganz! Blöde Kuh! Scheiss Kopf!* Her repertoire of insults poured out effortlessly, rhythmically. "Fania, come up here a moment. Where exactly is the wrong note?"

The musicians carried on. Standing behind Alma, I followed the score as it should be followed, which was something Alma didn't know how to do: vertically, from top to bottom, with a single glance taking in all the instruments. Then I checked every part. Most of my copyists transcribed badly, since they didn't know music and reproduced what they saw as mere dots on or between two lines, as they thought fit. So I corrected, explained, went to sit down again, and launched once more into Peter Kreuder, whose "Twelve Minutes" I had to reorchestrate with the help of the piano version, an adorable potpourri, particularly light and tuneful. It was rather urgent, as Ewa, Lotte, Clara, and I had to sing it at an imminent concert. Just at the moment when, once again, the tune was running in my head, everything started up once more. Alma would call me, lose her temper, or shout: "You've played it before, you ought to know it!" Then once again we would be treated to the list of despised animals: pigs, cows, and enough shitheads to befoul the globe. Baton blows rained down on guilty fingers, and it was Jenny who received the slap which Alma had been itching to deliver for some time now. As if swept off her feet by some devouring passion, Alma very soon lost her middle-class poise. I found it hard to get used to this method of punishing her players; here in the camp it seemed particularly displeasing.

A moment of calm again; I returned to my "Twelve Minutes," to escape into the wonderful, enchanted realm of music. Each section unfolded flexibly within me, one bar leading marvellously to the next. My hand transcribed rapidly; I loved this aerial, party music.

Outside, whistles blew, announcing the end of a selection. The *Blocksperre* was lifted.

A runner opened the door: "*Achtung*. Quickly. Herr Kommandant Kramer is coming!"

Alma blanched, stiffened. It was incredible; he wasn't even in the room and she was already standing to attention. Tchaikowska and Founia bawled frantically: Were we worthy to be in the presence of the master? Could anything in our appearance offend him? Was the room clean? And us? I half expected to have to show my hands and be told to go and wash.

Josef Kramer was the commandant of the camp of Birkenau; the face he showed when he came to listen to the orchestra was certainly not that known to the other men and women of the camp. The only one who had said anything about him at all was Ewa: he loved music, and it was he, with Mandel, who kept us alive; we depended on him. He always behaved correctly with us, but a Polish comrade who worked in the infirmary had told Ewa that he was not immune to the sort of collective hysteria that seized the SS when they loaded their trucks for the crematoria. On occasion he could be as wild as the rest of them, not hesitating to shatter a woman's skull with a blow of his club.

So this was the brute—I couldn't think of him as a man—who was about to make his entrance. I was curious to see him. I would have liked to talk with him, to understand. To understand—it was a mania with me. I continued to believe that there was something to understand, that this desire for extermination was motivated by reasons which simply escaped me. One didn't organize death for death's sake; there must have been another purpose, but what? Those men who, in defiance of all human laws, obeyed those perpetrators of monstrous genocide, behind what were they taking refuge so as to live with themselves? Of course I knew that they'd been taught that we, the Jews, were an inferior race, that morally and intellectually we were compared to a "beast driven by ungovernable passions, with an unappeasable desire for destruction and characterized by utter vulgarity," that the behaviour of the SS was ruled by the terrible phrase: "Woe to those who forget that everything that resembles a human being is not necessarily a human being." But for me, until my arrival here, despite the arrests made in Paris, these words were just theories; they didn't correspond to any reality. Now I asked myself: How could men and women actually apply it so implacably?

Petrified into an impressive position of attention, we awaited Kramer; he entered, two SS men in his train. This man was a force to be reckoned with; so stocky that his head seemed set directly on his blacksmith's body, he gave off a positively disturbing sense of power. His ears were huge; the cloth of his uniform was stretched taut over his broad chest, which bulged like a breastplate. He had the heavy yet supple tread of an animal; his presence was crushing.

He walked towards the seat prepared for him, sat down, took off his cap, and put it beside him. His chestnut hair was cut extremely short, accentuating the foursquare look of his solid head. Satisfied, he beamed from his chair and graciously addressed us: "Now, a moment's respite for all of us. We are going to hear some music."

Still at attention, the correct position for speaking to an officer, Alma asked nervously what Herr Langerführer would like to hear.

"Schumann's *Reverie*." Feelingly, he added that it

was a "marvellous, heart-rending" piece. Ewa, translating under her breath for my benefit, added: "Oh, so he's got a heart then?"

The violins seized the tune; it rose soft and distant, then broadened and expanded its elusive melancholy. The commandant had closed his eyes, letting the music wash over him. From the table behind which I was writing I could observe him without danger. What a delight to see him relax, leave all thoughts of his arduous work behind him. Big Irene bent her cheek, hollow but still pleasing in outline, to her violin and attacked her solo with talent. This was the supreme moment: the melancholy attained a melting sweetness which must have wreaked havoc with Kramer's tender heart. A few beats before the piece died away, slowly, as if regretfully, Herr Kramer raised his darkened eyelids; I noted in wonder that his codlike gaze was moist with tears. He had delivered himself up to his emotions and was allowing tears as precious as pearls to roll down his carefully shaven cheeks. What would the friends of the woman with the shattered head have thought?

Satisfied, he had relieved himself of his "selection" by listening to music as others might do by masturbating. Relaxed, the Lagerführer shook his head and expressed his pleasure to Alma: "How beautiful, how moving!"

Then his expression changed, his eyes dulled: he saw us. Lice exist only to be exterminated. He pointed to me: "What does she do?"

Alma explained to him that I sang.

"What?"

"Madame Butterfly."

I reflected that when I came back I wouldn't be able to listen to a single bar of Puccini's work.

He nodded. "Let her sing it."

I was going to sing; it was a simple, normal action. It was also simple and normal that I should cast an eye over my audience. I saw Kramer and my heart began to beat violently; my hands, normally perfectly dry, were damp now. It wasn't stage fright, the stakes were no higher than usual: it was quite as dangerous to comport oneself in such a way as to displease a warden as to embark on the great aria from *Butterfly* before the camp commandant. It wasn't that. For me, singing was a free act, and I was not free; it was above all a way of giving pleasure, giving love, and I felt a frantic desire to see those three SS men stuck like pigs, right here, at my feet.

Standing in front of those men with their buttocks spread out over their chairs, with that parody of an orchestra behind me, I felt as though I were living through one of those nightmares in which you want to cry out and can't. That cry would save your life, enable you to escape from the attendant horrors, and yet you lie there open-mouthed with no life-saving sound emerging. The kitchen lamp hanging at the end of its piece of wire had little in common with the warmth of a spotlight; and the grey walls with their ill-joined planks bore no relation to the soft gloom of a theatre with its suggestion of gold and velvet. Suddenly I had a vision of the nightclubs where I used to sing. Admittedly they were crammed with Germans, a positive mass of grey-green, but I was there of my own accord, willingly; singing was a cover, I was there only to deceive the better.

But that was in another country. Now our orchestra set to, and I began the countdown: three, two, one . . . Stage habits are stronger than anguish, and I sang, simultaneously freed and vanquished. No one would ever know how I struggled during those seconds. Certainly not Kramer, in whom I produced neither tears nor smiles. Turning towards Alma, he simply said, *"Ja, gut."* Then, with the same delicacy he'd shown me, he pointed to Clara: "And her?"

"She sings too, Herr Kommandant."

Relieved, sweating, I returned to my place behind the table, and Clara went forward; everything in her attitude proclaimed her pride, her joy at singing in front of the commandant. Was she to be envied or pitied? She sang "The Nightingale" by Alabieff in Italian; it was perfectly suited to her voice.

After having talked to Alma, who seemed satisfied, Kramer pointed to Flora, our Dutch accordionist, a large lumpy girl who carried her erstwhile fat in rolls of quaking flesh. His verdict, which Florette translated to me between her teeth, was alarming: "She's not a very good musician, she shouldn't be here."

Living with fear hooked into our deepest being, we thought we were prepared for a sentence like that. We were wrong: we reeled.

"She can come and work for us; my wife needs a nurse for our daughter."

Then he left his chair and padded towards my table like a mechanical bear; the whole room froze. Alma and her girls were standing, Tchaikowska, Marila, and Pani Founia were in the doorway at attention. I waited, seated in front of my scores, remaining seated; I put the right granted to our table to maximum use. They all held their breath. Beside me, Kramer examined my work. His thigh almost touched my shoulder; I could feel its warmth. He seemed immense; he leant over me, almost crushing me with the sheer volume of his flesh. I felt a violent desire to push him away so that I could breathe. His voice was loud and resonant. *"Was fehlt euch?"*

I understood but didn't answer. He repeated his question and Ewa translated: "He's asking you if there's anything you need."

"Ja, Herr Kommandant, this . . ."

I handed him a pencil: not just any pencil but the one marked MADE IN ENGLAND. I might as well be hung for a sheep as a lamb. He took it and looked at it, his sea-green eyes impassive. Then he gave it back and turned away, as Ewa translated his reply: "He says you'll get your pencils."

Now he was talking briefly with Alma, who was smiling at him. I was beginning to find her obsequiousness with this most monstrous of SS chiefs quite unbearable. At last she escorted the revered visitor to the door and he went out, followed by the two faceless officers who had remained silent throughout.

There was a general sigh of relief. The girls swarmed round me. When I informed them of my pencil gesture, Florette burst out: "Are you quite mad?"

The usual insults followed. "That's provocation," growled Clara. One of the Poles seized the scandalous object and held it aloft: "Look what she dared to give the commandant."

"You're completely mad!" Florette shrieked. "I hope you realize that he'll shove us in the gas chambers."

They were verging on the hysterical; there was hatred in their eyes. "You have no right to risk our lives."

They were really too stupid.

"Look, that'll do!" I burst out. "We'll end up there sooner or later in any case, and at least we'll have done it in style! Personally I find it very amusing to have put 'Made in England' under his nose. If we're going to be gassed, we might as well go smiling."

Only Ewa was amused, and she wisely pointed out: "Luckily for you he hasn't the wit to understand."

"It's Sunday, we're on concert duty. We'll have to get all tarted up," Jenny explained to me. "They don't let up, even on Sundays."

Everyone had a childhood Sunday in her memory to moisten her eyes. There was irony in Ewa's soft voice: "And on the seventh day, God rested . . ."

"While we're going to have to act the fool for the SS," groaned Florette. My stockings were torn; I sat there worriedly, a finger stuck in a hole in mid-calf. The possibility of mending it seemed remote. Wool, cotton, needle? Everything had to be bought, and I hadn't any bread. You could borrow a needleful of thread, but you had to wait your turn. I'd hardly thanked Anny, who'd just helped me out with one problem, when another arose. The washing I'd done yesterday in our little basin—I'd been waiting my turn for three days—wasn't dry yet. I wasn't the only one; at least a dozen of us were in the same situation, and we were resigned. "We'll play with nothing on under our dresses," concluded Little Irene. Mercifully the concert wasn't in the open air.

Our shoes needed cleaning and we rubbed them vigorously as best we could, with paper or a bit of rag. Some girls actually stole bits of my music paper despite my shrieks. They were willing to put up with any number of inconveniences to have clean shoes. The first thing Alma scrutinized was not our faces or our clothes, but our shoes: *Schuhe putzen*—Clean your shoes—was a well-known refrain, and the rule was that your shoes had to be cleaned and polished every day. With what? For our masters too, the most important item in our dress was the state of our shoes. I don't know whether this concern for appearance was part of Nazi ideology, but it certainly occupied a key position in their lives. Furthermore, their shoes and boots always shone and smelled: I shall never forget the smell of German leather. Despite its unpleasant odour, I would have liked to get my hands on some of their shoe polish. People must have brought it with them; it was a precious substance. There was no iron either, yet there must have been irons in the luggage. Perhaps there was a dearth of irons in Berlin. For the moment we smoothed our dresses with our hands, pulled at our skirts, and flattened the pleats with our nails. Part of this Sunday was spent getting ourselves clean and presentable; we mustn't shock the gentlemen, we had to be an agreeable sight rather than the reverse, and "correct" above all. In Paris, propaganda vaunted their "K"orrectness.

These little chores became miserably trying due to the

shortage, or absence, of everything. If Alma chose, she could have said a word to Mandel and our life would have changed, but for some reason she wouldn't.

The other evening, on one of her rare visits to our dormitory, she had seen me massaging the nape of Clara's neck and called me over. "Do you know how to massage?"

"No, not really, but I can soothe headaches."

With a romantic gesture she drew her long, sensitive fingers over her forehead. "I too have terrible pains; in French you call it . . ."

"*Migraine*, madame."

My reply was no longer of any interest to her: "Are you happy here, you and your friend Clara?"

I was amazed by the question, and even more amazed that she could ask me it. Had her life ever held anything other than music and German discipline? The rights of the conductor, the respect and obedience due to him? Did it enter her head that we might be something other than a sort of musical infantry, to be slapped and driven as the will took her?

It was a little before four in the afternoon when, Alma at our head, we made our entrance into the Sauna, where our concerts were held in the winter and when it was raining. My role as singer enabled me to be a spectator too.

The interior of the immense building known as the Sauna was odd and unpleasant. Its precise function remained unclear: showers, disinfection centre, a sorting centre when numbers rose too high. It had a concrete floor and its walls, also of concrete, were rough, a dingy greyish shade. The whole thing was about as attractive and cheering as a dungeon. It was lit by bare, swinging bulbs. There were no windows, only long narrow skylights lost in the upper gloom.

Up there on our platform, I had an aerial view of things, and this gave me a feeling of detachment. It was a

strange sight: I'd thought I was dead and entering paradise when I entered the music block; here, I might be in
the antechamber of hell. It was grey, colourless, sinister.

I closed my eyes and for a few moments enjoyed the
familiar sounds of a concert hall: the shuffling of feet,
the scraping of instruments tuning up, coughing, mum-
bling, a few discreet laughs, someone blowing his nose;
safe ground for me, a brief pause but so soothing. I
opened my eyes again and examined our audience. I
might have been in the Philarmonie Konzertsaal in
Berlin or the auditorium of the Paris Opéra. Seated on
perfectly aligned chairs, there they were, the officers
and gentlemen of the SS, wrapped stiffly in their heavy
greatcoats, some with an enviable fur collar. The long
leather topcoat of the lovely Frau Mandel opened
elegantly to reveal her silk-clad legs.

It was very cold; we were shivering, naked beneath
our dresses. A slip may not be much, but its absence is
certainly noticeable.

A little farther back, on roughly made steps, were
seated the aristocrats of the camp, marked with the
black triangle of the asocial; those delicate beings had
unshaven hair and sat at ease in comfortable clothes.
Regarded as regenerate, they were being punished and
not exterminated.

Set apart, another group: the nurses, doctors and,
with them, a few sick people whose eyes, too large for
their monkeylike faces, betrayed obscure alarm at being
there. An SS officer had turned round and his gaze fell
on the group from the Revier. He said something to his
neighbour, who looked at them in his turn; then they
both nodded their heads, clearly satisfied. It was indeed
satisfying that sick people should be present at these
Sunday concerts. And tomorrow, with the same striking
logic, they would consider these wrecks as superfluous
and would gas them.

Farther back still, isolated and penned in like cattle,
at the obligatory position of attention, the grey troupe

of deportees was half-sunk in shadow. I could see only the first few rows. I couldn't bear to look at them.

Stirring, lively, blaring, the Sousa march was belted out briskly and conscientiously by Alma. Whatever the artistic quality of the piece played, it still had to be played with scrupulous correctness.

For me, the real public was the teetering hordes of deportees. This morning, in their block, the door had opened and the blockowa had shouted: *"Achtung!* A hundred women for the concert!'' Some had gone voluntarily, those who still had the strength to remember that they'd once found pleasure in listening to music. The others had been ordered here.

Lotte sang, Clara keeping a jealous and worried eye on her. Some Germans got up and went out. Lotte noticed and began kneading her handkerchief furiously till it was a wet ball in her damp hand. She sat down, angry and alarmed. The inevitable ''Blue Danube'' uncoiled its romantic curlicues. Like refractory children, the ''black triangles'' began to rock discreetly. How charming the music was, what pleasure it gave. How lovely it would be to waltz . . .

Then suddenly something amazing happened: in the deportees' group, some women began humming. It was so inconceivable that the girls in the orchestra craned their necks to look; some officers, stiff-necked, chins lifted, turned too, presumably scandalized that they dared sing. But no! They had deigned this slightest of gestures not to punish the grey mass that had dared to hum, but to reward them with a glance. Not able to pick out any one in particular, they bestowed this proof of their satisfaction on all: approvingly, the SS smiled at the deportees.

How right Little Irene was when she said: ''You see, they're pleased. At last they've been given credit: they did something for the prisoners and the prisoners appreciated it!''

Alma Rosé

"THEY'VE FINISHED THEIR DAMNED RAILWAY!"

The girls went towards the windows and door. They moved slowly, as if unwillingly, but they went all the same, and so did I.

In the distance new rails gleamed in their bed, which rose above the mud. It was March; patches of snow melted slowly during the day and froze again at night.

"Well! We'll have a grandstand view of arrivals," remarked Jenny. "We won't be short of entertainment."

"They make me sick," shouted Florette. "Sick, sick! I refuse to see all this."

"We mustn't look," Ewa advised her.

Florette rounded on her like a wildcat. "You're above all that then, miss high and mighty, you have no memories, you arrived here in a carriage, were borne here by lackeys, eh? And of course you couldn't care less about us Jews, you won't be gassed . . . But it so happens that being a Yid myself, I do care."

Her hand searched desperately for something to grab and she came upon my arm. "Look, you see that smoke that smells of cooked corpses, do you know what that is for me?"

The girls had drawn away from us, out of weariness, perhaps, or indifference.

"I arrived here with my mother, my father, my

boyfriend, my whole family: twenty-one people in all. We'd been rounded up. I didn't know where they were going. When I saw them get into the trucks, I didn't understand. So when I arrived at the quarantine block, I actually dared to ask about my parents. Then the blockowa grabbed my arm, pulled me towards the door, and said in her foul German jargon, pointing towards the chimneys with her filthy finger: 'You see that smoke?—that's your father coming out of the right chimney and your mother out of the left.' I screamed like a mad thing, I was hysterical . . .''

She calmed down, her startling green eyes filled with tears. She lowered her head, suddenly humble. "Because of that, I think I'll rail against everything all my life. You don't get over a thing like that . . .''

Seated at one end of the copyists' table, Little Irene was drawing; head bent, she was concentrating, like a child absorbed. Her chestnut hair hadn't been shaved for three months; theoretically we were supposed to be shaved regularly, to facilitate Pani Founia's delousing sessions. She would march her heavy fingers over our skulls, her permanently black nails searching greedily for lice. As our gentlemen-taskmasters were extremely delicate flowers, these parasites struck terror among them. The women who were in contact with them—the girls in Canada, the interpreters, the women in the medical section and we, the orchestra—were not to cause them to run that shameful risk, the risk of catching lice.

I was moved by the sight of the nape of Little Irene's hollow neck, like that of an undernourished child. I leant towards her; she was drawing the cover of the Sunday programme. She was an even worse violinist than Florette, and to keep her place among us she had had the idea, which charmed Alma, of giving a programme to the SS "ladies and gentlemen." She drew quite well and they liked it: *Ach! gut! ach! schön!* We'd have done more than that to please our masters, our murderers, to live one more month, one more day . . .

On her paper were garlands of flowers, branches bursting into leaf, nests, birds—everything that was conspicuously absent here. Lovingly she touched up a sprig of lilac: "You see, Fania, the spring inspires me."

"How do you know it's spring? There's not a blade of grass, not a bud!"

"The days are longer, we're coming up to March 21, lilac will be flowering somewhere."

At these words, Jenny's imagination took hold: "I can't help thinking about the Porte des Lilas, it must have been lovely when it was all in flower."

Florette cut her down to size: "There can't be much left of it!"

"What do you know about it—it's not your part of town. My grandfather's got a little garden on the old fortifications and you ought to see the lettuce he grows, nothing but heart. He has two lilac trees, one of those fabulous purple ones and a double white. He always gives me the first spray. My husband's just like me, it affects him too; and emotions give him strength."

"We're fed up with these dreary records," Big Irene snorted.

In excellent humour, Jenny remarked firmly: "It certainly wouldn't be a sight for brats of your age."

"Ruhe! Ruhe!" ordered Alma.

It was a pity, because when they were laughing, they could forget their hunger. That night, Big Irene woke up suddenly. I wasn't asleep, and I heard her murmur miserably: "Mama, mama, I'm so hungry." Then she started crying. It was all the more irritating in that we could have suffered rather less. On various occasions Mandel had told Alma, in front of us, to ask for anything she needed. Well, we needed to eat! It was less inspiring than making music, but perhaps more vital.

Despite the orders she bellowed out so imperiously,

Alma seemed accessible to me today. Indeed, she was in a good mood: some new pieces had been sent to her from Berlin. "Here's some work for you: 'The Charge of the Light Brigade' and two Suppé overtures. The SS are fond of him."

I didn't share their taste, and by the time I'd finished I'd had enough Suppé for a lifetime.

"I thought we ought to put the *Butterfly* duet on the programme; you can sing it with Lotte. I must say I'm very fond of it; I think it's rather reminiscent of Ravel."

An unexpected comparison. Poor Ravel! Me singing beside Lotte would be a sight worthy of Dubout, my favourite caricaturist! My head hardly came up to her chest. The Germans might have no sense of the ridiculous, but I did. Despite my desire to laugh, I commended Alma for her marvellous idea, which earned me a smile. The girls welcomed these developments, which might presage a relatively peaceful rehearsal. I took a calculated risk and said boldly: "Alma, couldn't you ask Frau Mandel for a little extra, a parcel for the girls or something? They're so hungry."

Her face inscrutable, her lips pursed, she answered hissingly: "No! I refuse to ask for anything for them. They spoilt my concert last Sunday; I'd be ashamed."

And she turned her back on me. I didn't give a damn about her scores and her music. Internally, I apostrophized her: "You'd be ashamed? What of, you vain idiot? Helping women to survive? You've got a marvellous position in this monstrous place and yet you won't take advantage of it. What kind of person are you, you little German Jew? You're not a primitive animal. You're educated, intelligent, and you behave as if you saw nothing, as if you didn't know where you were. Doesn't the smoke from those charred bodies worry you? Don't you miss the ordinary little things of life? Aren't you a bit surprised by your audience of corpses, uniformed executioners, fat shrews? Where do you think you are, in the Albert Hall in London? In fact, do you as much as perceive these women? Are you aware of the dramas that go on in our seething block? Or are you thinking of your Uncle Gustav Mahler, of your father, of the men you've loved, if indeed there are any? Wrong notes seem to be your only recurrent nightmare.''

I didn't feel like writing music; it was going to be a long, unbearable day and I dismissed it before it had even happened.

How loathsome Alma was, lording it on her platform, masterful and self-confident. Or was she? Wasn't her ''I'd be ashamed'' an admission of pride and powerlessness? These three words haunted me; somehow I imagined that they were one of the keys to her character, that through them I would be able to understand her, to establish a relationship with the other Alma, the one who was taking her violin out of its case. Imperious but gentle, she proffered her chin to the side of her instrument. The careful way she placed her cheek and lifted her shoulder to support the violin bespoke a sensual pleasure compounded of tenderness and trust. Her agile fingers glided along the finger board in a possessive caress, her wrist supply bent like an acrobat's unstraining limb. Alma was transfigured when she played; she was incomparably beautiful. She gave off an extraordinary sensuality; her relaxed mouth softened, half-opened; her eyes misted over; her body trembled. Alma was in the throes of love. We were silent, we listened and forgot. When she stopped and put down her bow, the desire to applaud was irresistible. But it was very, very short, the length of a piece of music. Then, instantly, Alma became inhuman once again.

Her voice pulled me from my reverie: ''Fania, we'll rehearse *Ein Paar Tränen*. I hope you've learnt to pronounce *Lächeln?''*

I was afraid I hadn't. Florette had made me repeat the German word for ''smile'' twenty times and lectured me: "You must manage it, you're gifted for languages, you've already begun to learn German, so it's not that that's the problem, you're just not trying." Stubbornly I insisted that I couldn't pronounce the German *ch*.

Alma raised her baton. I launched into song and again came to grief on *Lächeln*. Alma lost her patience and so did I: "Listen, give me whatever word you like: *laugh, giggle, split one's sides,* anything, but not *smile*—I can't do it."

"You can. You must. All it needs is an effort of will."

"Well, I don't want to!"

This was effrontery; she was towering above me, her dark eyes dangerously bright with anger, her baton trembling in her hand.

"Do you know what you're saying?"

Silence.

"Yes: I don't want to say *smile* in front of the SS and I won't. I'd consider it the ultimate indecency."

Anything could happen now, endless *Scheiss Kopf,* a slap, her baton thrown at my head. Unpredictably, she was silent, turned away, shrugged her shoulders, and explained coolly to her musicians that they would have to play extra loudly at that point to cover my voice and render inaudible that offending "smile."

Lotte smirked; at least no one could reproach her with such failings: *"Ach,* those French! No sense of duty!" Clara pursed her china doll's mouth. I knew what she was thinking, I'd already heard it: "She taking my place, she's not satisfied with what she's got. And many would be, because she's really in charge here, after Alma. She knows that all I can do is sing, but she doesn't care, she only thinks of herself."

That was how things were now. Clara had changed quickly, very quickly. A month after our arrival in the music block, one evening at six o'clock, she'd said to me: "I've organized a box. I've taken my things out of yours. I won't share with anyone anymore." The next day, at dinnertime, I opened her box by mistake and saw a pot of jam. Clara rushed at me. "Leave that; I told you to keep your hands off it."

"I'm sorry, I wasn't thinking. All our boxes look alike. I certainly wouldn't touch that nobly earned jam of yours!"

There were tears of rage in her eyes, perhaps a last glimmer of a former morality, a remnant of dignity. The donor was probably a *kapo* from the men's camp. Only the *kapos,* the blockowas, all Poles, Slovaks, or Germans, could come to our block.

Had she been a virgin? It was possible, it wouldn't have been a decisive factor. Besides, the risk of pregnancy for internees was virtually nonexistent.

I felt sorry for Clara when I saw her twitching her large behind, almost as provocative as Lotte, but so different. Lotte was married; she always needed a man and became virtually hysterical without one. But for Clara, everything had been different. She had been an innocent young girl who loved her boyfriend and who still nourished childlike dreams. Living in a sheltered milieu she was innocent of life, like the adorable and naive Big Irene, who remained so, while Clara changed so quickly and so totally. She had become frighteningly selfish; she would do anything to get food. In the middle of all these painfully thin girls, her obesity was a wonder, a most effective lure for men, who paid court to her in butter and sugar. The successful candidate would pay Tchaikowska or another blockowa twenty cigarettes, a high rate, for the hire of her room for a quarter of an hour.

The environment, fear, and hunger had all done their destructive work. In Birkenau I had the impression that we were well on the way to suffering a sort of leprosy: bits of oneself rotted and fell off without one's even knowing they'd gone. Clara had lost her woman's dignity. What would I lose?

* * *

Pa-pa-pa-*pam*. It wasn't London, but our orchestra rehearsing the first movement of Beethoven's Fifth, which I'd rewritten from memory. The key phrase had given me a lot of pleasure. Normally it was the bassoons, clarinets, and strings which played it. For our orchestra I'd done my best with the mandolins, whose vibrato enabled them to produce a sustained sound. The guitars had the task of giving body to the arrangement, of reinforcing the mandolins, while the violins came in to swell the fourth note.

Alma had wanted some Beethoven; I'd claimed that all I could remember was the first movement of the Fifth Symphony and I suggested she put it on the programme. A rare pleasure for me. She didn't see any malice in it, nor did the SS. They saw no connection with the signature tune of the Free French broadcasts on the BBC. For them it was Beethoven, a god, a monument to German music, and they listened to it in respectful rapture. Their lack of a sense of humour was almost touching. There was intense jubilation when our orchestra played the piece. It was one of my most perfect moments.

Today the girls must have been in a state of grace because, despite our unlikely orchestra of mandolins and guitars, the clumsy double bass, the pipes and Frau Kröner's flute, Alma and her violins, the symphony soared, compelling and marvellous. All our table raised their heads and Founia and Tchaikowska stood transfixed in the doorway. The girls were transfigured: they understood what they were playing and I, eyes closed, was listening to the Berlin Symphony Orchestra.

Alma often asked me to massage her temples and the nape of her neck, claiming it soothed her neuralgia. I was quite prepared to believe it, but I felt above all she liked to emerge from her enforced solitude to find relief in talking endlessly about herself, like a queen confiding in her lady-in-waiting. There could be no intimacy between us. My only quality, in her eyes, was that I was a musician, a real one, guaranteed by my diploma from the Paris Conservatoire.

I knew a lot of things about Alma and yet I made no progress in getting to know her; she remained inaccessible, possibly because I couldn't feel those bursts of pity that might, in the circumstances, have brought her closer to me.

On this evening, she talked to me about herself in an almost methodical manner. I got the lot: childhood, adolescence, professional life. I had the impression that she was giving me a recital on herself, a solo there in her room, a monkish place which suited her to perfection, whose rigour and bareness she hadn't tried to soften in the least. Nothing was pinned to the white walls; everything was arranged in a military fashion, clean, tidy, cold. It was the room of a mother superior; it wasn't Auschwitz Alma was blocking out, but the world.

Seated on her chair while I gently massaged her head, neck, and temples, she gazed at her hands in a way I'd often observed—beautiful, vigorous hands which lay almost calmly on her knees. Then she began to talk, and her voice became gradually warmer, less harsh and metallic. "My mother always said that she listened to music or played night and day when she was pregnant with me, so that her child would be imbued with it. She wanted a boy and had everything ready, his room, his music, everything. Even his first little violin was there, lying in the red velvet cradle of its case. Everyone in the family assumed she would have a boy, and that he would be a musician. An uncle had prophesied his coming and nobody doubted it. But hopes diminished from year to year. I arrived very late, and I was a girl. My mother watched me grow and didn't even think that I was pretty. I understood everything that was said around me. The bitterness and contempt I met with everywhere made me miserable. I felt responsible for the dirty trick I'd played on them: I wasn't the genius they'd hoped for, only a very gifted and terribly shy little girl—but I'd sworn to become their pride and joy. I was gawky and clumsy, driven to desperation by my gangling legs and long hands." She paused for a moment to consider them. "Later, I changed my mind: I think they're my best feature. Very much alone and living such an unusual life for a child, I naturally had no friends. I played music all day long; for hours my mother would sit beside me, in front of the metronome, just listening to me. All my days were the same, all years identical. Except for one, when I entered the Conservatoire. I got my prize, and no one thought to congratulate me, it was so taken for granted. The contrary would have been a scandal which neither I nor my parents could have conceived of. From that day onward, I spent all my time on tours and concerts. One morning in my hotel room in Karlsruhe, combing my hair in front of the oval mirror, I realized that more than twenty years of my life had gone by—they were lying there beside me, shut up inside my violin, locked in that black case. I was a young girl and I had no lover; I felt so different from other young girls that I didn't even dare look at boys. That morning I wept for all those things I didn't know: tenderness, friendship, love. Then I saw that it was just a brief romantic urge; it was pointless to cry, because music gave me everything. If I was to devote myself solely to music, my life would have to be utterly uneventful. I gave more and more concerts on the Continent. I wanted to get to know Paris; it became an obsession. I learned French, which I found easy—musicians are gifted for languages—but the war put an end to all that!"

The life that Alma was recounting so blankly and yet so bitterly had certainly been monotonous. I too loved music, but with me it seethed, exploded, and blossomed. It was a flower, a firework, flaming within

me, white-hot. It was love, passion! It carried off my
life, inflamed it and transformed it, but it never demanded any sacrifice; the offerings I made it were the
first fruits of my new passions and my dead loves, which
it magnified! Alma's pathetically loveless youth struck
me as miserable and yet, strangely, it didn't move me.
Vague and distant noises reached us from behind the
door of the room; we might have been in a hospital or a
convent.

Alma gave a throaty little laugh, and suddenly I felt a
sense of closeness.

"I did marry, though. One evening, when I was just
back from a tour, I met a pupil of my father's, a well-
known violinist and a very good one. We talked music
for several days and then, one afternoon when we were
taking tea at Krauzer's, he talked to me of love."

She fell silent, her face expressionless.

"Were you surprised, were you pleased?"

"Surprised, yes. It was unexpected."

"Was he right for you? What was he like?"

"I don't know."

"I mean, physically."

"It seems to me now that I never looked at him, I
began to hate him so soon. When he was playing he had
a lot of presence, of style. He was dark, with rather long
hair—I don't like that sort of thing—and a very
pronounced Adam's apple."

"His eyes, mouth, hands?"

"He had grey eyes. I don't remember his mouth. And
his hands were good for the violin."

It seemed impossible that she should have noticed
nothing, felt nothing. I insisted:

"Did you like him?"

"Like him . . . I don't know."

"Did you love him?"

"I don't think so."

"Well, did he love you?"

Clearly, my questions annoyed and disconcerted her. Wasn't that what she wanted of me? Then what did she want?

"How could I know? He was poor, he knew that I really had something to offer him. By marrying me, thanks to my father's privileged position, he'd find any number of doors open to him. How could I say no? I let myself be pushed into it. In my family, girls have always obeyed, it's an established custom which I respect. This marriage pleased my family. My mother thought I was lucky—I wasn't pretty, I wasn't young any longer—and I thought she was right."

This passivity she was vaunting annoyed me and once again I felt as remote as ever. What could she have expected from this marriage of convenience?

After a pause she continued: "I think I felt grateful to my husband. I was surprised that he agreed to marry me and it made me humble."

That block of pride: humble!

"With him, I felt physically and intellectually inferior, I knew so little. I hardly read at all. Politics didn't interest me; that seemed men's business. I felt I was just a dead weight for him to drag rather gloomily along. We didn't talk much, only about everyday matters. I don't think we had anything to say to one another. Nothing changed when we married: we lived with my parents. The only difference was that I no longer went on tour alone. It was then that our relationship started to deteriorate: as we were both soloists, my husband became simply a rival."

Her nostrils flaring, Alma was trembling with indignation and retrospective anger. That was her real nature, which only music could reveal.

"Can you imagine, this musical upstart wanted to outstep me, Alma Rosé. If the newspapers said more about me than him, he'd count the lines and say meanly: 'If you weren't Rosé's daughter, you'd have nothing; it's all because you're Mahler's niece. What a family!

What a stumbling block for the young!' If the applause
for me was louder, he'd make terrible scenes. He'd say
I'd paid people to applaud. What do you call that?''

"A claque.''

That set off a new train of thought.

"He slapped me too, once, and that I really couldn't
take. It's fair enough in work, one can accept it, but not
just out of the blue. I hadn't deserved it. We had increasingly violent scenes. *Ach mein Gott, mein Gott!*''

Alma twisted her hands and started pacing up and
down the room again, her hair escaping the discipline
she imposed upon it; she was almost beautiful in her
desperate rage.

"Imagine him ranting, always ill-humoured, saying
cruel things, that I had no talent, that I played like a
machine, drily, with no soul, no—'' She fell silent,
looking for words, then went on regardless: "—without
those things in the stomach. He dared to say that my
playing wasn't sensual!''

I could have told her that that wasn't true, but I was
silent. These memories were costing her dear, but she
continued grimly: "He was so violent that I was afraid.
Divorce wouldn't have been possible in our family. One
morning, in the train coming back to Berlin, there was a
particularly stormy scene: he decided to forbid me to
play in public. He lowered the window, took my violin,
and hurled it out! I threw myself at the window—I was
out of my mind—and I looked: Its case had opened and
my violin had fallen on the embankment, shattered like
a body in a bombardment . . . my poor violin!''

She had tears in her eyes; it was as though she were
talking about a child. Her jaws tensed, contracted, she
clenched her fists. "I said to him: 'That's it.' He
shouted and threatened, but I left him, and that was
that.''

She sat down, calmer, and reflected.

"It was a very cruel experience. Perhaps I might have
thought that men were not for me had it not been that in

Amsterdam, at the beginning of the war, I met a very nice man, older than I. Everything was different with him, he did me good. He liked to hear me play, he encouraged me. He'd listen to me for hours—how he'd listen. His love warmed me like a thick coat. I felt very safe in his arms. With him I realized that at thirty-six I was as ignorant as a savage. I don't know if what I felt for him was love, perhaps it was more a very great tenderness. I think love could have come with time, if I could have divorced and married him. I cried when we were separated . . ."

Was Alma's pride perhaps just a facade? If she had given herself over to love, would her heart have opened to others?

"But why did you separate?"

"I had been arrested as a Jew, certainly denounced, though I don't know by whom. There's a lot of jealousy in our profession. It was a shock to me that it should have happened that way."

She crossed her long legs, too thin but still very beautiful, her hands round her knees, and leant backwards slightly.

"I hardly knew we were Jewish. For me, it was just a religion, not even a philosophy, different from that of other Germans. In my family, which had always been German, no one ever talked about it or thought about it. We thought like Germans. My father, who was first violinst in the Berlin Opera orchestra, had a privileged position, and the coming of the Führer didn't harm us at all." She gave a bitter little smile. "We were part of a minority that the Nazis kept for themselves. My father's quartet was well-known throughout Europe. Stories of arrests and deportation seemed things in another world. They didn't affect me or even interest me. Only music counted—I'd never had anything else. And my arrest cut me off from it completely. Losing music, I lost everything . . ."

Cooped up in that room, she reminded me of a trapped, quivering thoroughbred desperate at the knowledge that never again would he gallop drunkenly towards the winner's post amid the crowds and the sweet smell of success.

Alma the Kapo

I'D HAD A letter from Leon, my beau from Drancy, a few words on a nasty little piece of crumpled torn paper. This morning, ever since she'd woken up, Pani Founia had been making a tremendous uproar; incomprehensibly, her mattress was wet. She spat out insults, soliloquized, called Tchaikowska and her slave, Marila, as witnesses.

The affair had begun in a farcical vein but threatened to become tragic any minute. Founia proclaimed that if the filthy swine who had done it didn't own up in five minutes, it wouldn't be Alma she'd complain to, but someone much higher up!

"Five by five!" shrieked the abominable pair; like a general, Founia passed in front of us, stopped and spluttered at us full in the face in a Polish that was incomprehensible even to those who spoke the language. I was worried for Florette, the intended victim, when Halina grabbed Founia by the arm and showed her the ceiling. Heavily displacing her gelatinous mass, Founia went towards her bed, lifted her head, and began swearing again, but it no longer concerned us. Her wrath was now directed at the roof, which had had the temerity to allow rain to seep through onto her bed.

We'd hardly finished our soup when a runner announced the imminent arrival of a workman. He turned out to be a tall fellow with glasses (which was unusual, because people with poor sight weren't exactly cherished around these parts), impressively thin, which caused Jenny to say: "He can walk about on the roof with no danger of falling through; the only trouble is, he'll be carried off by the first breath of wind."

Dreamily, he examined the woodwork, nodded his head, and gazed around him with naive, shortsighted eyes.

"He seems to be looking for someone," commented Big Irene.

"Well, with his eyesight, he's unlikely to find her!"

Male deportees were forbidden to speak to us, and Founia was mounting inexorable guard. He climbed to the top of the *coja* and began to examine the woodwork.

Rehearsal time was approaching, and there was a certain amount of bustle. Suddenly Anny said: "That fellow's got something for you—you'll have to find a way to go up to him."

It would take just five seconds; I crept up to him and he slipped me a bit of paper and a murmured name: "From Leon; it needs an answer."

Leon had written: "Fania, I'm here in the camp and I'm making out all right, working in the factory, and I haven't forgotten you. Don't forget I'm here and that you still have your place in my heart. I found out that you're in the music block. Your boyfriend from Drancy who loves you, Leon."

Poor devil, what could he have done for me? I could just see his friendly Paris ragamuffin grin. He'd been thin as a rail, he must be virtually invisible now! We'd probably never have been really close—his mad gesture of slipping into the convoy at Drancy had been quite astounding. He must have hoped that we would travel together, that we'd make love, that we'd keep each other warm; a boy's dream in a man's head, an action from another era, the age of princesses, heroic vagabonds, magnificent adventurers. They knew how to do things in the poorer Paris suburbs. I felt a rush of sudden warmth and wrote back quickly, telling him that I was fine, that it was bearable, that I was delighted with his note, that I needed affection. I sent my love. How I would have like to be able to bandy more words with him on that subject.

His friend had a warm southern accent.

"When he knew you were here, poor lad, he went so pale that I thought it was the end. Then he began to talk and talk. He wrote this weeks ago, but he couldn't find anyone to bring it to you. He'd gone on about it so much that when I knew I was coming here, I brought the note for him, and that's the story."

The bridge of his nose looked as though it were about to tear through his skin, his striped cap made him look like a convict; he wasn't handsome now and he never had been. But he was bringing me everything I lacked—men, love, my country. I'd have liked to kiss him and my eyes filled with tears, which he no doubt misinterpreted; but he would pass the good news back to Leon and so, this evening, Leon would be happy.

Here, love was in short supply like everything else. Here one didn't love in a very romantic fashion. Clara, who'd lost all modesty, had become a *kapo*'s girl; Lotte, with her protruding stomach and hidden charms all too visibly available, sickened us all. In this setting, the few lines from Leon took on an unexpected value, became especially precious; I would have like to keep them, but it would have been risking death. So I opened the stove and, before destroying the letter, held it screwed up in the palm of my hand, warmed by my warmth. Then I threw it in; it caught fire almost immediately and turned unexpectedly into a bright vision of horror. The crematoria were so close!

Furious bellowing from Alma cut short my musings. What was happening? Once again, with long-armed violence, Alma had slapped Florette, who was standing defiantly before her, white with anger. Seething, our *kapo* declared that Florette's stupidity and ineptitude

made her head ache; then she marched rapidly back into
her room.

Florette's face was red and swollen, bearing the im-
print of Alma's fingers; she was weeping amid the
almost general hostility, snivelling like a little girl. The
day was starting off badly and everyone blamed her.

Alma called me to her room. She claimed that her
head felt terrible, and it must have been severe migraine
because she was lying on her bed. I didn't feel the
slightest desire to alleviate it. I'd rather have returned
her intolerable, unfair slap. Yet I began gently to
massage her temples with my fingertips.

She closed her eyes, her hands lying close to her body,
misleadingly relaxed. For some days now Alma had
been particularly edgy, oddly distracted. She would
leave us at attention for long stretches as if she were
unaware of our very existence. When I put a new score
on her desk, she would take no notice, then pick it up
mechanically; the girls would hardly have begun
sightreading it than she would raise her baton, shouting
"Ruhe! Ruhe! That's enough. Start again!" The result
was abysmal; it was as though sounds reached her with
delayed action, because she stopped the cacophony only
after a few bars. Then at last she would emerge from her
daydream, rant and rage, throw her baton at a player's
head, slap whoever might be playing worst, complain of
a headache, and stop the rehearsal. What could she be
so worried about?

"One can't make music without discipline. It's incomprehensible to me that that girl can't accept a slap
she's deserved."

"Why should she accept it from you?"

Alma drew herself up in amazement.

"What? But it's reasonable, it's my right. I'm here to
make music, not to indulge in sentimentality. You
French are so irresponsible, you seem to forget that
there's a time for everything; you confuse work and
play, you mix everything up, and worst of all you put

emotions in where they don't belong. It's not dishonourable to be slapped or hit with a baton by your conductor, indeed you ought to be glad. It's not an insult, it's a lesson. When I was young, I was often punished for wrong notes, and I always thought that that was right. In Germany, it is traditional for the conductor to mete out corporal punishment to his musicians. The great Furtwängler did so. Once, there was a great scandal, which I personally witnessed. The first violinist fell ill and was replaced by a Frenchman. Twice Furtwängler pointed something out to him and the third time, for the same mistake, he slapped him. The Frenchman slapped Furtwängler back. Now, how could that be right?'' The memory clearly still outraged her. ''The same mistake three times—some such action becomes inevitable, don't you think? The Frenchman didn't agree, but that's absurd. After all, we're the best musicians in the world. Without discipline, your orchestras will never be able to rival ours. One can't make good music without obedience. And here it's so difficult with these imbeciles, they feel no love!''

She meant love of music, of course. Did she realize what she was saying? Her anger mounted, her hands worked nervously.

''In a word, we must do our work properly; the officers must be satisfied. That's what we're here for, isn't it?''

No, Alma! We are here to die, we are all just temporarily reprieved, orchestra included. I was beginning to regard her as a real monster. I gritted my teeth to keep silent.

Alma got up and paced nervously up and down the room. Incredibly, her dark eyes burned with a sort of desperate passion which moved me despite myself.

''Sit down and listen to me. Do you think I don't see anything? You're wrong. I *won't* see anything. I refuse.''

She leant forward, took me by the shoulders, then let

me go and stood up. There was a moment of indecision. Then she began to talk and her French, usually excellent, began to fail her, becoming patchy and jumbled: "You don't understand! None of you understand! I mustn't be like the rest of you, perpetually softhearted, I have to be hard. *Ach,* if I spent my time pitying those who were being gassed, if I thought that all of you could go up in smoke just like that"—she clicked her fingers—"then I could sit in a heap and cry."

She clasped her thin hands convulsively till the bones whitened at the joints. I wondered whether it was the selections or the possible death of the orchestra that caused her the most despair. I was amazed to see her like that, no longer mistress of her thoughts or words. She sat down on the edge of the bed in front of me, her knees touching my own.

"The railway in front of our door is a horrible thing. They should never have done that, they should respect our block, respect music. These trains are a strain; if I looked at the people getting out of the carriages, as you do, if I cried at the sight of such young children, I'd never, never be able to manage my orchestra. Yesterday morning, during the *Blocksperre,* I stayed in my room. You were all at the windows, glued to them morbidly like flies."

It was my turn to become impatient: "Yes, we dared to look, and we were upset: three-quarters of the people were dead, taken out of the train by the shovelful. There were little children running around and crying for their parents. I stared like that so as not to forget what the Nazis have done, so as to tell the world! So that they'll be damned forever!"

"I've been keeping a close eye on the transports to see whether there are any good musicians," she said slowly. "You're as stupid as all the rest! If I let myself luxuriate in the general mood I wouldn't be able to hold out any longer and we'd all produce bad music. Commandant

Kramer and Mandel would do away with the orchestra. Now I'll come back to what you said about the Germans. When I arrived at the camp, I realized that Nazi society wasn't good, this aspect of it, I mean. Disorder was ruining my country; it needed a leader. As I told you, I didn't know anything about politics, but I did approve of the coming of Hitler. Only, when the Jews began to be hunted, I became worried. Why destroy us? We were Germans like the rest. The Nazis said nothing to me: I gave concerts freely, that was how I managed to go to Holland. And that's where I was imprisoned; I was almost immediately deported, without going back to Germany, without being able to inform my father. Perhaps he's still playing.

"My arrival at the camp was very upsetting. I didn't go through quarantine, they put me in the experimental block. I went into a huge room, very clean, almost like a hospital, with women lying on beds; I didn't understand, I wasn't ill. They made me undress and put me to bed. I still didn't feel too anxious. Why should I, I hadn't done anything wrong. One thing did worry me, though: the number tattooed on my arm, which seemed to me somehow ignominious. I was shy, I didn't dare question the women. I could see quite clearly, from the way they looked at me, that I was incapable of making myself liked. That's something I've never been able to do. Finally, without my having to ask, my neighbour on the right volunteered: 'Every morning an SS comes in with a list, he calls out numbers and the women on it get up and go through that door over there. Very few come back; in fact I've never seen any, but apparently some have managed. It seems that they all die, during or after the experiments: horrible surgical operations with anaesthetics.' What operations? She didn't know. Everyone was waiting and dreading their turn, I too. And yet I found it hard to believe. After the SS had been in, one was left in peace for the day. I don't know how many days I stayed there. I missed my violin, I'd have liked to have it by me like a baby. One day a new SS came in. He seemed to be looking for someone, and it was me. 'Are you Alma, the violinist?' 'Yes, Herr Offizier.' 'Then follow me.' I left that room without a backward glance, and entered a wooden hut, heated, with well-dressed girls holding musical instruments. We looked at one another in silence. It was all so odd. I hadn't known of the existence of this—well, orchestra. A coarse, hefty woman with an arm band displaying a white lyre informed me in bad German that she was the conductor, Polish, and a descendant of the great Tchaikowsky. Taken aback, I asked her to repeat herself; but after all, the whole thing wasn't so surprising. We Germans value music, we're a musical people, so why not an orchestra? The SS officer returned with a very fine violin for me. Fania, when I touched it, I was crying. Like you the day you ran to the piano.''

I was amazed she'd noticed and remembered.

'' 'Play,' he ordered. I played and played, oblivious of my surroundings, and totally happy. I was no longer among savages, I had a violin and I had been asked to play it. They seemed to appreciate my playing: *'Sehr gut,'* said the commandant. 'You'll take over the conducting. You'll be *kapo*, Tchaikowska will be blockowa. But now the orchestra must play pieces other than marches; we want concerts for ourselves and the prisoners. We want music!' Conductor—can you imagine how alarmed I was? I'd never conducted in my life, I'd never learnt to read a score; my position was more precarious than ever. The SS officers went out, Tchaikowska handed me her arm band. The girls were waiting, I had to do something. I ordered them to play something they knew. It was horrifying, frightful. Then I was afraid and I wondered whether there was anything I could do with them. Most couldn't sight-read; there were only four professionals, and the rest weren't even poor amateurs; and I had to create an orchestra out of this incongruous bunch. My life and theirs were at stake. I decided that strict discipline was the answer—they had dared claim to be musicians and they must prove it! I wouldn't let them massacre music!"

Her dark eyes shone with the fanaticism of a Judith. Her passion made her beautiful and inhuman.

"With me, you won't trifle with music. That I cannot tolerate. It's as if you were spitting in my eye, trampling on my soul. I've given my life to music and it's never let me down. Through music, with music, I've known happiness. Even here I've made sacrifices for it—do you think I was so different from the rest of you when Γ arrived here? They gave me this little room; I chose Regina, a very poor musician, to make my bed, clean my boots, bring me my meals. Have you ever wondered whether I might not prefer to sit with you, to chat, not to be so isolated? Only, if I'd done that, I'd never have been able to keep order. The conductor must keep his distance, he's destined to stand alone. He must be respected."

"And loved, Alma."

Astounded, she stared at me, head elegantly tilted. "You can't love a conductor without respecting him first of all. And anyway, love, here . . . from the very first, I noticed the incredible animosity that exists among these women. As soon as I'd turned my back, there'd be quarrelling, shouting, stealing, crying, laughter, fighting . . . it's a madhouse. So I have to shout the loudest, I insist on order in everything: in dress, in work—seventeen hours a day. Rehearsing must be done properly. I punish them or slap them for a single wrong note, and that's natural, essential as I've already said. I care about them all, though I prefer the good musicians, but that's natural. When they brought me Marta, a German born in Breslau, an excellent cellist although she was only seventeen, of course I was pleased. She is a well-educated girl and speaks very good French. She was brought up like me in true German fashion and was highly disciplined; she set an excellent example, and that was helpful for me. I looked after her, I got her sister Renate put in Canada: one plays better when one's mind is at rest.''

I'd scarcely had time to admire this humane action than I realized that it too had been performed solely in the interests of music. She was silent now, absorbed in her thoughts. Should I slip out discreetly? But there was something in this passionate woman that fascinated me. After hearing her story, I was more puzzled than ever by one thing: Was she more German than Jewish? Was that problem the source of her inner conflict?

''I don't know whether you realized it, Fania, but it's actually Mandel rather than Kramer who supports us. One can't ask anything of Kramer. Maria Mandel values the orchestra, it flatters her pride. She likes to think that Birkenau is the only camp in Germany, and indeed in all the occupied territories, with a women's orchestra.''

I wasn't too sure whether we were really the pride and joy of the SS, but we were certainly the apple of Alma's eye. Proud as a peacock, she wallowed in the idea of conducting that unique group. Her pride was leading her astray.

''I find the bad behaviour of these girls most upsetting—their disobedience, their irresponsibility. Here or elsewhere, what one does must be done well, if only out of self-respect. Sometimes Frau Mandel asks me if the girls are hungry. Of course they're hungry, of course I could ask for food. But when they play so badly, is it not my duty to keep silent?''

She posed the question but expected no reply; her notion of duty was a bastion against any sentimental weakness. So why did she glare at me so violently, as if she needed to justify herself?

''They shall have nothing! And they'd better pay more attention on Sunday. It's their interests I'm protecting, we have to please our superiors.''

There was a silence; perhaps she was vaguely disconcerted by my own.

''I have to act like this, Fania—don't I?''

On with the Music!

"NO!" SHOUTED FLORETTE. "I won't play, I hate music, it'll drive us all mad."

The girls had just come back from their evening session outside; I wondered whether something specific had happened, or whether it was a typical Florette explosion. Generally, comings and goings took place amid indifference and silence. This was the last chore of the day, and they usually returned more relaxed. This evening they came in dragging their feet, grey in the face. Without a glance, Alma went to shut herself in her room. Whiter than ever, Frau Kröner put her flute away in the music room, followed by several of the others, who were looking unusually vacant. Little Irene was gazing into the distance, Jenny was so pale that her freckles dotted her face with brown. Big Irene was looking positively pinched and staring worriedly at Florette.

"No! I can't, I won't go anymore. They can kill me, I don't care. It'll happen anyhow, it'll happen to all of us."

There was an almost tangible feeling of fear. Most of the girls were glaring darkly at Florette, hands itching.

"I can't bear to look at them, I can't bear their eyes . . . Fania, the dogs ate two of them today. They were going to piss or get a bit of ice to suck . . . The SS set their dogs on them. They tore them into little bits . . .

and those bastards forced their comrades to go and pick them up and put them on the pile of dead bodies, and I saw them, I saw them. Pieces of women's flesh turned into dogs' meat . . . They carried them as best they could, on their backs . . . and we went on playing, belting out that rubbish. Butchers with lumps of meat on their shoulders, they could hardly carry it, they were exhausted, and we were forcing them to march in step . . . There was such hatred in the eyes of those women . . . I can't bear it anymore. I won't go . . .''

In sudden solidarity, Hilde and Helga took her by the shoulders and pulled her away with the help of Little Irene.

"Come outside, it'll do you good."

Ferocious, oozing hatred, Hilde assured her: "We'll throw them to their own dogs, they'll tear them limb from limb in front of our eyes, we'll trample on their remains. They'll pay for this."

As they led the hiccuping Florette away, I asked Little Irene whether it was true that the SS set their dogs on people all the time.

"One or two prisoners die like that every day. We knew it, but we'd never actually seen it."

Never had I so appreciated being spared that particular duty; at that time the perverse SS mind had not yet been inspired to add a singer to the pseudo-fanfare.

Lying there on my bunk, I tried to rid myself of this incident, to detach myself from it, but the images persisted. That night the searchlights seemed nervous, sweeping over the camp and crossing our dormitory more frequently than usual. Physically and emotionally drained, Florette was sleeping in her favorite position. It seemed to me that our nights were becoming increasingly agitated; only the snoring of Pani Founia remained unchanged.

The ice and snow were melting slowly; here, April meant rain and mud that was continually whipped up by the wind. We were endlessly spattered, endlessly obliged to clean ourselves up with nothing, which was exhausting and irritating. The whole camp was in a ferment, as if spring were sending us scuttling about like edgy, frustrated animals. Rumours reached us of problems for Germany in Russia and Italy; there was even talk of a landing in France. Our block became a sort of turntable. Winter had sheltered us to some degree, kept us in hibernation; we had felt protected, segregated. Now once again there was incessant movement through the camp. We received visits from the women in Canada, the kitchen staff, the Revier staff, interpreters, clerks—our block was a general meeting place. People poured in from the outside, rumours buzzed. There was always something to alarm us. From our music room, nauseated, we watched the convoys arriving. The rate of selections had speeded up, the death factory was working at full blast; greasy soot stuck to our skin; women told us that corpses were piling up near the blocks because the ovens could no longer cope. Priority was given to new arrivals because they were alive, while those already here, dead or half dazed, could wait. They said that you could see an arm or a leg move among the corpses. We would have liked to block our ears, and yet we listened with morbid curiosity.

We had never played so much: there were two or three concerts every Sunday. Every day, and often several nights on end, the SS came to our block to demand endless musical desserts. Hell has many faces, and for us this was one of them. Yet I was grateful to this musical activity for granting me a respite and also for allowing me to oxygenate my brain by working on scores and orchestrations—it was like a few hours of mountain air. I was even able to enjoy myself, as I'd just done with an arrangement of *Cavalleria Rusticana,* whose first bars reminded me of our favorite song: *J'attendrai.* Written for those absent in 1939-40, it symbolized all returns for us, theirs and ours. Every time we played the arrangement we were secretly jubilant. It was amusing to be able to sing a song of hope under their noses. Guile is the revenge of the weak. I had organized other pleasures for myself. I had arranged *Josef, Josef* (a well-known fox trot, the work of a Jewish composer) as a march; in this way I'd seen to it that the women in the work groups marched off to the rhythm of Jewish music, and some of them clearly recognized it. Not a single SS ever noticed. They listened to it with evident satisfaction, beating time. Sweeter still to my eyes was the sight of them thoroughly relishing the first movement of the E minor violin concerto by Mendelssohn, a composer banned in Germany and the occupied countries. I had written it out from memory, and when Alma found it on her desk she turned to me: "Do you think that's possible?"

"Certainly. None of them is bright enough to notice."

"*Jawohl.* On the programme, just put 'Violin concerto.'"

And each time she played and conducted it, we exchanged a smile of complicity. We were running a real risk; but it afforded us such intense delight to see them beaming as they listened to that forbidden music. Such moments were all too short.

"On with the music!" Jenny jeered at every possible opportunity.

This had become our catch phrase. At Birkenau, music was indeed the best and worst of things. The best because it filled in time and brought us oblivion, like a drug; we emerged from it deadened, exhausted. The worst, because our public consisted of the assassins and the victims; and in the hands of the assassins, it was almost as though we too were made executioners.

The Sunday concerts were not always held in the Sauna; we moved around as ordered. One Sunday recently we had played in the block for the insane, which housed women who were mentally ill when they

were interned, women who hadn't been able to stand up
to the horrors of the camp or who had been driven mad
by the experiments they'd been subjected to. I don't
know whether our concert in this block was experimental, whether their reactions were to be studied
by the doctors of Birkenau and Auschwitz, but a large
number of them attended.

We played at the entrance to the block, in the central
aisle. The women sprawled on their *cojas* in an amazing
range of positions. Half-naked, some of them clung to
the uprights throughout the whole concert like skeletal
monkeys. They stared at us, holding out their hands,
perhaps begging for the crust of bread we couldn't give
them. Others seemed too dazed to see us, still less hear
us, so much so that I thought they must actually have
been deaf; some jumped up and down in a semblance of
dancing, lifting their tatters lewdly.

Alma was lucky enough to have her back to them, but
we had a chance to observe, particularly I, who had only
two songs to sing. At the end of a piece some clapped
frenetically, which in those surroundings was a gesture
of madness indeed. Throughout our whole stay in the
camp we were never applauded except by them. And
how Alma must have missed the applause; I could so
clearly imagine her bowing in her own way, haughty yet
exceedingly polite.

One of the poor creatures came forward grimacing
compulsively in a grotesque imitation of Alma at her
stand, then of Helga at the percussion. It was so funny
that I wondered whether she was indeed mad, or only
faking. The caricature was so unexpected that our
nerves gave and we laughed—like mad things.

I tried to reason with myself, to tell myself that after
all, our average age was only about twenty, that
laughter was the antidote to horror. It was laughter that
kept us sane, I knew, but I still felt that there was
something unhealthy about it. This laughter acted upon
us like an anaesthetic, and I was afraid that it might

hasten the gradual decline in respect for human life which was at work within us.

A few weeks earlier, Alma had asked me to compose a cadenza for the first movement of the Mozart A major concerto for Big Irene, our first violin. When Irene read it, she pulled a face and frowned. "It's too difficult, I'd never be able to play that."

"Don't worry, Alma hasn't seen it yet. I'll say I couldn't manage it."

Jenny butted in venomously. "It may be too difficult for her, but not for me." Her jangling Paris tones became a positive hiss: "Who do you both think you are? I played the violin before she did, at the Rialto theatre, every night, and my public was pretty choosy!"

Contrary to all expectation, Alma absently agreed that Jenny should play the cadenza. So for days she tortured us and exhausted herself with the piece; it was painfully bad. Alma seethed and raged, but Jenny persisted, repeating: "I've practised it and I'll play it."

On Sunday morning, turning her pointed little rodent's face ostentatiously towards me, she assured me that she knew her piece by heart, that it was extremely easy, that all she needed was a bit more time to touch up her interpretation, but that this afternoon we'd see all right. I didn't even shrug my shoulders; I was past caring. The only thing that interested me was to know where we would be playing. I feared another experience like the one in the block for the insane, and was relieved when I learnt that we would be playing only for the sick people in the Revier and in the afternoon in our own room for the SS.

Since I'd been in the orchestra—almost four months —this was the first time we'd given a concert in the infirmary. I was pleased really: to play for sick people seemed to me a perfect justification of our existence. I had an idyllic view of the thing. My imagination took wing and pious clichés crowded my thoughts: we would be bringing a moment's respite to the sick, making them

forget their suffering, and so on. It took me a moment
to realize that I was the only one smiling. Alma, in an
abysmal mood, did not seem to be touched by the slight
exaltation which usually enlivened her before a concert.
Furthermore, apart from Jenny, the girls seemed
gloomy. Ewa sighed: "I wish it were over. I hate singing
in the Revier."

"Why? After all, perhaps we can do something for
them—make them forget their state for a bit."

"We play in the morning," Florette interrupted
brutally," and they'll be gassed in the afternoon."

Unable to swallow, I stammered, "Do they know?"

"No, but Alma does, and so do we."

Cowardly, I too would have preferred not to know.
In my imagination, I had seen the Revier as a sort of
hospital, with beds, not really luxurious of course,
rudimentary but at least clean. I found myself in a
stinking, unheated shed, whose floor had, however,
been newly washed for our arrival. In the blocks of
bunks whose tops were lost in gloom, ghostly women,
half naked, shivering on sheetless straw mattresses,
some without covers, watched us with eyes bright with
fever.

Calmly, carefully, in the central gangway near the
open door, we installed our stands, arranged our scores,
then tuned up. Since on this occasion I was to sing one
song only, I would have given a lot to have an instrument in my hands, some absorbing task which
would have allowed me not to look at those women, not
to see them. Some of the less seriously ill came up to us,
stared at us. I wondered what we were contributing and
which ones knew that they were condemned. Suddenly
with a feeling of horror I wondered if we were fulfilling
their last request.

Alma signalled to her players and the orchestra
launched into the "Blue Danube." Some women started
to hum, others shrieked like suffering animals, some

laughed, blocked their ears, rocked in time. Some, oblivious to our presence, were praying, hands clasped. Very few were following the concert in the normal fashion.

The girls played arias from operettas, fox trots, waltzes, as if all this were none of their business. Near the open door there was a bustle of doctors and SS. An officer whom I'd never seen before caught my attention. He was very tall and thin, with a flat skull and tow-coloured hair. His glassy, expressionless eyes lay in deep, hollow orbits, like those of a corpse. He was examining us closely and I felt uneasy at his mirthless laugh. I asked Ewa who he was.

"Tauber, the adjutant general, the worst of all. He doesn't like music."

That much was evident; his cruel little eyes bored into us while his thin mouth curled briefly into a moue of superior disgust.

"What's he doing here then?"

"Just seeking a bit of distraction."

I was hypnotized by that vicious face, though I knew it was forbidden to look at an SS man. Near him there now appeared a superior officer, a tall, monocled SS colonel, greying at the temples and extremely elegant—you'd almost think he was corsetted inside his uniform. His crop tucked under his arm, he tapped his gilded cigarette holder against his gold cigarette case. Where had he sprung from and did he like music? Ewa didn't know. Apparently there had been some new SS arrivals and he was probably one of them. Fortunately, as it was now my turn to sing, this diversion had un-frozen my heart and throat a little and I sang the second aria from *Land of Smiles:* Taking tea *à deux* . . . it's wonderful . . ."

It was abominably incongruous.

Almost before I had finished, the fashion-plate colonel and Tauber turned on their heels. A few women listened, sniggering; one tried to join in the refrain, in a broken voice whose singing past was probably all too recent. It was pitiful, excruciating, but I carried on singing about love and cups of tea.

Now it was Jenny's turn. She floundered instantly, played whatever came into her head. She had forgotten everything. She was red in the face, sweating heavily despite the cold. Alma gave up conducting the cater-wauling that her bow produced, for it obeyed no conceivable time signature, but she kept her eyes fixed on Jenny and her stare was so derisive that Jenny could not fail to feel it as intensely as one of the famous slaps. At last Alma put an end to her torture with a sharp flick of her baton. Thoroughly humiliated, Jenny wept copiously while we, oblivious of time and place, laughed till we cried; affected by our own helpless giggling, the women too began to laugh. We were unable to control ourselves, yet each one of us was quite aware that Jenny's fault was so serious that it could have cost her her life.

We put our things away and left the infirmary like workers going off duty. After our departure a hundred, two hundred of these women would go to the crematoria. Had we already become brutes? How could one explain one's indifference? I thought of two recent facts, independent of each other, but which had succeeded one another chronologically: the return of Marta and Zocha's behaviour with the milk.

The morning had ended with the usual metallic clank of bowls which followed the arrival of the soup. Sitting round our tables, we swallowed the viscous liquid. Outside, it rained on interminably. Wet, head streaming, a girl appeared in the open doorway and the wind swept in. She was very thin, verging on the moslem, tall and almost without breasts. Florette and Jenny, in amazement, shouted out, "Marta!" So this was our longed-for cellist. She didn't smile, her greeting was

colourless, she came from another world. The girls'
greeting wasn't too warm either. She proceeded un-
steadily towards her bunk and sat on the edge of it.

"What was wrong with you?" asked Jenny nervously
from a distance.

"Typhus."

"And you pulled through? You lead a charmed life, I
must say."

Informed by Regina, Alma appeared on the scene.
Though different physically, they were members of the
same haughty and superior race. They exchanged brief
and rapid words in German. As far as I could judge,
because by now I could speak it fairly fluently, Marta's
German was very pure. Her hollow orbits made her
wonderful almost golden eyes larger and darker. When
Alma had gone, she sat there dreamily for a bit, then
murmured in excellent French: "Alma would like me to
accompany you at the next concert, but all my things are
dirty . . ."

I warmed some water on the stove in our little bowl,
which was fortunately empty, and said, "Give them to
me, I'll wash them for you."

She seemed surprised. I didn't wait for an answer,
took them and washed them. Exhausted, Marta
stretched out on her mattress. I put her things to dry on
the stove, expressing the hope that they would be dry by
four o'clock. She acquiesced vaguely, looked at me
oddly but didn't smile. Marta was very proud, and independent. The girls, curiously angry, seemed critical of
my action, which I regarded as a gesture of ordinary
solidarity, but which was incomprehensible to them.
They confronted me: Clara, Jenny, Florette, Helga,
Elsa, Anny, backed up by the vigilant chorus of Germans and Poles. The Russians always kept aloof. The
two Irenes and Ewa merely observed me. I was judged,
condemned: "You're cracked. So you've taken to doing
other people's washing nowadays?"

I defended myself: "She's just come out of the Revier, she can hardly keep upright. I don't see why I shouldn't help her."

"Because we don't do that here." Jenny's explanation was precise. "Whatever her state of health, she's got to manage on her own."

"If you think anyone would do the same for you, you've got another think coming," was Clara's contribution.

"I don't expect anything in return and that's not why I'm doing it. I do it because it's natural."

They were staring at me, disapproving and incredulous, a stupid blinkered herd; for them, I was mad or pigheaded.

Jenny, who had become the spokeswoman, attacked: "Who do you think you are? A führer? We don't take lessons from anyone, and particularly not from you."

They were all too stupid, too selfish.

"Look, you poor idiots," I burst out, "if you carry on like this, you'll never be able to go back to real life. You're lost! To live with other people you have to have a minimum of solidarity. You may get out of here alive, but inwardly you'll be deader than any of those poor things they burn every day!"

Eyes closed, taking refuge in her weakness, Marta was remote from the commotion she was causing.

The others smirked at me, convinced of the protective strength of their egoism. I was the crank, the simple-minded one, the madwoman spouting gibberish.

I felt that their sarcasm was teetering dangerously on the verge of hatred; and once again the group of Poles, both Aryan and Jewish, struck me as the most fanatical and odious. Was I going to become a racist, here where that was the most monstrous of sins?

I turned away and went to the window, pressing my nose against the pane for a moment; the rain had stopped, and something resembling the sun was trying to pierce through the cloud of smoke no longer driven

our way by the wind. A few yards from our hut the
enormous, well-fed silhouette of Zocha was blocking
my horizon. I saw her gesture before my brain translated it to me: she was raising her arm and, from the
bowl she was holding, she was pouring milk into the
mud! She had had enough so, from her lordly height of
five feet nine, she was throwing it away. About thirty
miles from Auschwitz her parents, Poles who hadn't
been displaced, had a farm. Each morning they brought
their daughter a parcel which actually reached her. She
was big and fat and as strong as a man—a monster! One
would have been hard put to it to find any human traits
in her at all.

Presumably that day Ewa's thought had followed a
similar course to my own, because that same evening,
while we were sitting round our stove, she talked to me
about the problem:

"The first trip I'll make, afterwards, will be to Paris,
and you must come to Krakow; I'll make you love my
country." A fleeting apologetic smile passed across her
face. "You must have such a bad opinion of us. I saw
Zocha pour away that milk this morning. I'm ashamed
of the way some of my compatriots behave. I must admit that I wasn't overfond of the Jews, but here, how
could one continue to hate them as those stupid girls
do? How can they feel loathing for people who are so
mercilessly massacred? What right have they to despise
a race when there are people among us like Zocha who
throw milk away? That really upset me. She's a heathy
young girl, she eats all day long, and she wouldn't even
offer her surplus to someone less fortunate than herself;
that seems to me scandalous. Then there's that brute
Danka, who bangs the cymbals fit to deafen us. I've
caught a look in her eyes which shows that she actually
enjoys making those poor creatures drag themselves off
'in time' to our music. Irena's a frightful creature, too,
vicious, hypocritical, and cunning. Kaja is a solid
peasant type, but perhaps the worst of all; she leaves her

bread to go mouldy. Then there's their horrible patron, Tchaikowska, who brought them here in the first place—fancy usurping the name Tchaikowsky. She's completely unpredictable, stupid and hysterical, and she seems to be fuelled by spite. I suffer when I think that women like these are my compatriots. They're not all like that, I know; but here, the majority are.''

"Perhaps it's that one notices it more because they're *kapos,* blockowas.''

"Yes, but why them?''

"They're pretty tough physically, and you need to be, in their job. The SS know it and get the message across. Some of these women have been here since 1942. When a young girl is flung into this atrocious atmosphere, her instinct orders her to react. She learns very quickly that you have to please the Nazis in order to survive, and that to do that you have to act like they do—it's only then that they trust you. That's the only guarantee of survival one can have here. It's true for people like Tchaikowska, Founia, and Marila. They've ended up thinking like Nazis, feeling that they too are a master race. The Nazis obliterate all traces of humanity in the internees, they appeal to the lowest instincts, set prisoners against each other, arouse all possible forms of savagery, crush the weak, protect those who become monstrous like themselves—and that's how they attain one of the aims of National Socialism: the destruction of human dignity. And of course with some underprivileged people born in a socially impoverished milieu, where there's no education of any kind, the ground is already prepared; all you need to do is alternately beat them and reward them for them to become torturers in their turn.''

"You're probably right,'' Ewa said thoughtfully. "But I still see them as Polish, and I wonder what will happen to them when they leave here—after all, they have a better chance of survival than the others. So how

will they readapt? Will they ever be able to live like
everyone else? What will society do with these women
who have learned to live on other people's corpses? Will
they have husbands and children? And what will their
place be in a different Poland, freed of the horrors of
Nazism? Perhaps it's not entirely their fault. Is it ours,
the fault of the privileged classes? It's very painful to
have to feel partly responsible for them. Before coming
here I knew nothing of this kind of feeling, I'd never
have talked like that. But I knew practically nothing
about society or about the world. I knew only my own
milieu, that of the Polish aristocracy, another sort of
ghetto! I'm thirty, I've got a husband and a son, Mirok,
who's nine now, whom I adore. I'm one of the most
successful actresses in Krakow. My life was just like that
of any girl born into my sort of society. My father was a
count, my husband a member of the aristocracy too. I
was brought up in a castle, and learnt French and music.
I did what used to be called the 'humanities.' This
education led me into the Resistance—could any member of the aristocracy have acted differently? There was
no choice. The invader came, and I did what I thought
right for my country. That brought me here. I don't
regret it. My Poland—bled white. I'm Polish first of all,
I put that before religion or family. I hate the Germans,
I hate the Russians; they've made all of us into permanent rebels!''

She was beautiful: Ewa, our grande dame! Like a
wild creature, nostrils flaring, she was breathing the air
of those heady escapades which led heroes cheerfully to
their deaths. Yet here she was without glory; cheeks
flaming, she continued:

''When I see those chimneys smoking day and night, I
can say that I regret nothing of what I've done, and that
I'd do it again. If I had to be part of the work group or
shut in Block Twenty-five, taken to the gas chambers,
I'd do it all again, because I'm certain that this night-

mare will end in the defeat of Nazism. It can't be other-wise. Then what will happen to my country? Shall I still be alive to see it? Though even that hardly matters, because my son will live to see the Liberation; he will live freely in my Poland!''

Marta

AT ATTENTION, heads erect, five by five, our gaze apparently fixed on the middle distance, we saw Frau Drexler approaching a bed in my row. This was the first *Bettkontrolle*—bed check—I'd witnessed. The SS woman twitched the cover off sharply. Tchaikowska and Founia didn't wait for orders, they zealously yanked off the mattress; hidden underneath were a towel, a slip, some soap, a tin plate, a fork, a spoon, all painfully "organized." "Confiscated," barked Drexler. It was devastation. All mattresses were overturned, bedclothes thrown to the ground. Drexler accompanied her purifying action with vigorous *"Verfluchte Juden!"*—damned Jews. She didn't speak her words, she spat them. The girls were shattered by this general search; gazing into space, they didn't bat an eyelid. To attract Drexler's attention could mean death.

She was delighted by her pathetic booty: it represented weeks of privation and she couldn't fail to know that. Astonishing to enjoy lording it over such a feeble lot. The grace of the Führer, who like God the Father reigned over great and small, had raised her to this exalted post, while in her native Swabia she would have been, perhaps, a waitress. If the well-loved Führer, through the medium of the SS, had recompensed her by putting her here in this camp, the largest and most efficient, she must have deserved it. You could read that in her eyes, in her manner. But this awareness of her

justly attained rank didn't prevent her from being
furious with the cold, the boredom, furious because the
days and months were so long, because there were too
many Jews in the world and she would never manage to
exterminate them all! Anyway, she was afraid of getting
lice, which were rife everywhere except in our block.

Like the other SS women, she lived in a state of perpetual rage. And now she was taking it out on us,
probably because she had recently been subjected to the
rudeness of a superior. A posting in Auschwitz rarely
struck the members of the SS as an agreeable
promotion; this token of trust, this nod in the direction
of their high sense of duty and devotion, was the reverse
of welcome. Only the camp commandants, the really
high-ranking officers, the genial organizers of death,
Himmler's henchmen, could hope to obtain promotion
in the Hitlerite hierarchy this way.

Triumphant, with the tip of her toe, Drexler poked
about in our belongings—nightdresses, towels, bras, all
forbidden things; with a vengeful heel she crushed bits
of bread, some biscuits, a miserable bottle of scent.
Which of us was going to have to erase the traces of this
havoc? Frau Drexler left us, smiling complacently,
followed by Pani Founia and Marila bearing off the
remains of our fortunes.

After their departure, the girls gave way to their anger
and despair. The most important of my belongings—my
toothbrush and my precious notebook—had escaped
the catastrophe because I always carried them on me. I
could no longer remember where that horrible little
notebook had come from, nor of course did I know
what its original purpose had been. Here everything one
got hold of had a past that was best ignored. Already I
cared more about that notebook than anything else.
Within a few days it had become essential to me, a real
friend; I would caress it lovingly like the silky fur of a
comforting animal, a warm, familiar, well-loved skin. I

kept it to the end, and it was to be an invaluable aide-mémoire.

The loss of their property, whose replacement they would now have to spend weeks "organizing" with their bread rations, depressed the girls utterly. Now hunger would rack them further still.

Marta passed haughtily in front of us, carrying a bucket. She went out into the wind and rain—we got water from outside, from the taps of the hut opposite, the lavatory block. She came in again with the same expression of icy indifference. The full bucket tugged at her thin arm, transforming it into a gaunt vertical line, a sort of rod of bone ending in a bucket slopping with water.

"Ah, it's Marta who's going to wash the floor," I commented automatically. "Who punished her, and why?"

"Why, does she interest you?" muttered Florette.

"Yes, look at her. She can hardly stand and yet she's carrying that bucket as if she couldn't care less."

"Don't you worry about her. With what her sister brings her from Canada, she'll soon be back in form."

"You don't seem overfond of her?"

"Well, she's a great faultfinder, and her pompous way of talking High German annoys me. She's been brought up like a princess; she's probably never done any dusting even. She's the kind who doesn't like to soil the tip of her little finger."

On her knees, Marta certainly looked very clumsy; she had plunged her cloth into the water and hadn't wrung it out enough, so that it spread enormous puddles of water. I'd have liked to help her, but the girls wouldn't have allowed me to, and I had no desire to provoke another lecture on charity. Her lovely statuesque face expressed nothing except a real weariness.

The call of a runner announcing an SS warden—we

were being treated to the works this morning—immobilized us. I'd never seen this one—she was a real Kraut: gaunt cheekbones, a heavy jaw, deep-set blue-green eyes with sharp brow ridges, blond but lacklustre hair. What did she want here? Her attention was caught by Marta, still on her knees amid her spreading puddles. A look of satisfaction crossed the bony face. Towering above her, legs apart, hands on hips, she planted herself a yard or so away from the toiling Marta; her whole mass of flesh and bone seemed to judge her work reprovingly. Her look expressed such disgust that a shudder of concern passed through us all. Was she going to bawl: *"Aufstehen! Raus!"* and take her off to Block 25? That was her right: Marta didn't know how to wash this floor; unable to perform her task, she was botching it, and that merited the death penalty. For this Nazi, it was evidently more important to be able to clean a floor properly than to play the cello.

We didn't have to wait long; with a violent kick of her boot, the SS sent Marta to the other end of the room. I saw Little Irene go pale. Marta stood up coldly.

With a swagger, the German declared, "I'm going to give you a lesson."

Then we were treated to an astounding spectable: the virago tucked up her skirt and knelt down. Head high, looking superior, she seized the cloth in both hands and squeezed it powerfully into the bucket; then, with quick skilful movements, she mopped up the puddles and embarked on a masterly cleaning of the floor. We had to admit she knew her stuff, the bitch.

In stunned silence Alma, Tchaikowska, Founia, and Marila didn't miss a moment of the sight: it reversed the established order of things. There was absolute silence, broken only by the sound of the rubbing of the cloth on the floor. Petrified, we contemplated this woman who had the power of life and death over each of us, on her knees in front of Marta, serene and erect but not at attention. Marta was only seventeen, but she was observing the SS woman at her feet with utter insolence. Her expression fascinated me. I wasn't the only one; there was admiration in the eyes of Little Irene, a tender admiration I wouldn't have thought her capable of.

When she came to the end of the room, squeezing her cloth for the last time, the warden got up, and the pitch of our anguish rose. She pulled at her skirt and looked Marta up and down contemptuously, then said, chin high: "That's how you wash a floor; now you know."

"*Ja,* Frau Aufseherin!"

There was such arrogance in this reply that I saw Alma swallow desperately; one didn't confront SS, or attempt to stand up to them. Calmly, the German turned her back on us and went out. Our room had never been so clean.

The laughter we'd been holding back burst out all the more violently for being triggered off by fear. The event had indeed been exceptional, not only because we had seen an SS on her knees washing the floor, proud of having perfectly accomplished such a "marvellous" task, but because something had occurred between her and Marta, even though we'd have been hard put to it to say what. Coldly, with the overweening air of a member of the Prussian gentry, Marta informed us: "That woman was the maid of all work in my father's house."

Then she calmly took her cello and went to sit in her place.

The news was astounding, and naturally required some comment.

"All I wonder," Jenny said in amazement, "is why Mrs. Mop didn't send her to take the air in the crematorium."

"My God," Clara cut in, "she'll send us all to Block Twenty-five. Just because of that idiot."

"Don't be crazy! The woman's so dazed by her own propaganda that she thinks we were lost in admiration of her, scrubbing the floor like a loon!"

"Come off it, though," Jenny persisted. "Did she

take what she saw in Marta's peepers for admiration? She'd need to be even stupider than she is!''

"I must say I liked Marta's courage. To brazen it out with that SS woman when she had more to fear from her than any other. What nerve!''

This praise, coming from Little Irene, brought a gleam of jealous disquiet into Florette's eye.

We never ceased bickering over this incident; it entered our mythology, and as we gathered round the stove at night, chewing our bread, each of us would tilt it to suit her own particular purpose. Jenny turned it into a sort of cardboard cutout of the mock-heroic type, where Marta, in the triumphal attitude of the noble explorer, received the obeisance of the conquered chief cowering at his feet! With Big Irene, we entered the sugary domain of the novelette: the former maid flew to the help of the mistress she'd always secretly admired. Lili used it as the basis for a tragedy, whose first two acts we were acquainted with but whose third was to be devoted to the vengeance which was going to wreak havoc among us all.

Observing Marta, I thought how irritating she must find these commentaries. Silent, haughty, self-absorbed, she was visibly elsewhere. I tried to imagine her walled domain: did her dreams encompass an unknown partner or did she enjoy a romantic solitude?

Marta manifested a distrust of everything that wasn't her own world, and this limited her relations with the girls. "She doesn't even meet us half way," Florette would complain, exasperated by this attitude. I realized that shyness had a lot to do with it, that she was ill at ease in this odd world which was ours; she found it as worrying as everything else that hadn't been codified by her milieu. Even the long conversations she had with her sister Renate, two years older than she, were reserved: they might have been figures in a painting by a minor master of the English school, "Young Ladies in Conversation.'' Renate too was very beautiful, but Marta had some special promise, as of imminent incandescence.

Beside her Little Irene was strangely silent, taking no part in the interpretation. I'd been waiting for some sort of clear statement from her, Marxist in tone, on the concepts of serfdom, proletarian revenge, something incontrovertible; but she seemed absent, so distant that she made a clumsy movement causing her neighbour's bread to fall from her hand.

"Oh, I'm sorry!"

"That's all right," said Marta, bending down.

Quicker on the draw, Irene picked it up and handed it to her. She murmured thanks and her cheeks darkened.

The brown moss that did duty as hair gave Marta the look of a little boy. Her mat complexion, long-lashed dark eyes, clearly defined mouth and the proud way she held her head reminded me somehow of those Berber adolescents one sees leaning meditatively against doorposts in pictures of Moroccan medinas.

She raised her head towards me, and her thoughtful look came closer to home. For a moment I thought she was going to smile, and that reminded me that I still didn't know what sort of effect that would have on her face. What a strange girl; her hidden frailty was apparent to me, fleetingly, at that moment.

I was alone by the stove. As usual, Ewa and I had been reciting poetry to one another: it was our way of keeping in contact with the other world. Florette, chin on knees, Anny and Big Irene had listened to us. Clara, in a corner, a scrap of mirror in her hand, rehearsed her songs to herself, studying her expression. I had told them an installment of the *Picture of Dorian Gray;* each evening, from memory, I "read" them a chapter before they went to bed. The dormitory was now asleep, with an odd sigh, a groan, a childish mutter from the depth of a dream. Numbed by the warmth of the stove, I was daydreaming; when I left its circle of warmth it would be cold, and I dreaded that moment.

A piece of music I wanted to write—a symphony, no less—was taking shape inside my head. How one could feel the urge to create in such a place I don't know, but then how could one want to do anything at all?

"Am I disturbing you?"

It was Marta; in the long nightdress which her sister had given her, she looked like a demure schoolgirl, but dreadfully thin. Furious gusts of wind were driving the rain against the windowpanes.

"To think that a few days ago Little Irene was drawing lilac and talking about the spring!"

Marta was enthusiastic: "She draws very well, don't you think? I'm better off with a bow, myself!"

"Better than with a cleaning cloth!"

She gave a quick, reticent little laugh.

I continued: "You were marvellous. What a wonderful reversal of roles. You were the queen and she the slave."

"You know, in our house, she was never treated like that. We looked after her well, very well. We had a cook, a nurse, and a chambermaid. Actually, I might not have recognized her—I didn't see her much. She did only the rough work."

She gave another unobtrusive little laugh. "She's right, I certainly don't know anything about housework; I wasn't brought up that way. How could my father have thought that such things would be useful to me? I went to the University and the Conservatoire. Music took up much of my day. My parents used to entertain a lot; my father is a successful lawyer. We felt sheltered, protected. We wore the star but we'd never been worried. My sister and I were arrested in an unexpected way, in the street, in a roundup, and as we were Jewish, we were deported."

A slight smile softened the cold lines of her face. I

could easily imagine her with a chignon at the nape of her long, fragile neck. Women grumbled: "Quiet! We can't sleep."

"Marta, we'd better go to bed or she'll come down on us like a ton of bricks."

Unconvinced, she nodded, wished me good night. I almost expected her to hold out her hand like a well-brought-up young girl and, thinking of this gesture, I realized that we were totally cut off from it, that it was something forgotten, a movement for a civilized world. In bed, I thought of Marta; this evening she seemed so totally different from the heroine of the other morning. I didn't know why, but I felt she was somehow slightly pathetic.

A furtive shuffling, the wood of my bed creaked, and a head appeared: it was Marta.

"Fania, are you asleep? Am I disturbing you?"

"No, not at all, come up here beside me."

She climbed up and sat at the foot of what served me as a bed. "I can't sleep, I'd like to talk to you for a bit."

"Lie down here, we can talk more quietly." Long and thin as she was, she occupied almost no space. The fact that she had dared to make this approach didn't seem to me in keeping with her distant manner. She must have had something to say to me. She sighed slightly.

"When I came out of the Revier, I was glad that there were French girls here—you have a lighter way of taking life, you laugh easily, and I thought I'd be able to speak French. I've grown fond of your literature, particularly your poets."

I doubted whether she had climbed up here to talk to me about poetry. Lying slightly stiff at my side, she continued in a more worldly fashion. "I'm very fond of Little Irene, she's very intelligent. One can talk about so many things with her. I'm not so fond of Florette—she's hard, there's something uncouth in her that inhibits me; she so easily loses all sense of proportion. One person who strikes me as remarkable and well educated is Ewa; she's intelligent, too. But Irene's intelligence is more positive, more concise; Ewa's mind is made for poetic speculation, whereas Irene's is constructive. The sort of mind we're going to need after the war!''

All this was chatter of no importance and I let it pass. A silence fell; Marta moved slightly, breathed a bit more nervously, then gently asked: "I may be disturbing you, but I'd like you to talk to me about Irene."

"Which one?" I asked provocatively.

Suddenly cool, she answered: "You know which one." There was another silence.

I told her what I knew about Irene: that she belonged to the Communist Youth movement, about her action in the Resistance alongside Paul. When I told her that they'd both been taken to the fort of Romainville to be shot, that she'd been in the death cell and known those uncertain dawns when one waits for the door to open on the chaplain, I sensed that she was moved. She was living through Irene's anguish; this daughter of the upper classes was burning with the unknown faith of political martyrs. I talked to her at length about Irene's positive character, about her sense of duty imbued with dialectical Marxism, her exemplary behaviour in our block, her imperviousness to our bursts of ill-humour and our collective hysterics.

She was satisfied; her heroine had passed the test. "That's just as I imagine her. I like her way of behaving with the SS. She's not big physically, and yet she has a firm, unprovocative way of looking them in the eye, of standing in front of them, which impresses them. They respect her. Also, I love her face; she's so beautiful, so much more so than I am . . .''

"Tell me what you don't like about her, it'll be quicker!"

Touched, she moved at my side. "You're right, but you see, Fania, I'm worried, something's happening that I don't understand."

Now, as if in sympathy with Marta's tale, the wind had dropped and the rain was falling gently and regularly on the roof of our hut; there was a moment of calm.

"I love my sister Renate very deeply, but when I think of her I don't feel any of those contradictory feelings I have when I think of Irene. The other evening, when she made me drop my bread, her hand brushed mine and I wanted to seize it, to kiss it. I'd never want to do that to my sister—or anyone else. When she talks to Florette, when she listens to her nonsense or reasons with her I really suffer, I almost hate her. How can anyone of her calibre waste her time with such a crude, limited person? Irene is so marvellous. Since I've discovered her, I'm less unhappy. All I think about is her. Knowing that she's asleep not far from me, that tomorrow she'll be there, makes me extraordinarily happy. Do you know what I dream of? Irene puts her hand on mine, and we never leave one another again. Yesterday evening, for a moment, she took my fingers in hers, and it was so tender and violent that I hoped I'd faint. I kept the feeling of the warmth of her skin all day. This evening, I put my cheek on my hand where she'd touched it, and . . ."

It was perfectly clear: Marta was in love with Little Irene. It didn't surprise me: a thousand little signs had told me that there was a sort of complicity or understanding between them; but I hadn't thought of love. If it had been boy and girl I'd probably have sensed it immediately. I wasn't shocked, particularly because Marta was only seventeen, and her need for love was utterly natural. At her age, you didn't make love, you craved it. You dreamt of tenderness and endless kisses. But love needed a setting, a decor. What was offered to Marta here, what face did love have? The discreditable couplings of whores with *kapos* and block superintendents whose physiques were often closer to those of beasts than men.

In Birkenau, one couldn't long remain ignorant of

homosexuality—it was rife; it offered the women
satisfaction for their fantasies, allayed their solitude,
their sexual needs. If, for many, it was just a way of
cheating reality, for some it was a revelation, and Marta
was possibly one of those. In the music block, the only
homosexuals I knew of were a strange and repugnant
trio, Wisha, Marila, and Zocha; I'd learned about their
intimacy in circumstances so colourful that they continued to make me laugh for some time.

One evening, at about seven o'clock, mad yowls burst
from the Polish corner. We rushed over: Marila, her
face swollen with fury, hefty legs apart, clinging lim-
petlike to Wisha's arm, was shaking her fist at Zocha.

"Now we'll see some fur flying," Jenny said jubi-
lantly. "Domestic row brewing. Not to be missed. They
all sleep with one another, but not together. Wisha's the
boss, the fellow!"

For the moment she certainly didn't look it; her red
hair gave her the look of a pale, wizened little boy.
Wisha tried to disengage her arm and to put a distance
between herself and Zocha, who was clinging to her
neck. Jenny completed the picture: "Marila, that fat
shapeless cow, is the legal wife, and Zocha, who's not
exactly a dish either, is the mistress! And it's the real
thing, I can tell you. Do you get the picture?"

"Just about, but why is Marila shrieking fit to
burst?"

"Because she didn't know that her darling was un-
faithful to her. Everyone else knew, but not her, that's
the way it goes. A pity they talk doubledutch; otherwise
we could really get our money's worth."

Marila continued to shriek; she was foaming at the
mouth and showing the whites of her eyes.

"What shall we do? " babbled Founia, her little piggy
eyes expressing a glimmer of concern.

"Lie her out flat on a table," I nipped in smartly.

Her body arched, head thrown back, Marila, scarlet,
continued squealing like a stuck pig, a thread of saliva

running pleasingly onto her chin from the opening that did duty as her mouth. Then suddenly her body went limp, her eyes closed. I took her big black-nailed hand and patted it. I'd gladly have slapped her to help her regain contact with her life and its misfortunes, but the gesture might have been misinterpreted. Then inspiration struck:

"Anyone got a piece of sugar?"

A pause. I insisted on its curative virtues for someone in her condition. As I was well thought of by Mandel and Alma, Tchaikowska and Founia respected me. I was well on the way to being omniscient. Dreadfully panicked, Wisha handed me a chunk of the precious substance; firmly, I ordered the sufferer to open her mouth and stuffed in the first piece. The result was instant: she began howling again. I promptly stuffed in another, a third, a fourth—their devotion seemed unbridled—while tenderly, lovingly, Wisha caressed her fat legs. It was shameful wastage, but what joy to thrust this Polish treasure into that dribbling aperture. We positively sobbed with laughter; uncomprehending, her comrades were now laughing confidently. Marila was choking and we were splitting our sides.

What did the doings of this sordid, hysterical group have in common with the love that Marta was hesitantly confiding to me?

Marta gave a sort of dignified chortle: "I couldn't sleep, I was thinking about her so hard. Fania, I adore her."

"No, little one, you love her."

I could feel her body trembling beside me; she was worried. What she was experiencing was upsetting her ideas above love, her upbringing, her whole conventional outlook. Did she even know that such a thing existed? Perhaps I'd been too precise, too brutal. Already that love that she didn't yet know was bringing her its tithe of worry, and becoming reality.

"Oh, Fania, it's not possible!"

"Of course it is, and it's no disaster . . ." And I explained to her that to the pure all is pure; she so needed reassurance.

"So, Fania, it's not wrong to love as I do?"

"In the camp one might really call it a blessing."

"Thank you. You've done me so much good."

Was it wrong to love here? If I believed in God, I would say that to feel a pure, clean feeling in this place, where Evil reigned supreme, was a sign of His blessing. Loving wasn't wrong, it just seemed amazing to be able to isolate oneself sufficiently for it. The camp had entirely sterilized the need in me, and I wondered desperately whether it would ever return.

The next day, while my copyists were lazily working, made languid by the late spring which gave the air a certain unaccustomed mildness, I observed Little Irene: pencil in hand, head raised, she was wrapped in some distant dream. That in itself was surprising, because this small positive person usually worked away at her current task as though it were part of a specific programme carefully drawn up by herself. She must have had a considerable reputation for efficiency in the Party. Not far off, Marta was thoughtfully resining her bow. In my mind I heard her worried questioning—"Do you think she loves me?" I tried to imagine this self-centred rationalist Irene, organized almost to the point of fussiness, plunging into this love—and what love: a quicksand uncodified by Marx! She made no secret of her future plans. She was so sure of herself, of her judgement, that they couldn't but be excellent: she would marry Paul. They would graduate from the Communist Youth to the branch, then to headquarters; they'd militate just as they always had. She'd have a child—it was necessary for a woman—but only one; she had no vocation as a mother of a large family. These were not new decisions. She and Paul had always been in agreement on this point. The Party needed them, they must devote themselves to it entirely. She would draw, write, perhaps she'd get a couple of diplomas—she was so gifted—German, a bit of politics and economics. To build the new society, they were going to need educated people, competent and capable. The future didn't worry her, it posed no problems. Her path was clear, she would start off on it by a triumphal return. Not for one moment did she doubt that she would find Paul waiting for her and that they would be received like heroes. Listening to her speaking with such assurance, so serenely, I wondered about the nature of her love for Paul. Indeed, did she really love him? For her, above all, he symbolized the militant, a worthy companion, and that seemed to be enough.

For me who had always been fed on love, this conception of marriage seemed very bourgeois, something like the system of tactical marriages which strengthened the great families of France. For Little Irene, he would strengthen the future of Communism. There was not the slightest trace of doubt: "When I came to Birkenau I understood that, even more than in ordinary life, one could count only on oneself, one's own intelligence, one's own authority, and that the most important thing was to know how to assert oneself, so that as soon as I learnt that there was an orchestra here, I went to find Kramer; I told him that I played the vioiin and I was taken on as a musician."

How she had managed to go and see Kramer I didn't know. She had a way of telling one the essentials that made it impossible to ask questions. I knew very little about her: her father was a tailor and had been deported. She had told me quite calmly that "he probably disappeared up the chimneys," no trace of emotion in her voice. A hard light in her black eyes told me that Irene was not the kind of person who forgot, but the kind who noted down debits and credits and demanded their due from people and from life. She was going to extract the price of this death from the Nazis, from those SS whom she impressed, despite her small size: "You see, Fania, they despise sycophants and cowards. I'll never let myself be insulted by anyone at all, no one in Birkenau has ever bullied me. Perhaps they feel that I'm certain to get out of here alive. Perhaps it's because the moment I arrived, I decided not to let myself go, not to let myself be 'had' by the horror, the misery, and all the rest. For me, the Nazis will lose and we shall know a Socialist world that will be free of them forever."

I too was convinced that when the world knew what "they" had dared to do, it would crush them and reject them down to the last man. It was impossible to know whether there was a place for love in this highly organized being; the only experience she'd ever had had been carefully thought out, the "intoxication of the senses" had had no part in it. "I was imprisoned in the fort of Romainville when I learnt that I wasn't going to be shot—that's probably an honour denied to Jews—but deported. I'd never slept with Paul; we didn't want to take any risks—a child would have hindered our work in the Resistance, our struggle against Nazism. But I didn't want to go off to a work camp or a deportation camp without some degree of experience to arm me against the possibility of rape. From Romainville I was taken to Drancy, and there it was easy to put my plan into action. You know me, you know how methodical I am. Accidents can happen; I couldn't bring a child with any moral or physical blemish into the world, so I chose my partner carefully, and we made love. I felt nothing—no pleasure, rather the reverse. Was that love? I don't think so, so I'll wait."

In the evening, Little Irene and I were sitting chatting by the stove. For once she had left the fertile topic of rebuilding society and was talking to me about her family, as if she felt a sudden rush of nostalgia. I learnt that her mother, whom she'd never mentioned before, had died a long time ago, that her sister was married and had a string of kids, nice but riotous. Then, out of the blue:

"Here there's no one I can talk to about it, you're the only one who could listen to me and give me advice. Something has happened to me that I was totally unprepared for."

This was a new tone! She hesitated a moment, then suddenly sidestepped towards Florette.

"You must have noticed the rather childish admiration Florette feels for me. She's in a permanent state of rebellion and I'm the only one who can calm her down, the only one she'll listen to. In fact, you could say she adores me. There's nothing odd about that, I understand it quite well—I represent everything she'd like to have been. But that's not the case with Marta. She has nothing to envy me for—she's intelligent, highly educated, a wonderful musician, beautiful. Have you noticed how beautiful? Politically we appear to be at opposite ends of the spectrum: her class loyalties should make her fear Communism and therefore fight it; at the very least, she ought to distrust me. But since she's been back, her eyes are on me all the time. She always manages to be next to me, she blushes when I go anywhere near her. The other evening, I did a little experiment: I put my hand on hers for a moment, and she was so obviously agitated that I was embarrassed. So I tried to analyse the feelings I arouse in her, and I arrived at the conclusion that it couldn't be compared with what Florette feels for me. It's something else, and it goes beyond sympathy and friendship . . ."

Usually so sure of herself, Irene was hesitant now. I was thoroughly enjoying myself: to receive the confidences of two young girls within twenty-four hours was not without piquancy and humour; it took me wonderfully far from the camp. At least I was hearing about things other than death, eating, and sexual intercourse. Absorbed, her small solid hands with their square nails crossed on her knees, Irene was looking for words.

"I think she's very pure, very innocent, unaware of what she's feeling, which could well upset her, frighten her. I don't think I'm a Lesbian. I knew there were such people, but I had no reason to concern myself with them. Here, conditions are different. I admit that I'm as involved as she is, but she's the prisoner of her education, of her bourgeois morality, so perhaps she'll refuse to admit it!"

I could have told her that Marta loved her, that she was prepared to face this love, but I was silent. There was something in Irene's rationalism which annoyed me, she was so complacent and clear-sighted. A bit of uncertainty might humanize her.

"To tell the truth, I've noticed how interested she seems in you, but you never know. At her age, it's natural to be exaggerated and romantic in the way you show your feelings; after all it could just be friendship."

"Yes, it's possible."

Now for the first time I caught a glimpse of concern in her eyes, which darkened with something that began to look like anguish.

"You know, I'm really afraid I may be wrong, it's all so new and unexpected. Unreciprocated love wouldn't be at all right for me. I'm amazed at what's happening to me, Fania: I love her and . . . I desire her. I want to caress her boyish body, to be caressed by her . . . I want . . ."

"To make love. And so?"

She fell silent, a Puritan deflated and vaguely shocked by my realism. Was she going to talk to me about good and evil like a little bourgeoise?

"Do I have a right to embark on anything? I'm older than she is."

"Four years older. Don't be ridiculous, don't have absurd scruples. Father always used to say to me: 'If you are square with your conscience, there's nothing you can't do.' If she's sincere, if you are—"

"Fania, can you doubt it?"

"Well, what are you waiting for? If you can seize some moments of happiness in the midst of all this horror, I don't see that anything should stop you."

"But, Fania, what if I'm wrong, if she doesn't want me?"

Death's Bookkeeper

A RUNNER BURST through our door and collapsed on our bench, breathless, brandishing a shred of packing paper. A parcel? Between gasps the girl managed to utter the name of Big Irene. It was an important event. All that remained of the original packaging was a bit of stained, greasy, sticky wrapping paper. Judging by its size, it must have been a big parcel. Big Irene took it doubtfully, looked at the writing and began to cry, kissed it, put her cheek against it—it was the writing of her Jean-Louis.

Like an animal scenting quarry, Jenny pounced: "Well, I must say, your bit of parcel isn't very brilliant. Look what they've left you. It stinks!"

Irene's trembling hands picked ineffectively at a remaining bit of string.

"Let me do it," said Anny, always a watchful friend. She quickly removed the paper; inside, an utterly rotten herring lay on an envelope stiff with oil. Unable to believe her eyes, Irene murmured: "A letter!" Seized with respectful wonder, we gazed awestruck at the letter; her tears fell faster. "It's from him, from my darling."

Typically, Jenny commented, "The scent of your love letters isn't exactly aphrodisiac. My man uses Evening in Paris, it works better."

The girls surrounded Big Irene, full of envious respect

for the object of this miracle. Bending her pretty, childish head to read, she escaped from the circle and took refuge near the window. Fascinated, we kept our distance, not daring to go nearer; but none of us assumed the various activities interrupted by this incredible event.

Her face silhouetted against the sooty sky, she read it through once, twice, then gazed dreamily into nothingness, a big tear rolling down her cheek.

Jenny was our spokeswoman: "Well, what's the verdict?"

Irene turned to us a face which spelled love and resolution. "It's marvellous. He tells me he loves me, he says, 'Live for me, I'll wait for you.' I'll hold out till the end, for him."

Then her expression changed to one of anguish, and she asked pathetically: "I will come back, won't I?"

Her look had the entreaty, the desperate intensity of a child asking: "I will get better, won't I?" Ewa and I assured her that she would.

She sighed. "At night, to get myself to sleep, I imagine this return. Time's going by, but luckily I trust him. This letter is already six months old, and so many things can happen in six months! Do you think I'll get another?"

"Deliveries aren't exactly regular, you may have noticed," jeered Jenny. Eager hands stretched out towards the letter. "Let us touch it. It will bring us good luck."

Now the inevitable commentaries started to flow: How had he got the address? Why had the SS responsible for parcels let this one through? Could we start to hope? Then each of us began to rave about her own case: why not me, too?

As she left, the runner was still expressing amazement at having been the bearer of such an extraordinary thing. "I never take parcels with letters anywhere—you're certainly privileged!"

Privileged! The adjective provoked chain reactions which temporarily obliterated interest aroused by the letter. We couldn't fail to know that there were a number of unflattering stories circulating about us.

"Privileged—what does that mean?" Jenny objected acidly.

Her mouth pinched, Lili answered: "They say we're Kramer and Mandel's pets."

Florette saw red. "It's those idiots from Canada who've spread the rumour that we get parcels. In fact we had the last one, which was also the first, three months ago."

Calmly, Marta relayed the Revier rumours: "They say that the 'orchestra girls' get food supplements every day."

The girls choked with indignation when Anny revealed that the work groups claimed we got half a loaf of bread after each concert. The statement sounded so fantastic that silence fell, and the general outrage fed, for a moment, on that improbable dream: half a loaf!

"If I had half a loaf a day . . ." Clara murmured through her tears.

Once again the floodgates were opened, and bitter recriminatng phrases flowed. Jenny said to Clara, who went scarlet: "You wouldn't need to go with your *kapos* anymore!" Then, viciously: "Oh, I see! Look, fatty, it's not by chance because of your farm horse behind that they think all this stuff about us? When the 'others' see it, they can hardly think we're living on air!"

No one went to Clara's assistance, and she went off, swinging her huge behind, to take refuge in the music room, followed by the hostile stares of the girls.

Ewa changed the subject. "Let's be fair, we do have privileges."

Disapproving attention focussed on her.

"Yes, we have showers every day with lukewarm water, while the 'others' have to go to all manner of lengths and risk being beaten just to wash in ice-cold water. We're decently dressed, we're not cold. Our room is heated, we have a blanket and a sheet while they have quite inadequate rags. We can go out when we want to go to the lavatory. But they . . . you remember the lavatories in the quarantine block!''

I preferred not to.

''With these very real advantages, some of which are actually visible, how do you expect the other women not to think that our soup is different too—that there's more of it, and better? They're wrong; not only is it the same, but we're actually rather unlucky in this respect. As we never go out of the camp, we can't steal an odd carrot or some other vegetable from the fields and we've nothing to barter while every time they go out, they manage to bring something back!''

''I think you're right,'' agreed Little Irene. ''But I'm sure that this difference is intended by the SS: divide and degrade! Only 'they'll' stick to that idea, and they'll still feel resentment even when we're back.''

I lost interest. Little Irene's arguments were becoming political again; she was laying before us for the nth time a future blazing with social justice from which Fascists and Nazis were excluded. Four words filled my mind: *them*, the *others, us,* and *after*. Would the gulf that existed between us and them be spanned, or would it widen? Would there be enough survivors from the orchestra for the truth to emerge, or would all that would be known come from some few survivors of the camp who had cast a shocked glance in our direction and retained, in all good faith, only a subjective vision reflecting their feeling of the moment: envy, jealousy, anger, bitterness, or black humour?

Here at Birkenau no two five minutes were alike, and in that sense life in the camp world was more intense than in any city open to the world outside. And the world made itself felt here in so many ways: Paris was liberated; the Russians had won the war; Moscow was occupied; like Carthage, London had been destroyed! For a moment anything could be true, anything false. These pieces of news, whether true or false, had one point in common: they were always punctuated by selections. Thus the information which promptly followed the arrival of the letter that morning was staggering: "Girls, no more selections for us!"

It was so marvellous that it took us a few minutes to react. "What do you mean?"

"That they're only gassing the new arrivals, the ones in the convoys."

"Who said so?"

"A doctor, Dr. Mengele."

"Where's he breezed in from all of a sudden?"

"From the camp at Auschwitz."

"Do we know anything about him?"

We didn't yet, but the news wasn't to be long in coming.

Mistrustful, like a fox sniffing poisoned bait, I turned this news over in my mind: of course, it had been specified that this statement concerned only selections made within the camp, and more especially those among the sick. That it should have been a doctor who said it didn't strike me as an absolute guarantee. After all, it had been in the name of science that the Nazis had embarked upon the most abominable experiments on Jewish deportees; we were members of an inferior race, along with the Gypsies, just about good enough to act as guinea pigs. But there were some among the Germans who were not absolute monsters, and this one might be German rather than Nazi.

While my mind teased at this information the better to give itself over to enjoyment of it, the others had already abandoned themselves to joy unconfined.

The following days the news, retailed by the runners and Renate, Marta's sister, was very good: Dr. Mengele had thoroughly cleaned, disinfected, and repainted a barracks and equipped it with real beds with sheets for the convalescents!

I might have still had my doubts had not Marie confirmed it all: Marie, whom I hadn't known long, was a French Jewess, a young doctor of twenty-seven or so. I had met her at the end of a concert given in the infirmary, and we immediately took to one another. She was small, slight, with long chestnut hair and marvellous eyes à la Michèle Morgan; her patients adored her.

For three days, happiness reigned; one piece of good news followed another: all the convalescents were going to be transported, were being transported, had been transported into the new Revier. You should have seen them, washed and clean, in their gleaming white beds. You should indeed: because, at the end of the transport, on the third day, Mengele, the marvellous Mengele, had all four hundred of them gassed!

Hardly had we had time to react than we received news of the arrival of the SS, in full force: Kramer, followed by two lieutenants whose names we didn't know, then Mandel and her two acolytes Drexler and Irma Grese, plus the astounding SS colonel I had first spotted at the Revier concert whom I now immediately felt inspired to call Graf Bobby. This was the name of a well-known character in Germany, the creation of a cartoonist of the kaiser's time; corseted, monocled, he was elegance and snobbism personified. Beside my Graf Bobby, supremely elegant and indeed wearing a monocle, Kramer, squat and red-faced, looked like a butcher.

Accompanying them but standing apart was a tall, beautiful girl who must once have been marvellously slender but was now, naturally, too thin. I sensed that she was Jewish: she reminded me of the biblical Judith, with the addition of the tender gaze of the bride in the Song of Songs. Reasonably dressed, she wore neither triangle nor star, but an arm band saying "Chief Interpreter." She looked very pale. Perhaps it was she who had ticked off the four hundred names of the women who'd just been gassed. In the camp, the chief interpreter acted as death's bookkeeper, helping the officer in charge and crossing out the names of the condemned.

Faithful to their policy of disunion, the SS forced some prisoners to work against their comrades. Camp or block chiefs and work organizers, block overseers and administrators, food servers—these were all positions you could retain only by demonstrating great conscientiousness in the execution of orders, and exemplary zeal generally. Not to meet SS standards was to risk returning to your original position or being gassed. There was also a staff of prisoners, generally Polish and fifty in number, who shepherded people into the gas chambers. Their presence reassured the new arrivals, who reasoned as follows: "They're not soldiers, they're prisoners like ourselves leading us to the showers, so we can trust them." For these people, the hands that took their garments, that helped their children and their old relatives to undress and handed them towels and soap, were brotherly hands. It was they too who loaded up the dead and threw their bodies into the ovens. Prisoners who refused these jobs were immediately gassed.

To recruit them the SS promised them an easier life. Their barracks was clean, the food better and more plentiful, their clothing adequate. All contact with the others, who despised them, was forbidden. On Sundays, weather permitting, they could be seen playing football.

One day a Pole belonging to this specialist group saw his wife, his son and daughter go into the gas chamber. Like a madman he galloped over to Kramer, managed to speak to him, and those present had the privilege of witnessing the amazing spectacle of Kramer tearing across the camp followed by the Pole, going with him into the gas chambers, and bringing out wife and children just in time. This was just one of innumerable incomprehensible gestures; it didn't prevent the Pole from being gassed in his turn. Those who accepted this position to save their lives were in effect condemned—they knew too much and their reprieve lasted two months.

Observing the unbending stance of this interpreter, I wondered how much her task weighed upon her. How could she accompany someone like Tauber? We'd just learned one of his recent exploits: a couple of months previous he had brought a thousand women out into the snow, lined them up, entirely naked, in the freezing air, then, moving along their ranks, lifted their breasts with the tip of his whip. Those whose breasts sagged went to the left, those whose breasts remained firm went to the right and were spared a little longer, except of course for those who perished from the cold.

Learning about this form of selection, we compared the relevant portions of our anatomy. Apart from Little Irene, whose breasts were ravishing, with nipples like rosebuds, and Clara, whose breasts were full but still firm, the rest of us were flat as the palm of a hand. It was a fleeting form of security; Tauber might easily decree that this evident lack of femininity was a blemish.

I'd had plenty of time to think about this and other things too as, behind Alma, we waited at attention while the SS sat down and gave the order to play. Did they notice that we were standing up? Would they take any notice of a troop of monkeys presenting arms? That was about it, though of course monkeys would be more amusing.

For the moment, contrary to custom—generally they didn't tarry in our parts—they sat around as though waiting for someone. Mandel gave each of us a brief inspection, and we were seized with anguish: were our shoes clean, our dresses decent? Who was coming?

Sharply, Mandel ordered Alma: "You'll do the duet

from *Butterfly*, Schumann's *Reverie, Mattinata,* and
'The Charge of the Light Brigade.' Oberarzt Dr.
Mengele is coming to hear the orchestra.''

After a perfectly calculated pause the head surgeon
made his entry. He was handsome. Goodness, he was
handsome. So handsome that the girls instinctively
rediscovered the forgotten motions of another world,
running dampened fingers through their lashes to make
them shine, biting their lips, swelling their mouths,
pulling at their skirts and tops. Under the gaze of this
man one felt oneself become a woman again. The
elegance of Graf Bobby in comparison seemed affected.
Dr. Mengele wore his uniform with incomparable ease
and style, like a sort of Charles Boyer. A smile played
over his lips. Insouciantly he laughed and joked, conscious of his charm. He was even civilized enough to fall
silent when Lotte-Suzuki and I-Butterfly started our
duet, and he showed even greater consideration in omit-
ting to laugh at the unusual couple we made, she so
enormous and I so minute. Actually it didn't seem to
worry anyone, and particularly not Irma Grese, who
rested her blue gaze on me and, in the way one might say
of a monkey, "what's more, it talks," commented in
surprise, "How come she's got such a good voice, being
Jewish?''

The doctor didn't appear to like "The Charge of the
Light Brigade,'' because he left the room almost at the
first bar, followed by Graf Bobby. Alma blanched. Had
she failed to please? Kramer got up in his turn and ordered *"Schluss!"* The SS filed out; the last to go
through the door was the interpreter, and it seemed to
me that she hesitated for a split second before going out.
Who was she?

Alma could rage away, hector us, throw her baton at
our heads, trample on it if she liked; the orchestra didn't
care, because now one name was going the rounds,
holding us all in thrall; that of the interpreter, Mala.

More than a name, she was already a legend, even for

me who was not very well informed. Little Irene filled me in:

"Mala is our hope of salvation. She was in the Belgian Resistance and arrived from Brussels with one of the earliest transports. Immediately, with five of her friends, she was selected. That evening the crematoria couldn't take any more. For several days the men had been shovelling corpses in but the mound never seemed to get any smaller. Mala and her friends were locked in Block Twenty-five. No one had ever come out of there alive. The internees whose huts open onto the courtyard of Block Twenty-five tell horrible stories; they say that you can see a succession of women staring at you madly from behind the bars, that it's unbearable. Naked too—why go to the expense of clothes, since they're going to die?—they're thrown down in the stinking straw. The SS toss them something to eat when they remember; they may be there days, weeks, or a few hours. You couldn't even call it hell, there's no name for it. When the truck stops and the door opens, the living set off for the gas chambers, the dead for the crematorium. One night Mala and the five girls managed to escape by climbing through an air vent. They ran towards the camp entrance, went out of it, and found themselves in the place we call *Vorne*, near the houses of the SS who live outside the camp. They were sitting in front of their doors, smoking and chatting; one was even playing the harmonica. The evening was sharp but fine. Commandant Höss was talking with his officers when suddenly these naked girls appeared before him; they were so surprised they burst out laughing. Höss asked them where they came from and who they were. Mala, as cool as if she'd been fully clothed, answered: 'From Block Twenty-five, Herr Kommandant.' The SS looked at one another in amazement. Her courage impressed them and the interrogation continued:

" 'What's your name?'

" 'Mala.'

" 'Where are you from?'

" 'Belgium.'

" 'Have you a profession?'

" 'No, but I can speak French, German, and Polish.'

" 'How old are you?'

" 'Nineteen.'

"Silence. The commandant paused for reflection, then gave the order to have them dressed. 'Find them some work. This one'—he indicated Mala with the tip of his stick—'shall be an interpreter.' That was no sinecure; Mala immediately realized that she would be able to use this position to help others. Soon she was occupying a post of some importance in the camp and became chief interpreter. For some reason the SS trusted her without her having to give the kind of pledges they usually understood: denunciations, zeal during selections, etc. Perhaps it was because she's brave, silent, calm, efficient. In fact, without their realizing it, she controls them, impresses them. The internees respect and love her. We all have total faith in her. It's got around that Mala omits a name on a list whenever the circumstances of selection allow it. When they have difficulties, the deportees go to her. Despite the fact that she's Jewish, even the Aryans respect her and don't dare mock or insult her. And that's not all. Mala has a lover: Edek, a handsome lad in the Polish Resistance. They are able to arrange meetings because they both hold positions which allow them to go out, even when the camp is confined to quarters. He's an administrative assistant. I don't know anything else about them, but people who've seen them together say there's no doubt about it, they love one another."

Outside it was pouring; the rain bounced on the roof as hard as hail, struck the window aggressively. The stove was glowing red, the wind's whisper had become a roar. Most of the girls, the Poles, Germans, and Russians, were already in bed, but our little group, seated round the stove, was prolonging the evening.

Little Irene concluded: "I've never talked to her, I've just seen her walking through the camp, head high, looking aloof; but one senses that she's burning inside, and today, at last, she came here. Perhaps she'll come back."

I felt a desperate desire to see her, to talk to her; she struck me as a classical heroine, a living archetype.

"Well, we certainly can't count on it," Anny remarked more calmly. "Anyhow, what could she do for us?"

Mala

THE FOLLOWING DAYS, Mala did come back to see us. Not out of love of music—there was room in her life for two sorts of love only: love of freedom and love of Edek. They sometimes met in our block and each time it was a unique moment. She would come in, a few moments later he would enter, they would look at one another but keep their distance, and this distance seemed to unite them; they didn't touch one another or speak, yet around them the air would begin to hum. They looked at one another and everything caught fire. For a moment their love recaptured the beauty of the world for us.

This evening, at the end of a particularly long *Blocksperre,* Mala appeared, looking drawn. The circles around her lovely eyes looked dark in her pale face, like a tragic mask. Little Irene and Ewa asked: "What's the matter? Are you ill?"

"Yes. After a selection I'm always ill, ill with disgust, rage . . . it's got to end! I can't take it any longer. We must do something, the world must know, it must put an end to this horror."

Nervously, I asked: "But how? What will you do?"

"I don't know yet, but Edek will find a way!"

There was such faith in her eyes that I too believed her. If anyone were to succeed, it would be she, they.

"We shall tell men the truth and they will believe us!"

We were all staring at her now. It was so glaringly

simple: if the outside world knew what was going on here, they'd stop it. It was so obvious that we agreed: "Yes, they'll believe you!" How could anyone not believe her?

We began to ramble: if the camps still existed it must be because no one had managed to escape and inform the world of the truth! Someone even claimed that when the pope learnt of our existence, he would mobilize all Christendom in an unprecedented crusade. It was all becoming so definite that we asked Mala, "How will you do it?"

"I don't know, but I shall!"

That was enough for us. Everything was settled now.

One morning there were rumours of an Allied landing, apparently in France. Florette and Jenny shrugged. "Just another fairy tale!"

"No, this time it's Mala who says so."

It was she who fed us news; we awaited her arrival feverishly. Her position as interpreter enabled her not only to move around freely, but also to glean information of all kinds from the SS, since she was constantly in their company. We didn't dare rejoice yet, but we all observed the Germans closely. It might be our imagination, but they seemed more jumpy than usual, more tense.

A few days later, Mala confirmed the information. Our group stayed up late into the night. In the morning we scanned the sky, looking towards the Carpathians. Sometimes, wind permitting, when the crematoria were less busy, we could see those mountains where the Polish Resistance had their hideouts, and we were certain they would bring us freedom.

But days passed, our impatience gave way to somewhat disenchanted resignation; it was a long business.

One morning there was an interminable roll call. The orchestra had been waiting for an hour for it to end in order to go out and play, but no whistle had yet been blown. The SS were counting and recounting the women, sirens were lowing, soldiers rushing about. There had been an escape. Time passed, a rumour went round: Mala had escaped, and probably Edek too, because the deportees in the men's camp had also been standing at roll call for hours.

When the whistle finally blew, emotions had reached an unbearable pitch of intensity. Everyone knew the truth, or was prepared to invent it. One thing was certain: Mala and Edek had escaped. That evening we brought together everything we knew and managed to reconstruct the escape in a way which turned out later to be accurate. Thanks to the complicity of some German and Rumanian SS whom Edek had bribed—stolen "organized" gold circulated in all the camps—Edek had obtained some men's clothing for Mala and an SS uniform for himself, and false papers for both of them. Mala, wearing men's overalls over trousers and sweater, carrying a stoneware washbasin on her head, had gone out escorted by Edek in SS uniform, revolver at his belt. He was supposedly accompanying a workman to another camp. Since his pass appeared to be in order—the names had been scratched out and replaced—they had both set off towards freedom as they'd sworn.

We were insanely gleeful. Our reasoning was oversimple but heartening: "Since they're out, we'll be freed!" We were beside ourselves, but on our guard. The SS fury could redouble, indeed there was nothing to prevent them from gassing the whole camp if they felt like it.

So we behaved discreetly, nurturing our hope in whispers. No one slept. In each barracks, on each tier of the *cojas*, everyone waited for a miracle. Days passed; sometimes we pricked up our ears when we thought we heard strange noises, cannon fire, rifle shots. Our imagination ran riot: we could already see Mala and Edek returning at the head of millions of soldiers, who would enter the camp and put out the SS men's eyes, bayonet them in the stomach. We were drunk with images of gory revenge. For the first time since our internment we lived and breathed hope. We'd never sung or played with a lighter heart. Furthermore, we were singing and playing for ourselves; the "ladies and gentlemen" had other things to think about. Morning and evening, when the girls played *Josef, Josef,* the women in the work detachments gave them a wink of complicity; a different wind was blowing over the camp. The crematoria were pouring out their black smoke and masking the approach of summer, but we didn't care: summer with its harvest of victory was already singing in our hearts.

Rumours pullulated: there were vicious searches throughout the camps, interrogations in the SS building, accomplices were sought. But everyone claimed ignorance, and it was true. When you made a plan to escape you didn't confide in just anyone. The cold eye of the SS was inquisitorial, they observed us and each other. There were two or three traitors among them, perhaps more.

Early one morning, furtive and rapid, the news spread through the camp: Mala was back.

With bellowings, whistle blasts, and baton blows, the SS, *kapos,* and blockowas drove the women furiously out of the barracks, even us. Thousands of prisoners were out on the central square, in the alleyways, motionless, holding their breath. In the middle, on her own, was Mala, half naked and covered in blood; we learnt that she'd been tortured and hadn't talked. Standing, head proudly high, she looked at us and smiled. Tears came to our eyes, tears of love and gratitude. She was what we would wish to be: pride and courage personified.

An SS officer addressed her in the habitual ringing tones; I could hear every word and I would never forget them:

"You see, Mala, no one escapes from here. We are the stronger and you're going to pay for it."

He took out his revolver, loaded it and said:

"I'm going to shoot you as a reward for your exploits."

"No!" shrieked Mala. "I want to be gassed like my parents and like thousands of other innocent people. I want to die like them. But where we've failed, others will succeed, and you'll pay, you'll pay—"

The SS cut her off with a slap. I was standing about thirty feet from Mala and I saw something shining in her hand—a razor blade, with which she slashed her wrist.

The SS rushed forward, threw her down, trampled on her, put on a tourniquet; they wanted her alive. They tied her hands behind her back and dragged her off; she stumbled, picked herself up, and shouted to us: "Revolt! Rise up! There are thousands of you. Attack them—they're cowards, and even if you're killed, anything's better than this, at least you'll die free! Revolt!"

The SS man hit her, she fell; she was just one mangled mass of blood, a disjointed puppet, but her expression, her eyes . . . I would never forget them. They carried her off. We didn't know whether she was still alive.

Silence hung over the camp. Behind the crematoria, the sky was red as Mala's blood.

On the other side, in the men's camp, a gallows had been put up. Like us, the men prisoners were there, motionless, silent. Edek Kalinski appeared, hands tied behind his back, unrecognizable. He who had been so handsome seemed no longer to have any face at all: it was a swollen bloody mass. We saw him climb onto a bench. A snatch of the verdict in German, then in Polish, reached us; but before it was concluded I saw Edek move: he himself put his head in the noose and pushed back the bench. Jup, a camp *kapo*, intervened, took his head out, made him get back on the bench. The speech was resumed, but Edek didn't wait for it to end to shout: "Poland isn't yet—" We would never know the end. With a kick, Jup, his friend, tipped over the bench. An order rang out in Polish and thousands of hands were lifted to raise their caps. In final homage, the inmates of the men's camp bared their heads before Edek, who had been their hope.

We learnt the story of their recapture gradually too, piecing together a patchwork of whispered information.

They had walked three miles, Mala with the sink on her head, its weight making her legs tremble, Edek following. This was how they arrived at Kozy, a little village nearby. There a Polish accomplice sent them to a friend's place and they spent the night under a bale of hay.

I imagined their two bodies together; what a current of love must have joined them that night. Fear must have dropped from them, forgotten. They were alone for the first time, reunited. It was probably their first night, and their last. They had to make contacts in the town. Mala exchanged her blue overalls for a pullover and trousers. For reasons which remained unclear, she went to wait for Edek in a cafe. Germans, mostly in uniform, came and went. A Gestapo officer sat down nearby and stared at her—did he find her beautiful, or odd, or both? Though far from lacking in sangfroid, Mala was uneasy. She decided to leave, got up; quicker than she, he grabbed her by the arm and turned up her sleeve. The truth was revealed in the form of a tattoo. Upheaval in the cafe. Edek appeared at the door in SS uniform; he immediately grasped what was going on. He could have mingled with the other uniforms, turned calmly on his heel and gone away. He went towards Mala; without her, he would give up, without her he couldn't live, even as a free man. Despite her desperate glance, he joined Mala and let himself be arrested.

The rest we knew.

What piece of recklessness, theirs or their friends', had led them to this tragic end? Days passed, rumours died down, but the yeast of hope had brought up great bubbles in us which burst:

"They were out long enough to see friends, to talk to them, to tell them what we're going through; the world knows now, so why don't they come rushing to our aid?"

"I don't understand, what are the Allies waiting for?" complained Big Irene.

Florette was bitter. "It's not difficult to understand: What are we to them? What do a few thousand condemned people more or less matter? They've got their war to win, their power to assert. Nothing else interests them. They've got the world to carve up!"

I limited the scope of her cynicism. "I don't believe the Russians can think the way the others do. I'm sure help will come from the Carpathians."

My enthusiasm convinced no one. Everyday life had now resumed. Once again, the girls were swamped in their own self-centredness. Fear laid down its law. The monsters were now more powerful than ever and already people were jibbering at the idea of the reprisals that would inevitably follow this escape. There was no shortage of criticism either: "We're the ones who'll have to pay!" Mala and Edek were blamed. The girls spoke disapprovingly of their thoughtlessness, their impulsiveness, some even dared to say "stupidity." They became utopians, madmen, egoists.

Ewa, Little Irene, and I repeated firmly that the girls were wrong, that we had been given a marvellous example, that living wasn't a question of resigning oneself but of struggling, that we had to help one another, show solidarity, form a block ready for anything . . . We talked and talked, and no one listened. Life went on.

Our Beloved SS

SEATED ON A sort of gate, one leg dangling, his whip in his hand, Graf Bobby was preparing for "work." The doors of the railway carriages were open, and out of them tumbled men, women, and children. Few got up. Others came out shrieking, leaping over the dead. The transports, it seemed, took several days, standing on sidings to give priority to military convoys. These deportees had been travelling for twelve days; twelve days without air, food, or water.

Graf Bobby raised his face gracefully, thankfully, towards the sun. He was smiling, he always looked smug as a cat, pleased with himself and life. The others had hard, closed faces, but not he, though I doubted that that made him any the less deadly. He'd crossed his legs and the tip of his boot gleamed like glass, catching the sun's rays. The SS soldiers grouped the survivors five by five. His long cigarette holder in his mouth, Graf Bobby, with an airy flick of his switch and as the whim took him, separated those who were to enter the hell of the camps from those who were to make a hasty entrance to paradise. What a noble métier!

Outside, whistles blew more frequently than ever. Tchaikowska, squawking throaty *Verbotens*, crossed our room and went to close the door. What was so special about this *Blocksperre* that we couldn't have our door open?

Today we were rehearsing the quartet from *Rigoletto*.

Despite its somewhat unusual makeup and comical appearance (Lotte, contralto, Maddalena; Ewa, tenor, the lover, the Duke of Mantua; Florette, baritone, Rigoletto, the court jester; me, soprano, Gilda), the SS adored this piece, which meant that we performed it regularly. Hardly had the last note died away than we heard bursts of laughter so violent that, despite orders, we went to the windows and opened the door a crack: a young man, entirely naked, very tall, very thin, with a long nose, was singing and prancing outside the open door of a carriage, his hands flapping in the sunlight. The SS, from the humblest to the highest, were having fun, Graf Bobby among them.

The madman's tones rang out joyfully. All we could make out was a series of *"Hurrah! Bravo! Bravissimo! Bonjour, bonjour!"*

The procession of victims filed slowly past; heads turned towards the madman and some laughed. When they had disappeared in the direction of the ramp which led to the gas chambers the madman was alone with the dead from the carriages; and while the prisoners, in their striped rags, piled them onto the trolleys, he laughed and clapped his hands and capered grotesquely. The empty carriages slowly backed away and new ones arrived at the platform. The simpleton continued with his joyous number, he danced on. The SS continued cackling, slapping each other on the back. Then, doubtless deeming that enough fun had been had by all, Graf Bobby sent him, with a wave of his cigarette holder—how elegant it all was—to join the others on the ramp.

The diversion was over, but not the *Blocksperre*. It was still on at suppertime. It was so stifling in our room, heated for hours by a blazing sun, that Pani Founia and Marila had left the door open when they went to the kitchens to get the supper rations; almost automatically some of us looked out at the platform. Behind barbed wire the hopeless, monotonous cohort of the selected flowed by. A runner had told us they were Belgians, and Big Irene and Anny were looking intently at the new arrivals, as if all this sadness nonetheless brought them a whiff of their own country.

"You know," remarked Anny, "they really look Belgian." Then, violent, irrepressible, a strangled shriek rose in her throat: *"Maman!* It's my mother, my sisters!"

She threw herself forward. Down there on the ramp, her mother and sisters didn't look round. Brutally Florette planted her hand over Anny's mouth. Ewa, Little Irene, and Lili pulled her back. Anny struggled desperately, wrenched away Florette's hand, shrieked, "Let me go. I want to go, I want to see them—to die with them. *Maman, maman!"*

Florette landed her a well-judged blow and groggily she allowed herself to be carried to her bed. We took turns mounting guard beside her. She cried all night and fell asleep at dawn.

At rehearsal time, sitting on a chair, she was still stupefied, vacant. Gently Big Irene put her mandolin in her hand: "Play. It could be your turn soon, so play!"

From that day, Anny was never the same again. Always secretive, she withdrew further, closed in on herself; at the same time she became more outspoken, less conciliatory in her judgements, but above all, so much colder.

An hour later, this tragic episode was thrust definitively into the past. Word was going round that Kramer and Mandel had left Birkenau. We didn't know where they'd gone, or why; what concerned us most, of course, was whether they would be back. They loved their orchestra, they were proud of it, they were our most faithful clients, our protectors. Without them, our future was at best uncertain.

I caught Alma carefully inspecting our premises, her worried air betraying her train of thought: our block was clean, well-kept, adequately heated, and louse-free.

Other services could well be installed here; the camp was perpetually short of space, the teeming hordes poured in incessantly. The SS might decide to take it over, and we would land up either in a work detachment or in the gas chamber.

Not having been officially informed of the absence of our patrons, Alma decided to pretend she didn't know about it. We would rehearse as usual. The Sunday concert, by which time perhaps they'd be back, had to be perfect.

It was a real rag-bag: Viennese waltzes which they loved, a medley of Dvorak which they enjoyed without realizing that it was forbidden music, some Brahms Hungarian Dances, Schubert's "Lilac Time," snatches of *Tosca, Whitehorse Inn, Song of the Volga*. They were very eclectic, our SS. In fact they loved music but knew absolutely nothing about it.

This rehearsal gave us a glimmer of hope and we threw ourselves into it wholeheartedly, too much so in fact—it might perhaps have been better to have courted obscurity. A runner came to give the order to stop all rehearsals—the concerts had been discontinued, only the morning and evening sessions were to be kept up.

Discouraged, Alma put down her baton and went to shut herself up in her room, but reappeared almost at once. She strode across the room and went out. Was she going to attempt to intervene? But with whom? Exhausted by a bout of dysentery which had lasted several days, I went to lie down; we'd soon see!

Alma's return was somewhat unexpected: she came in with her arms full of balls of wool, followed by a runner similarly laden. She plunked the multicoloured harvest down on my table. Now we were a knitting factory!

"You see," Alma said to me, "I must show them that we're capable of doing something other than music. If they come in here and see you all nicely turned out sitting hands in lap, they're going to think you're useless. So I asked Frau Schmidt for suggestions; she suggested I go to the sewing block for work. They had nothing to give us; they're far too frightened of having nothing to do themselves. But I saw this wool and asked for it. So that's it, we'll do knitting, anything, but a lot of it!''

One hour later, except for Alma, Little Irene, and myself, who didn't know how to knit, all the girls were hard at work; scarfs and pullovers were the favorites, apparently in great demand. The SS could come along whenever they liked, they would be most edified. I stayed on my bed, ravaged by awful tearing stomach pains. From high up on my perch I could see them all, and I still had enough sense of humour to enjoy the sight: my copyists around their table, and the musicians at their usual places were clicking away busily. Alma passed among them, irritated and irritating; her total lack of expertise preventing her from actually directing operations but her air of chief-warden-in-a-prison-workshop exasperated them. Florette knitted quickly without lifting her eyes; Ewa was more leisurely, examining her work, measuring it, smoothing it with her hand. The Polish Jews knitted madly as if their lives depended on it, and indeed perhaps they did. Here the most extreme commonplaces took on strange resonances. The Aryan Poles worked slowly. Clara was constantly unpicking what she'd managed to do. The German needles clicked with positively mechanical regularity.

Two or three days went by punctuated by the varying rhythm of the knitters. We were in constant dread of a visit by Tauber, who, in Kramer's absence, seemed to be fulfilling a number of roles, too many for our liking.

Tauber, a long, angular man, was a melancholic ravaged by ennui. He sought the freakish, the novel; the routine of the ''right-left'' selection bored him, depressed him. In fact, the convoy routine didn't interest him; it left no scope to the imagination and he had plenty to spare. What he liked was selections that took place within the camp.

It seemed that we had nothing to fear from him in the immediate future, so absorbed was he in perfecting his latest brain wave, which consisted in putting the whole of the women's camp outside, with the exception of the Aryans and the staff of the special blocks, Canada, the sewing block, and the music block. He would review them, naked in their ranks, choose fifty or so from among the less sturdy so that they would collapse all the sooner, and order them to dig a ditch. The trickiest feature of this task was not the depth but the width, which had to be neither too great nor too small. When this work of art had been completed, the other women who'd been waiting, naked, at attention, had to run and jump the ditch; those who fell were good for "special handling"—the gas chambers.

Tomorrow perhaps we too might serve to distract him and he might be highly inventive in the use he put us to. Anything could happen. We knew he detested Mandel, and we did not doubt that part of his wrath would fall on us useless creatures. He had already forbidden rehearsals and concerts.

Most of the girls found the interlude agreeable. It reminded them of old times, when they used to knit sweaters, a bright scarf, or thick socks for "him," or for the children. Some knitted in the evening around the symbolic presence of the burnt-out stove.

On Sunday, collective anguish rose a few notches. No concert. This negative fact would be remarked on and observed by other SS, by Graf Bobby, though we still weren't sure how powerful this upstart was. And what could one expect from Dr. Mengele, who was the only other music lover in Birkenau? Probably nothing. Why should he, who exterminated them every day in the name of racial purity, under cover of science, now defend a handful of Jews who had had enough of a good time as it was?

This evening, everyone addressed their own gods to pray for the return of Kramer and Mandel! No one seemed to note the extraordinary paradox, the bizarre humour of the thing: the victims clamouring for their executioners.

In our block overt religious practices were usually badly received, with jibes or snarled invective. Apart from these moments of stormy piety, the most powerful manifestation of religion here was a degree of intolerance which would certainly have made a thoroughgoing atheist of me if I hadn't been one already. The Aryans had not the slightest hint of Christian charity and the blinkered Jews rejected everything which was not Jewish. For the Zionists, there was no salvation outside Israel. German or Polish, their claims were identical, their statements peremptory: "The Jews are the greatest people on earth. There can't be any Jewish murderers, because Jews do not shed blood. Nor can there be any Jewish whores, parricides, or infanticides." They always ended with the complacent aphorism that the Jews were the salt of the earth, the chosen people, to which Florette was always quick to answer bitingly that they were indeed, chosen for the gas chambers!

What exasperated me about these fanatics was their sectarianism. Never, even at Birkenau, was I lured into the murky excesses of blaming a whole people for the faults of a few of its representatives, and yet how tempting it was! Provided one could ignore the existence of those Aryan German internees—Communists, Resistance fighters, opponents of the Nazi regime—who had been shifted from camp to camp since Hitler's coming to power, one could indeed state with impunity that all Germans were murderers. Could one claim that all Poles were universally infamous, just because of the existence of a Tchaikowska or Zocha? Admittedly I didn't always show such equity; I often consigned them mentally to torments beyond belief.

This evening there were no jibes, and believers were left to pray, whatever their religion, as if obscurely the nonbelievers were thinking that perhaps there might be something in it after all. Only Florette, always vehement, and Jenny, always aggressive, declared roundly that the supplicants made them sick and that we had enough problems as it was without being forced to listen to all that jabber.

"I understand how you feel," said Big Irene, ever conciliatory, "but it clearly does them good. We must be tolerant."

There they were, narrow and sectarian in their own ways, and I understood them. In Birkenau, they were paying the price so that others might have the right to be Jewish openly. In that sense, they didn't like me not to be wholly Jewish, wholly on their side; they wanted me to be like them, particularly now, this evening, when concern was growing. Anny, her knitting abandoned on her knee, shook her head. "This lack of interest on the part of the SS can't last; they'll wake up with a jolt one day."

For a week, instead of the raspings and wailings of strings, the reedy whine of pipes and the thunderous banging of percussion, we'd heard nothing except the diligent click of needles, interspersed with classic exclamations: "I've gone wrong with my decreasing!" "Damn, I've dropped a stitch!" From outside, worrying noises reached us. It was quite clear that our current SS didn't like music, and what if they didn't like knitting either? We hardly talked anymore; no more arguments, jealous scenes, dramas, love affairs, nothing. We were so tolerant now that believers were left in peace. We scarcely dared to breathe. We had gone to ground, in terror.

The joyful and breathless child who opened our door was barely fifteen.

"Girls, they've come back!"

We were seized with something like delirium, we hugged each other, yelled, danced, clapped, we were happy, *happy!* Our beloved SS were back!

That was the state we were reduced to on learning that tenderhearted figures like Kramer and Mandel were back. When I grasped what had happened I was deeply alarmed. It required incidents like this for me to realize that, gradually, my judgement was deteriorating. I was beginning to accept the perpetual presence of horror, of death, the incoherence of the camp; my rebelliousness was weakening, it needed the whiplash to stir it to life. What kind of state would I be in when I got out of here? If only it didn't last too much longer, if only I didn't have to leave too many more bits of myself on this barbed wire! Never, not once, not even in the worst moments, did I doubt that we would be liberated.

When Mandel came to see her cherished orchestra and found it knitting, her surprise was evident.

"What's all this?"

Alma explained.

Mandel reacted instantly. "Drop all that, I'll have it taken away. Get back to playing at once. I want to hear music all day."

She took Alma aside and addressed her vehemently; clearly Frau Mandel's cool behaviour was a thing of the past. We were delighted, and even more so when Alma, in excellent humour, informed us, "She was incredibly angry when I told her that we'd been ordered to stop rehearsing. Really livid. She won't have anyone interfering with her protégées as long as she's alive!"

Alma, who had not been unaware of our "pious" evenings and was not totally lacking in humour, added: "I think perhaps we ought to pray for her!"

Music for the Reichsführer
Heinrich Himmler

SUMMER HAD COME. For a few days now it had been really warm, though the heavy cloud of smoke from the crematoria was hanging motionless in the warm air. The camp was seething like an ant heap disturbed by a giant's foot. The SS were nervous, though for once they didn't take it out on us but among themselves: officers barked at noncommissioned officers, who, as was only fair, passed it on to the soldiers. The civilian staff, interned or not, were all on edge; everyone, whatever his rank, was rushing about. This incomprehensible excitement affected the orchestra, too. Particularly tense, Alma rehearsed us frantically. We plucked and scraped and banged, making more noise than music, a screeching festival of wrong notes. My head was splitting. I no longer knew what I was writing, and when I sang it was mechanical, without any heart. Our only escape from this madhouse was when we went "shopping."

There was a sort of illicit market up against the side of one of the blocks, provisioned by the girls from Canada with merchandise filched from the consignments and by the women of the work detachments who managed to pull up an odd carrot or turnip and sneak it through the routine search. Fresh vegetables were real treasures, both for us and for them. We were all short of vitamins, and these vegetables were more essential than meat.

There was a throng just like at an ordinary market, with some women seated on the ground, others standing, and there was often lengthy discussion; but the actual physical transaction took place in the twinkling of an eye—the bit of bread, the soil-covered carrot flew from hand to hand. Runners kept guard; as soon as they saw an SS cap they would give the alert and the women would scatter like a flight of starlings. In a second everything would vanish, sellers, buyers, and above all merchandise—under skirts, in bodices. The SS were certainly not fooled, but for some reason, provided the evidence was not spread out before their eyes, they agreed to see nothing.

Trading activity was equally intensive around the kitchens. This bustle was normal, part of our everyday life, just as much as the trucks with their cargoes of dead, of half dead, of condemned. What wasn't normal, though, was the particular tension we were feeling, stirred up by the unusual activity of our masters. We came upon detachments of workmen running in all directions pursued by the barked orders of their group leaders. Huts which had never seen water were sluiced now with torrents, fellows in striped garb repaired roofs, unblocked pipes, laid new ones, checked electric circuits. The appearance of unknown SS aroused unfavorable comments: "They're not going to give us different ones," the girls grumbled. "There's precious little chance of improvement, they'll just be worse than ever." Even more worrying than the arrival of new SS was that of the black shirts of the Gestapo, the security police, who prowled around inspecting.

A rumour spread around the market, the Canadas, and the lavatories: we were going to be visited by a top SS man. "A supershit," commented Florette. It was worrying news, and we chewed on it with the same care we devoted to our piece of bread before the evening rehearsal; for three days now Alma had added three extra hours of music to our daily seventeen.

"Flora probably knows something about it," remarked Big Irene.

"We haven't seen her for some time; since she's become Kramer's maid, she's very choosy," observed Jenny. Oddly enough, that same day she turned up in our block, "as nicely turned out as an English nanny," as Jenny put it.

Since her French was abysmal, the niceties of Jenny's remarks escaped Flora. All she could grasp was the admiration; flattered, she explained that she hadn't forgotten us, but that she was so busy, she had such a lot of work to do!

We were glad to hear that the commandant's villa was impeccably clean; apparently Frau Kramer had a lot of time on her hands. There being few amusements in these parts, she did some very lovely crocheting. She had embroidered *Gute Nacht* on the pillowcases, for instance. The children were very well brought up, and the youngest was a beautiful baby. She also gave them music lessons. The girls hooted with laughter.

"He'll be a happy man if his brats play like you do!"

Ignoring Jenny's comment—she never could grasp sarcasm—Flora sailed on: "There's a front garden with flowers—it's nice for the children. We aren't in the camp; it's so much pleasanter not being inside the barbed wire—"

"One of the roads leading to the crematoria runs right in front of the house, doesn't it?" interruped Little Irene.

"Yes," she answered blankly.

"Well, so you can always see an endless procession of dead bodies?"

Flora was scandalized. "But I'm working, I haven't the time to stand and stare!"

What a marvellous answer! We listened to her in astonishment. She simply wasn't aware of what she was saying. "Particularly not just now," she went on. "We're expecting a visit from someone very important.

The commandant is very busy; there's going to be a reception at the Auschwitz headquarters and perhaps at our place too. Frau Kramer is in a great state. You see, here it's not like Berlin, she can't get hold of anything."

No indeed.

"But who is coming?"

"I don't know. They haven't mentioned a name."

Volubly, she resumed the panegyric of her esteemed master: "You'd never think, to look at him, that Commandant Kramer was such a good father and husband, and so thoughtful!"

Jenny told her to shut up if she didn't want us all weeping with emotion.

Flora blundered on complacently: "For her wedding anniversary he gave his wife such a pretty handbag, so original, with a rose stamped in it. I commented on what lovely leather it was, and she said it was human skin, tattooed, which is very rare."

My disgust rose to my lips. Elsa stared at Flora in horror; her parents, who had managed to escape to Belgium, were dealers in leather goods and she had been learning the trade herself. She burst out: "How could any leather workers have agreed to do such a thing?"

Well she might wonder, but obedience was all. To make a handbag out of a comrade's skin was anodyne compared with the work of the "volunteers" who led the selected to the gas chambers; of Jup, Edek's friend, to whom Edek had given his and Mala's locks of hair, Jup who had removed the stool from beneath Edek's feet, who had hanged his friend in order to preserve the great hope: to get out alive. To survive, what could one do but obey?

Our souls were weary and our bodies likewise. We were hungry: the soup was less and less solid and anything might turn up in it, bits of paper, cardboard, string. It was so revolting that we could hardly keep it down. The very smell of it turned the stomach. Without much enthusiasm we were preparing for the last rehearsal of the day. The days seemed endless, the evenings were longer now, and our memories served us impossible dreams: heads raised to starry skies, strolls down deep flower-edged lanes—inaccessible things, things which perhaps some of us would never know or feel again.

"Ruhe!"

Authoritarian, harsh, Alma's voice made me jump. Exhausted, instruments in hand, the girls raised their heads.

"I want your full attention, please. I have something very important to say."

You could have heard a pin drop.

"A very important SS leader is coming to visit the camp. I want a really conscientious performance. He is one of the most important men in Germany. He's very interested in us; the orchestra is known about even in Berlin. It must be faultless. I will not stand for even the slightest mistake."

The orchestra, her orchestra! There was hatred in the sidelong looks the girls exchanged, exhausted as they were by this enforced music.

Who was this great man? we wondered—hardly Hitler himself, surely?

It wasn't Hitler's name which was finally pronounced, but one even more terrible for us: that of Heinrich Himmler. Alma expressed her amazement: "Do you realize the implications—Himmler, an absolutely top-rank man!"

She said that as though suddenly all vestiges of power had fallen from Goering, Goebbels, and all the rest.

Heinrich Himmler the arch-enemy, the inventor of the camps. Horror, hatred, and a sense of powerless rebellion seized me. The mastermind of death, of our death, was coming here. The executioner was coming to gloat over his victims. Words failed me then and they fail me now; as with love, one needed new words for hatred, freshly minted, never used before by others for other loathing!

My friends looked shattered. Even the Russians and most of the Poles were registering some kind of emotion. It needed Alma's lack of awareness not to be deeply disgusted. Then, as the girls digested the news, an insidious fear crept among us. A faceless fanatic, Himmler was something of an unknown quantity: a priggish zealot, a Savonarola of anti-Semitism. He was the Reichsführer of the SS, one of the party's highest positions; the creator of the SS, which had become the elite of the Nazi movement. It was he who had conceived and realized this colossal and monstrous organization whose main aim was the annihilation of the Jews. In Auschwitz, people still remembers his '42 visit. Transmitted orally, these memories reached us from all sides: he had been present at the extermination of a recently arrived convoy of Jews, had given instructions enabling selection to be even more efficient, necessarily entailing the death of those whom it was more economical to kill than to feed. It was said that, during all the phases of the operation, he had examined all those taking part in it: all signs of pleasure, of repulsion, of any emotion whatsoever had to be absent from their faces and behaviour. The SS, a crack unit, had to do their duty scrupulously, and keep their feelings for the Führer, the Reich, and their families. Were they not the foundations of the society of tomorrow, cleansed as it would be of all rotten blood? Commandant Höss, at that time in charge of the Auschwitz complex, had complained of the "sensitivity" of some of the officers, and Himmler had then advocated an increase in the use of dogs, impervious to any form of pity.

He had also made a point of being present at the corporal punishment of a woman internee and, on leaving, had ordered that the whip should be administered on the bare backs of men and women attached to a wooden support, that that particularly educational punishments should be intensified, that prisoners incapable of working should be sent to the gas chamber. He had also complained about the inadequacy of the installations (although they had in fact reached a pitch of very considerable perfection), expressing regret that they could annihilate no more than six thousand a day. This limited number, in his view, was seriously hampering the purification of Europe. This bureaucrat of extermination made provision for everything.

It was for him that we were going to play.

Then we went through a period of hell; some days we worked for twenty hours at a stretch, deadened, faltering, on the verge of collapse. Alma's implacable baton hypnotized us, conducting us with a frenetic beat we could no longer follow. We rehearsed the programme *ad nauseam:* by way of an opening, a medley from *The Merry Widow,* then Peter Kreuder's "Twelve Minutes." My throat was sore with so much singing, and I'd gladly have lost my voice altogether. To end up with, Lotte was to sing an aria from *The Gypsy Princess.* If the Reichsführer was satisfied and wanted an encore, Clara would sing Alabieff's "Nightingale," a most apposite bucolic number! A Suppé march was to be in reserve. This programme caused a certain amount of ill-feeling between Lotte and Clara. Clara kept repeating that she should have been chosen, but that "the German woman" favoured Germans. This petty bickering increased a tension which was nerve-jangling already.

Alma had forgotten everything: camp, setting, gas chambers. Her concert had to be perfect. She was German, Himmler was one of the great leaders of her country. She was proud to play for him. We all shared Florette's view: "But my God—what would she do for Hitler?"

Never had Alma been more alien to us. At last, D day

arrived. The camp had been scoured, the roadways had even been raked, gravel had been thrown down at the last moment so that the mud, which never dried completely, wouldn't have time to absorb it. Ever since early morning we had been polishing ourselves up, like sailors for an admiral's review. While we were busy cleaning up our clothes and shoes, Alma called us yet again: "Any minute now you will be in the presence of the Reichsführer; it's vital that you should know that he appreciates music, indeed he plays the piano. You must perform perfectly so as not to offend his ear. Don't look at him, don't talk among yourselves, sit up straight; he is most concerned about posture. And above all, play in tune."

"It makes me sick, sick," repeated Florette. "She's just panting with excitement at the idea of playing for this monster."

The girls could hardly contain themselves.

"If only Alma were aiming at getting better food for us we might understand it, but not at all. It's just for her, to get a good mark, like a child, a compliment. It's pathetic!"

Tchaikowska and Founia examined us; Alma inspected us once again and off we went, carrying instruments, stands, and music. Our stultified state acted as anaesthetic to any desire to rebel. We climbed onto our platform and waited, trembling beneath a merciless sun. The SS looked edgy; dogs panted and yawned. The air shimmered with heat. Our armpits moistened and we hoped desperately that it didn't show; the ultracorrect Himmler was unlikely to relish sweat marks. He probably sent people to the gas chambers for less.

An hour went by. My throat was so dry that my thickened saliva stuck to my palate. Lotte was scarlet. Clara was streaming. Alma remained haughtily dry; she couldn't be Jewish, she must belong wholly to the superior race, there must have been some mistake on nature's part! From where we stood, the camp—entirely emptied of its occupants, who were confined to their blocks—looked so clean that I hardly recognized it. It could almost have been a different world had it not been for the smoking crematoria chimneys, the unremitting blast furnaces of death.

At last a group of uniforms emerged from the main thoroughfare. I could hardly distinguish Himmler from among the other officers—smallish, pale, puny, slightly bent, dark-haired. This savage defender of the superiority of the German race was a surprising advertisement for blond, blue-eyed Aryans—no doubt another of nature's little slipups. The thought amused me for a moment; this implacable führer, this king-sized assassin, was positively lost in the crowd, a negligible little fellow with a shifty gaze behind his old-fashioned pen pusher's glasses.

Now he was about twenty yards away from us. Hardly had she seen him than Alma snapped to attention. A sign from her and the orchestra launched into *The Merry Widow;* under this sun, on this platform, beneath watchtowers, amid barbed wire, in front of these men in uniform, it seemed to me incredible, ridiculous, grotesque. Ewa firmly averted her gaze; she was looking towards the Carpathians in the direction of our Polish rescuers. Little Irene had elected to look the visitors in the eye with a disdain, an insolence that alarmed Marta and would have made Alma seethe if she had seen it. But she saw nothing, she was conducting her orchestra, which was playing for the Reichsführer Heinrich Himmler, whose insignificant face is engraved in my mind: His moustache, modelled on that of comrade Hitler but with a slight respectful difference in style, topped a lip which wasn't even thin—the lower lip was positively rounded; but the gaze was fearsome, a sharp, inquisitorial gaze devoid of all other expression.

The official group remained standing—there weren't any chairs; they hadn't come to hear a concert, and that must have worried Alma. Himmler looked bored, but he stood there in the sun, presumably because he was so "correct." Standing near him, Mandel watched me as I sang my part in "Twelve Minutes." I hoped desperately that she wouldn't feel moved to ask for *Madame Butterfly*. I felt I wouldn't be able to sing a solo, that no threat could move me to obey. Luckily, hardly had we finished the piece than Himmler said something to the officers, who clicked their heels, wheeled round, and marched away, while an SS signalled to us to stop. Alma interpreted this very badly, and we barely had the time to heave a sigh of relief before she exploded: "You played badly, abominably out of tune! Of course he didn't like it. He'll gas us all." ("And quite right too," one could almost hear her adding pettishly.)

And so, ingloriously, we went back along the deserted alleyways to our block. No sooner had we crossed the threshold than the whining began. Lotte shrieked that it was the girls' fault she hadn't been allowed to sing; if they'd played better, Himmler wouldn't have left. After all, she was German, and it was her right. Clara complained that if she didn't sing on such occasions, her presence in the orchestra would no longer seem necessary and God knows what would happen to her. The girls bickered, blamed one another for the fact that Himmler had walked off. In my opinion one would hardly have expected him to applaud and ask for an encore.

At first their mindlessness amazed me, then anger took over: "Are you all completely oblivious to the fact that he invented the gas chambers? He's the head of the SS, their creator, they obey him blindly. It's he who suggested to Hitler that he should get rid of the inferior races, he's the instigator of the massacre of the Jews, and you, Clara, you poor idiot, you'd like to sing in front of him . . ."

"It's not for my sake, but for the orchestra," she answered haughtily. "If he'd liked my singing, we might have had a parcel."

"A parcel! You'd do anything for food. Sleep with whom you please—what you're selling is of no value—but don't grovel in front of that rat-faced bastard, whatever else you do!"

"Why don't you go and say that to Alma? She's barking at us because he didn't congratulate her."

My anger had passed; all I felt now was disgust and great weariness. It was true that Alma had dreamed of receiving a compliment from Himmler. The stupidity, the childishness of it all when one thought of the millions of murdered, was so clear to me that I now had only one desire—to be alone, out of earshot, and to cry my full, the pent-up tears of weeks.

Something special was required to round off a day like this, and Alma supplied it. She summoned us, and unexpectedly her voice was bright with happiness: "I want to tell you how pleased I am with you."

Flabbergasted, we looked at one another: had she gone mad?

Jenny tapped her forehead discreetly.

"And now by way of a little relaxation I'll play you the *Zigeunerweisen* by Sarasate."

We were baffled. Playing for us was her way of thanking us. She took up her violin and then, just as she was about to start, stage-managing her effect with maximum skill, she added: "I've just been told that Himmler liked the orchestra. He smiled!"

The following morning, though, catastrophe struck. Coming in from the morning session outside, Helga, our drummer, collapsed and was taken to the infirmary. Tchaikowska, who had gone with her, told us that the verdict was typhus. That meant, at best, weeks of orchestra with no percussion and, at worst, its disappearance altogether. Alma was pale: this could mean the end of the orchestra. How could one give rhythm to marches without drums? It would be impossible to play the Suppé overtures the SS were so fond of, and it would be good-bye to "The Charge of the Light Brigade."

We learnt the news in the music room. Alma let her baton fall onto her desk out of sheer discouragement.

"What will become of the orchestra? I'd give three guitars and six mandolins for the drums!"

Mandolinists and guitarists paled.

What would become of us was more the question. Disconcerted, we fell silent. The announcement of Frau Mandel's arrival added to our anguish. "Just what we needed," remarked Florette.

The Lagerführerin found us at gloomy attention. Our depression surprised her sufficiently for her to question Alma, and she nodded understandingly throughout Alma's explanation. She uttered a phrase indicating that in no circumstances would she dream of dissolving the orchestra; this assurance convinced no one who understood German.

Then she stated resolutely, "We must find someone to replace her."

As no one had told us to be at ease, we all remained immobile. Head high, she cast a soldierly glance over the assembled company. We followed her gaze impassively. Everyone was afraid, even the Poles, even Founia and Marila. Suddenly her face lit up—her eye had just alighted on me. *"Meine kleine Sängerin,* my little Butterfly, you shall play the drums!"

This enormity traced its path to my brain with the utmost difficulty.

Timidly, Alma expressed her nervousness: "But Frau Lagerführerin, she's never played the drums."

"Well," said Mandel briskly, "she'll learn. Then she'll know one thing more. It's always useful, isn't it?"

Alma, who grasped the situation perfectly, replied with an unenthusiastic *"Jawohl."*

"In fact tomorrow I'll send someone over to teach her." Airily, she added: "After all, it can't be difficult to bang on those things!"

Only Alma and I could see what this all meant: not only did I know nothing of the instrument, which required great dexterity, but I was going to have to play an instrument I knew nothing of without any music—Helga being a professional, I had written no part for her.

The girls looked at me nervously, animosity gone: they were dependent on me. I felt no pride, but considerable concern. They were sizing me up: Was I going to be able to rise to the occasion?

Florette concentrated on such humour as there was in the situation: "They'll send us someone from the men's camp. Clara'd love to be in your position."

"Don't be ridiculous," Jenny protested, "he'll be a rag like us. She'd send him flying! What she needs is a real man, someone who lashes out good and proper, who can make her see a few stars. It sets her dreaming when she's covered with bruises; she thinks she's in a field of periwinkles!" Then, directly to Clara: "How many pots of jam does that booby of yours give you for your services?"

I never got used to these jokes, which drove Clara into an appalling state but which she was obliged to swallow, because she knew that she was little loved and unlikely to find a champion, even in me. To think that it was Clara with whom I had sworn eternal friendship, friendship unto death, in the fashion of incautious schoolgirls. And secretly I was worried that I might have been in some small part responsible for the change in her. Perhaps I should have been more vigilant. From a well-brought-up girl, engaged to a boy with whom she was still in love, she had become this *kapo*'s girl. Swinging her hips, complacently proffering her pallid fat, she would go towards the highest bidder, steering a course between her two main concerns, guzzling and singing. Occasionally she would go through phases of trying to revive our old friendship, attempting to flatter me: "Get me singing work. You can do anything with

Alma. If I don't sing enough they'll say they don't need me, and . . ." All her anguish lay in the dots that punctuated her sentences. She hated Lotte, Ewa, and probably me too; every singer was usurping her place.

She exaggerated when she brought up the possibility of being thrown out of the orchestra; she didn't really believe it. It was a way of insisting on first place: she needed to shine. In the evenings, since she couldn't make any headway in our circle, Clara sat apart learning new songs which would enable her to supplant the others. She refused to admit that there was no longer any hope of that: her voice, which had been very lovely, had been affected by the conditions we'd been living in and it was losing its strength and subtlety. She would have to give up her ambition to be a singer at the Opéra, which was a shame because she might well have succeeded, everything being in her favour: she was very gifted, very beautiful, and so absolutely self-centred that she would have been able to cast aside anything that might have hindered her progress. In normal life, all this could have remained quite *comme il faut,* but the camp, exacerbating all needs and all desires, had thrown a cruel light upon her. So many people who would normally have been pleasantly unremarkable became monsters in Birkenau.

Clara's latest lover was an enormous flat-skulled brute of a German with a frightful reputation; he was said to be a sadist of a calibre that aroused envy even among the SS. When he had come to the block, his little grey eyes sunk between two folds of flesh and his enormous hamlike hands had made me feel positively unwell. Apart from his duties as *kapo,* he also lent a voluntary if professional hand in the exemplary executions that took place in the camp. I had asked Clara whether she realized exactly what sort of a man he was and what his profession had been before he'd been interned: "He was an executioner," I said, "an assassin, and here he doesn't even kill for money, but for pleasure. Clara, don't do it, don't go with him. When you go back home, you won't be able to face yourself, your friends, your fiancé, your family. The memory of that brute will poison your life. Stop—there's still time. It's better to die of hunger than be a prostitute!''

Her eyes became cold. "Leave me be. He brought me a bra, do you hear, a bra! And anyway, there have to be executioners. If it wasn't he it would be somebody else.''

There was nothing surprising about delight at that particular present. Bras were rare, forbidden objects, and Clara set store by them, particularly as she knew the way Tauber had made one of his recent selections. The said treasure had already suffered one indignity: poor Yvette, who had dysentery, had organized herself a chamber pot for the night, and very early in the morning she would empty it discreetly in the lavatory. She slept on the third tier. One morning Clara, who slept on the lowest tier of the same *coja*, began howling insults in her direction. In the night, the pot had fallen on the bra. The girls laughed heartily while Clara railed on. "It's nothing, just wash it," I kept repeating, but Jenny added insult to injury by saying that ill-gotten gains never did anyone any good.

Two hours after Mandel's departure, an SS wearing the distinctive arm band of the music block came up to Alma and announced that he was the drum teacher; we were certainly witnessing some strange happenings. An SS as teacher—I savoured it in advance, but my pleasure was short-lived. Firstly, there was nothing of the Siegfried about him; he was faceless, neutral, uniform grey from head to foot, with expressionless pale blue eyes. Only his hands were alive, blessed it seemed with a life of their own: rapid, efficient, incisive, they flew from the big drum to the small and from the small to the cymbals.

I didn't know what instructions he'd been given, but not once during the course of my training did he utter a word, not even a yes or no. If I hadn't heard him talking with Alma, I'd have been convinced they'd chosen a mute. He took my hands almost squeamishly to correct a position, or else sat in my place and demonstrated.

The first movement was the alternate beating of two drumsticks, which was easy; this then became more complicated with a two-one, one-two system. But even that was a mere nothing until the foot came into it; tapping hands and feet at the same time and to the same rhythm but with different movements required a whole period of apprenticeship. I had no time for that. Mandel would never have accepted that I, her little wonder, couldn't play the drums. Every night at six thirty my percussionist would arrive, automaton-like, to give me my lesson; I drummed as if I were mad, day and night, but more particularly as if I were deaf—unluckily for the others, who weren't. Founia, apoplectic, choked with impotent fury; all the girls were on the verge of hysterics and talked of killing me. I didn't even hear them. My head was a big drum; I beat away like a machine and when I tried to grab some sleep, to everyone's relief, I heard a beating in my skull. Then I would leap up and go to drum some more. I realized desperately that though I'd grasped the principle of a drum roll, I still couldn't do it, and drum rolls were crucial, the basis of all percussion playing.

When Sunday arrived everyone had dark circles around their eyes as though our entire block had been on a real binge.

"The Charge of the Light Brigade" was on the programme. It was marvellous weather and the concert was to be held outside, on the square at a sort of crossroads, a wide corridor between the barbed wire of camps A and B. Chairs were grouped around our platform. There was a holiday bustle; the SS were looking particularly dapper, whips tucked under their arms, boots gleaming. The first impression was of a concert in the bandstand of a small garrison town surrounded by electrified wire. But today I hadn't time to observe the spectacle—I was too busy drumming, performing a positive dance between the drums; hands and feet flying, I leapt around sweating heavily, which was most unusual for me. Luckily I had a sense of rhythm and it was that that saved me, because the rest was random. I left my instruments to go and take my place among the singers, then went back to drum as best I could, but at least in time. Then it was the duet from *Butterfly*—what a fiendish idea to have put *that* on the programme—and off I went to sing again. My performance must have been fairly exceptional, a positive marathon, and my small size did nothing to lessen the comic aspect. The girls had difficulty keeping straight faces. The SS smiled, Graf Bobby cheerily tapped his boot with his whip, adjusted his monocle. Mandel beamed; she was right, her *Sängerin* could do anything, even act the clown. Mengele, who had apparently dropped in, also seemed to be enjoying the spectacle. Kramer was frankly amused; I suspected that I'd be applauded at the end. Only here, in the camp, one could never know in advance how things were going to turn out in the end.

Alma was playing the violin; it was a big concert with a solo performance, and I had a moment's respite before the last piece. There were a lot of SS women, Drexler, Grese, even Frau Schmidt, whom we rarely saw at our concerts, nurses and secretaries of all kinds, presumably brought out by the fine weather, the summer air. Alma really was a virtuoso; I seized the opportunity for enjoyment and relaxed.

Behind the barbed wire, at a decent distance, were the deportees, in considerable numbers. Under the brutal light they looked thinner, more pathetic than ever, though the summer sun ought to have dealt more mercifully with them than the winter frosts, which had given

some of them frostbite. We were fairly near the electrified fence and suddenly I saw one woman run up to it
and grip the metal. Violently shaken by the current, her
body twisted and she hung there, her limbs twitching
convulsively; against the light she looked like a monstrous spider dancing in its web. A friend rushed forward to detach her, seized her, and was welded to her
arms by the current, writhing spasmodically from head
to foot. No one moved, the music played on; the SS
listened and talked among themselves. Another girl ran
forward and tried to pick off the two twitching bodies
with the legs of a stool. No one helped her; we continued playing. The SS laughed and patted one another
on the back; Graf Bobby shook his head, adjusted his
monocle, and stared through it at the women, faintly
disapproving. Silhouetted against the brightness, the
crooked bodies formed grotesque swastikas. At last the
girl managed to detach them from the deadly current
and they fell to the ground motionless, rigid; we didn't
know if they were dead. The SS turned away with a final
laugh, a last amused comment; the show was over. Ours
too was almost ended. I drummed furiously. The
women dragged off the tortured creatures by their arms
and legs, like ants bearing off a corpse of one of their
own—a funeral to the strains of *The Merry Widow*.

As Jenny said, "That sort of thing gives you a turn."
None of us was shocked by this reflection, we found it
natural.

Heads lowered, we went in. With a broad grin which
did nothing to restore the balance of her twisted face,
Pani Founia handed me—an egg. Ewa translated her accompanying message: this present wasn't just for me,
but for everyone! It was to thank us for our lovely concert.

An egg for the whole orchestra—and furthermore, as
I cracked it, Jenny observed that it was "as suspect as
the rest of us." I would have liked to laugh, but I
couldn't.

OUACHITA TECHNICAL COLLEGE

The two hours that had just passed seemed to me a sort of synthesis of life in the camp: the grotesque comedy of the drums, a concert in a barbed wire enclosure for sinister uniformed puppets, the woman's suicide, the other woman's heroic solidarity, and to cap it all, Pani Founia's reward: a rotten egg.

It was enough to make one laugh till one burst.

Luckily, a few days later, since she hadn't had typhus after all, Helga came back; I vacated my place at the drums with some relief.

In Memoriam

FOLLOWING HIMMLER'S VISIT, as if in chain reaction, there was a further marked increase of activity in the camp. Enormous numbers of transports arrived from Hungary: gas chambers and crematoria were at the saturation point. We were enshrined in a thick smoke which hid the sun and half-choked us with its awful smell of burning flesh. We stifled, we could hardly eat. To try and get a little air in the evenings, we would sit at the door. One evening at dusk Florette commented on the magnificent sunset.

But the distant red glow wasn't the sun.

Night had fallen now and there was no coolness in the air; the sky was still red at the horizon and the smoke hung over us like a huge lid. Ewa sighed: "We're in the devil's cauldron."

Later we learnt that the cause of those flames had been a ditch filled with the corpses of gassed Hungarians, which had been sprinkled with gasoline and set alight. In the morning the sky was still glimmering; they had burned all night.

The convoys continued to pour in, stopping in front of our door, just fifty yards away from us. We could see the selected walk up the ramp from the platform and disappear from our horizon to the gas chambers. It was a haunting sight. We were separated from the new arrivals only by barbed wire. We could see every detail, we could have talked to them. It was appalling to see those calm people, mostly dazed with exhaustion, neatly lined up awaiting death without knowing it. Florette couldn't stop staring at the endless rows; she had been born in Hungary in a little village now part of Romania.

"Do you think we ought to tell them where they're going?" she murmured.

"Why? What good would that do? They don't know, they're still happy."

The Hungarians had brought plenty of food and clothing with them. The girls in Canada were swamped with possessions of all sorts; the harvest had never been richer. Overwhelmed by the avalanche, they allowed their friends to benefit: on this unprecedented occasion they "gave things away." Through Renate we all received nightshirts, so that in the evening we looked like girls at a boarding school A few hours earlier we had been sobbing desperately; now we were padding around in pink nightshirts and pomponned satin slippers.

What an inconsistent, paradoxical situation we were in, with abundance and luxury at one extreme and unparalleled wretchedness at the other.

There had been a *Blocksperre* since dawn. For five hours the camp had been confined to quarters. The door of our dormitory had been locked, and only the door of the music room left open. I wondered whether the strains of our orchestra reached the deportees in the convoys. It seemed possible; they sometimes turned their heads in our direction. They must have thought that they were in a place with some semblance of humanity since there was music. We tried not to look in their direction, telling ourselves we mustn't and doing so all the same. It was hard to know whether this compulsion was morbid curiosity or worry that one might see someone one knew.

The *Blocksperre* was over. Graf Bobby, without prior

announcement, sauntered through the open door as was his custom. The girls leapt up. He smiled. "No, no, sit down, girls!"

He sat down too and gracefully gestured us to carry on. *"Weitermachen!"* He corrected himself: "Or rather: do continue." He spoke impeccable, even mannered French. He asked Alma whether we couldn't learn some Mozart, a great favorite of his, and added that only Wolfgang Amadeus could bring him the calm of spirit required by his work. His work: left, right, life, death! It must indeed have been a weighty task to choose and kill in the place of fate. Still, he was resigned to Alma's answer; he would listen to our orchestra another time, today his nerves were too fragile for anything other than the divine master.

Coolly he stood up and came towards me, leant over my work, took my score, peered through his monocle: "Curious! Excellent! Amusing! Your orchestrations are very good, but so funny." And he began to laugh. Alma was following this disturbing scene from her stand; it was hard to know what the laughter of an SS colonel presaged.

"You actually manage to make music with such an orchestra," he went on, "to produce musically possible orchestrations. Congratulations!"

Now it was Little Irene's turn.

"You have a nice touch, were you a professional?" (in civilian life, he almost seemed to say).

He can't have noticed her expression because his worldly air remained unchanged. Then he turned back to me: "It's odd, today I asked if there were any musicians in the transport from Hungary, and no one came forward; such a talented people, it's curious, don't you think?"

I couldn't gauge the expression of the eye behind the monocle, but the other one fixed me provocatively. Irritated, I answered, "Well, perhaps they thought they'd misheard. It probably seemed unlikely to them, arriving at a work camp, that anyone should ask for musicians.''

"That's possible, but I find it astonishing. The Jews are very musical, as we all know." Mechanically, he tapped his shiny boot with his stick. "Perhaps when they get to the camp we're sending them to, they'll understand and try their luck.''

I had to keep quiet. We weren't supposed to know that they were sent to the gas chambers. Still, faced with such cynicism, I couldn't completely conceal my feelings: "Perhaps they'll lose their fear!''

I amused him. Casually, with the tip of his whip, he poked through the papers on the table.

"But tell me, if you were in our place and we in yours, would you send your enemies where we send ours?''

The orchestra was listening, all the girls nearby had heard the insidious, provocative question. All those who understood French had their eyes on me, and I answered calmly: "Certainly I would, Herr Oberfuhrer" (and it was a rare pleasure to tell him so). "But definitely not women, children, old people—they're not my enemies.''

He tapped the table and smilingly replied: "What a curious answer. That's good, you're not without wit.''

And off he went again, twirling his stick.

Hardly was he out of the room than the girls exploded at me: "Lunatic, idiot, imbecile, fool! Do you realize what you said to him? It certainly won't be long now before that truck draws up outside—''

"Ruhe! Ruhe!" shouted Alma.

It was less Alma's order than the arrival of a ravishing girl of about twenty that cut short their vengeful reproaches. A real beauty, slender, well built, long legs, a marvel! Her curly hair fell softly to her shoulders, perfect teeth were revealed by a dazzling smile. It was a pleasure to look at her and she knew it.

"Where's she blown in from?" Jenny asked nervously.

We soon knew: from Hungary. Ewa, as she was called, had a very pretty voice, a pure, ethereal soprano. How she had managed to sail straight into the music block we did not learn, because Ewa the Hungarian despised us and scarcely spoke to us.

Perhaps it was sheer charm that had wafted her straight here, avoiding the quarantine block. She had even managed to save her mother, to have her taken on with us: Mandel decided that she could help Pani Founia in the kitchen. If this Ewa had been ugly and deformed, however good her voice, she would have gone the way of the crowd. Bravo, I thought; that was two more snatched from the jaw of death—at any rate for the moment.

Not everyone shared my way of thinking. A block of hostility formed around mother and daughter; their presence was a threat to the girls' comfort and security. Our room was somewhat cramped already, and there weren't enough beds. If there were too many "new" girls, might they not have to get rid of the "old"?

Lotte and Clara were openly hostile to the lovely Ewa. They were afraid: she was younger than they were and sang better. Here, one soon lost one's voice. Lotte's had lowered in pitch and now, too often, she forced it and shouted rather than sang. Clara refused to admit that her voice was less clear than formerly. Both were racked with jealousy when I wrote out *Una voce poco fa* from the *Barber of Seville* from memory for Ewa to sing in Italian, and very well she sang it; her voice, her beauty, and her pride delighted the SS.

The emotion caused by her arrival was almost immediately forgotten though, swept away by the entry, in mid-rehearsal, of a runner. "Girls, get ready, you're going for a walk!"

I wasn't sure I'd heard correctly, and I wasn't the

only one; Alma asked her to repeat herself and in a clear, joyful voice the girl reiterated: "It's a fine day. Frau Mandel has said you must go for a walk! They'll come and get you."

A walk—that meant going out, through the gate of the camp. The idea made us dizzy; we sat there nodding our heads like old crones. "Well, well, fancy that," we mumbled incredulously.

"Hurry up, get dressed, correct dress, *schneller,*" ordered Alma.

Within a few seconds the block was topsy-turvy. We pulled our navy blue skirts and white tops from under our mattresses—our method of ironing. People were rushing in all directions:

"Lend me your needle."

"Damn, I've got a stain."

"I can't find my stockings."

It was like a hen run in turmoil; but our twittering ceased at the entrance of an SS soldier, an inoffensive-looking blond lad with his rifle slung and his dog on a lead.

"Well, here's nanny."

"Get an eyeful of our chaperone."

His mate, from the same mould, was waiting outside; they looked like twins. Alma informed us that we weren't to talk to or question our guards and that we were to walk in our usual rows.

And off we went, without either our *kapo* or the Poles. We couldn't imagine why we'd been granted this astounding privilege, but we didn't need to know. Sandwiched between the soldiers, we left camp B. Drexler, riding past on a bicycle, could hardly believe her eyes. The women we met stared at us, astonished by a procession directed not towards the crematoria, but towards the entrance of the camp. We crossed camp A, stopped in front of the gate which opened before it, and went out. The deportees were staggered, and so were we!

We turned left at the entrance. We didn't talk, we were not yet really sure that it was happening. The road became a path. We no longer walked in rows; in front of us was the fair, well-shaven neck of the SS boy, his uniform-grey back, his machine gun and panting dog. Behind us marched his double. There were about thirty of us, all in a state of disbelief. We didn't dare laugh or smile or sing. When we stopped being incredulous, we became serious because happiness is serious, particularly in such circumstances. It was marvellous weather, and there was grass, a thing we hadn't seen for months. "Grass," said Jenny rapturously, "like at Vincennes. No, more like on the fortifications."

"So it still exists," murmured Big Irene, whose eyes now reflected the colour of the sky. We turned our backs on the crematoria and inhaled air without smoke, air too strong for our eager, deeply breathing lungs.

Timidly, Florette said: "It smells . . . it smells of . . ."

At the head of the group, someone had stopped. "Sniff—it's lovely!"

"It smells of grass, new-mown hay," said Anny ecstatically. "It smells of freedom."

Tears came to our eyes. Our SS, who had paused with us, continued their march.

In this magical grass were flowers—buttercups, harebells. We gambolled around like lambs.

"I never thought I'd see them again."

"I knew I would, but I didn't think it would be before I got back."

The phrase caught at our emotions for a moment, like a splinter, but today we didn't dwell on it; we were happy. After almost two miles we passed a work detachment of women. We weren't allowed to speak to them or even to look at them. But they looked at us, flabbergasted at first, then, as recognition dawned, enviously. They always had the same range of reactions to us: jealousy, hatred, incomprehension, complicity. I wondered how they would describe us later; in their eyes we possessed everything they longed for. What resentment and hatred would they heap upon this, our only walk? It would be the measure of the pain, the suffering that they had felt at the moment we passed by. Then we passed a detachment of men; their eyes betrayed no more indulgence than the women's had, but no hatred either—only disgust. One of them spat in our direction, and I wished we'd never passed either group; my joy had turned sour in my mouth and I was obliged to chew on it like a cow chewing the cud.

After about an hour's walking, we came upon a small, clear pool, as blue as a patch of sky. Water, grass, some stunted trees—not very beautiful, but trees all the same: a paradise! We sat down in the grass and the SS settled down some way off, in the shade. Their dogs sat at their feet, ready for action, their open snouts revealing teeth like great white almonds. I suddenly felt something approaching pity for them—after all, they were not responsible for the jobs men made them do.

Jenny looked at them enviously. "Those hounds must live on the fat of the land—they've got coats like goddam mink!"

Her mind ground on a bit in that direction, and she added: "They could have given us a picnic, as a bonus."

Little Irene was quick to reply. "We can't stop you dreaming, but reality's enough for us."

Jenny lay back on the grass and made some faintly risqué remark about there being certain other things missing too. We laughed; we'd have laughed at anything.

Florette looked longingly at the water. "Could we bathe?"

Anny was enthusiastic too. "Shall we? Should we ask permission?"

"It would be better if a German did the asking."

Marta and Little Irene were sitting together, their shoulders and arms touching, holding hands; their whole bodies proclaimed their oneness. Despite what they imagined to be their total discretion, malicious rumours were going around. But how could they disguise the brightness of their eyes, their glowing skin? In spite of their aloofness, the bubble in which they'd shut themselves, Florette's suggestion had reached them. Marta got up and went to speak to our guards. *"Ja, ja,"* answered one of them.

"We can bathe," announced Marta.

"What shall we do? We don't have any bathing suits."

"Do without!"

My brutal advice alarmed them; they looked at the SS—could they bathe naked in front of them? They were men, after all. So they kept on their underclothes and rushed into the water like children, swimming and splashing. How pathetic their bodies looked in that harsh summer light!

For some reason I couldn't bring myself to join them. I was pleased at their happiness but I remained remote from it, uninvolved. Almost immediately Little Irene joined me. We looked at each other in silence. We couldn't explain the root of our sadness, and perhaps it was better that way.

The swim, the sun, the air had positively intoxicated the girls. When they came out of the water they ran about just like little girls out of school, doing a sort of ring-a-rosy on the grass under the impassive gaze of the SS.

"May we pick flowers?"

The soldier flapped his big ears in an affirmative nod and went off to give his dog a drink, followed by his friend.

To pick flowers: it was an incredible action, with all the pointlessness of a vanished era. They made little bunches which they clutched in their fists like children on Sunday walks. Some broke off branches from the trees, just to have something green to hold in their hands.

Big-ears and his friend got up, slung their rifles, and off we went, arm in arm. Florette began to sing and we joined in.

A peasant, bent double, straightened up, sickle in hand. He looked at us in astonishment, and would doubtless say, later, that we hadn't been as badly off as all that—a bit thin perhaps, but well dressed, and that we went about singing and laughing. And that would make a lot of people feel better. That's what eye-witnessing is all about.

It must have been late because, on the way back, we didn't meet any work groups. The light was golden. On the horizon, in front of us, lay the dark cloud of Birkenau. As we approached, the frightful smell came forward to meet us. Silently we went through the gate, then crossed camp A in our lines, our flowers in our hands.

Now of course we met other prisoners; they stared after us, disgusted, poised for insult. Yet one of them smiled at me. She held out her arms and I gave her my bunch of flowers. Incredulous, she stared at her hand where the blue harebells quivered, closed her fingers over them, and ran off. That image remained for me the symbol of the walk.

Our guards, still silent as graves, supervised our entrance, then turned away and went off, followed by their dogs. It had been a marvellous day.

Pani Founia greeted our late arrival with raucous disapproval. Exhausted, the girls collapsed onto their beds and fell asleep. We had to sleep off our day as one sleeps off wine.

I drifted off to visions of branches and water and sun.

But the vision faded as the following day got going; in the music room, a runner was asking for Alma, who had to go immediately to the main SS office.

"Rehearse while you're waiting," she instructed us primly.

We did so, but our thoughts were elsewhere. Alma's visit to the main office was an act that put our fragile, uncertain life in the balance. It was Kramer and especially Mandel who were generally concerned with us. Anything taking place at a level other than theirs, above theirs, even with their participation, didn't seem to bode any good at all. Was it somehow a result of Himmler's visit? After the walk, the oven? That would certainly be typical of their approach. Everyone was worrying away at the problem and their preoccupation was visible in their faces. The singers were always the most concerned, because they knew that they were the least indispensable and the most easily replaceable.

Time passed and Alma didn't come back. Tension mounted and we were on the verge of hysteria when she positively sailed in, radiant, transfigured, walking on air. She vouchsafed us nothing, but went straight to her room. We sat there, all eyes riveted questioningly on her door; suddenly it opened, and Alma called me in.

"I wanted you to be the first to know the news." She breathed deeply. "You see, I'm leaving . . ."

Now it was my turn to catch my breath.

"Yes, you heard right, they've just told me I'm going to be released."

Stunned, I repeated: "Released? You can't mean it . . . But why?"

She gave a short laugh. "Well, I'm not going to be absolutely free to go where I want. They said that it was a pity to keep a musician like me in the camp, so I could go and join the Wehrmacht. I'm going to join the troops, to entertain the men at the front. That means that I'll be able to play the violin as I like, what I like. Fania, I'm getting out of here . . ."

"You're leaving here and going to play for soldiers who are fighting against people who are going to liberate us."

She wasn't listening.

"Alma, I can understand that you're happy to be

leaving the camp, but you haven't been released, you still belong to them, you're at their mercy like a slave. They're sending you to entertain their men. Those men are your enemies. Wherever they go, they take war, tragedy, and death with them. They are the instruments of Nazism, racism. And you're delighted to be entertaining them!''

She looked at me uncomprehending, and then beyond me—the symbol of the reality of the camp—to see rapt audiences: She was on a stage, her violin tucked lovingly under her chin, its precious wood warmed by the contact of her cheek. Her vision was stronger than mine, and she wasn't convinced by my point of view; she barely heard me.

"They've got you in their power; they can still kill you whenever they feel the time is right, because you're Jewish. No talent in the world can remove that defect.''

She smiled at me vaguely. "Don't worry, death isn't important—it's making music that matters, real music, and freely . . .''

"But you won't be free.''

Alma's gaze became reproachful. "You don't understand me. You're not pleased for me about what's happened—I shall no longer be playing inside a prison.'' Suddenly vehement, she added: "I'm German and I'll be playing for the soldiers of the Wehrmacht. Do you think they're all Nazis?''

It was true, there were good Germans, but they'd almost all been shut up in prisons and camps. The others, the ones who were raising their arms in unison, were probably just cowards. Could one anathematize a whole race just because part of it was rotten? In Birkenau everything within me rose up and drove me to total hatred of everything German.

Alma was beginning to get impatient. "It's playing here, for the SS, under this sky, which is degrading; it won't be degrading to play for men who may be going to their deaths. Why try to spoil my happiness?''

Already she was gone from here, she had reached another world—the world she had come from in the first place, a world where people issued invitations and entertained.

"When I told her the news, Frau Schmidt asked me to dinner. She's pleased for me, she's a real friend!"

A friend, Frau Schmidt? The führer of Canada, who reigned over the murderers' treasure, who had the power of life and death over her girls and wielded over them the authority of a brothel keeper (her former profession, so it was said)? Interned since '33, apparently she had entirely created and organized her particular department. A tall woman, all her elegance lay in her spareness; fat, she would have been vulgar, but thin as she was, she could deceive. Her pale grey eyes had a birdlike fixity, her carefully drawn back white hair, tucked into a small dingy bun, bore witness to past blondness. No one knew why she had been arrested; rumours varied between criminality, Communism, and procuring, and any one of these suppositions could have been correct. She might have been attracted to Alma, possibly rather flattered that she who probably came from a fairly ordinary background should be the only friend of this virtuoso. Sometimes she came to listen to us, and none of us liked that; she was much hated. Jenny said she "looked about as sincere as a snake getting ready to give you a mortal bite."

Alma was unconvincing. "Yes, a real friend. Do you know that since she's been here, she's sent petitions to the successive commandants of the camp asking for her release, because they've got absolutely no reason for keeping her here; furthermore, she's the oldest woman in Birkenau. They don't answer her, yet they release me. She could feel that it was unfair, but instead of resenting it, she asks me to dinner."

For some reason the charitable feelings of the head of Canada left me cold.

That evening, shortly after Alma left for her

"friend's" house, a *Blocksperre* was announced.

"What's up?"

"What did she say?"

"Nothing, they liked her concert."

"Do you mean she was strutting around like a loon just for that, the poor idiot?"

I don't know why I didn't answer their questions; I didn't want to let them feed their imaginations on this rich piece of information yet.

It was a very long *Blocksperre*. Alma came back late after her dinner. I heard her crossing the music room and shutting her door just before I fell asleep.

Regina's voice woke me: "Fania, Fania, Alma is asking for you."

What a cretin! She wanted to expatiate on the glories of her dinner, damn her.

I found her astonishingly pale, her nostrils pinched, her forehead clammy with sweat, complaining of frightful headache and nausea, pains in her limbs and stomach. Her hand was hot and moist, and she clearly had a high temperature. I massaged her temples, which were covered with cold, slimy sweat. She was seized by bouts of nausea, vomiting, and diarrhoea. She was clearly very ill.

"Go and wake up Tchaikowská."

Regina ran to get her. Her face swollen by sleep, looking catatonic, the blockowa stood in the doorway and assessed the situation. "I'm going to get Frau Mandel."

A long quarter of an hour went by. Between two bouts of vomiting Alma looked at me like a frightened child and murmured with difficulty: "Fania, will I not get out of here after all?"

"Of course you will, it's just some temporary upset. It'll all be better tomorrow. They're coming to see to you."

I heard Mandel's rapid step, and she glided into the foul-smelling little room accompanied by an SS doctor.

He took her pulse, felt her over rapidly, covered her up, and told Mandel she must immediately be taken to the infirmary for stomach pumping. A few minutes later our *kapo* was taken off on a stretcher—the stretcher used for the dead, because in the camp, as long as you were alive, you walked. They took her out of the music room door.

The girls didn't seem to have noticed anything, so I told them in the morning, "Alma is ill, you'll rehearse with me."

"What about the morning and evening marches?"

"Big Irene will conduct them."

They said, "Oh, all right," and didn't ask any questions. Alma ill meant a bit of respite in the regime of "forced music" she imposed. No shouts, slaps, baton raps. A feeling of half-day holiday floated through the block.

The next day, the mood had changed. Little Irene asked me reproachfully why I hadn't told them that Alma was seriously ill.

"I thought it was nothing much."

Marta intervened coolly: "Which made them take her to the Revier, to a separate room. Renate says the SS doctors have been to examine her. They're doing all they can to save her!"

"Perhaps it's typhus?"

"No, they don't know what it is."

It was very hard to get them to rehearse. Their minds were elsewhere and they kept wandering off and walking about looking gloomy and lost.

"Alma's no malingerer," remarked Florette. "It must be serious."

"If she croaks, what'll happen to us?" wailed Jenny.

That evening, Renate informed us that Alma had been unconscious since the morning. The next day, before roll call, a runner shouted from the doorway:

"Girls, Alma's dead!"

Never before had the block known a silence like that

one. Then the lamentations began: "What will become of us? What will they do with us?" Generally the girls were somewhat indifferent to death. It no longer surprised them, it was the inevitable outcome of one's stay here, the end of the road. But Alma's death seemed incomprehensible. Florette summed up the general view: "I can't believe it, she seemed invulnerable. The orchestra *was* her."

Word quickly spread that her death hadn't been normal, that the SS had ordered an autopsy. Jenny harboured no illusions: "Whether they open her up or not, they'll throw her in the crematorium without any further ceremony. They're not too gentle with corpses around these parts!"

Wrong. In the afternoon, Frau Mandel came into the music room to tell us the news officially: "Your conductor, Alma Rosé, is dead. You may go to the Revier and pay her your last respects."

We dressed in silence, carefully, very clean shoes well polished, and all went off together. It was a fine day outside.

We expected to see Alma's body stretched out on a mattress in the infirmary. But a positive mise-en-scène awaited us: in a sort of recess next to the medical room the SS had put up a catafalque covered with white flowers—a profusion, an avalanche of flowers, mainly lilies, and giving off an amazingly strong scent. To get those flowers the SS must have had to get into vehicles and go into town, to florists—there were such things in Auschwitz; it was incredible. We stood there, immobilized with amazement and emotion. With the German sense of the dramatic, Mandel had separated us into two groups and we framed the bed of state: the conductor and her musicians. We stood there, herded together, unable to think, lumps in our throats, looking at Alma. Her face, very calm, very relaxed, looked refreshed. She was very beautiful; her long hands, crossed on her breast, held a flower. I wondered who had had that delicate thought.

I don't know who started it, but there was a sudden sob, and we all began to cry. Some SS came in, removed their hats, and filed past the foot of her bed. All were visibly moved and many were crying. They included officers whom we'd never seen. Mandel's eyes were full of tears; in honour of Alma, we mingled our tears with hers—we were in complete communion! An unforgettable scene.

While this moving march past was taking place, transports were arriving at the camp, people were being gassed, burnt, exterminated. Here, tears in their eyes, the SS bowed down before the corpse of a Jewess they'd covered with white flowers.

Depressed, we went back to our block; without Alma, we were lost.

"What I wouldn't give to hear her bellow," sniffed Florette, who goodness knows had never liked her.

"Alma was lucky, she died of an illness just like in ordinary life," Big Irene remarked gently.

"Still, it wasn't a very ordinary sort of illness."

There was no exact answer to the question of what she'd died of; after the autopsy, the SS doctors diagnosed poisoning. At midday, she had had the same soup we had. That evening, she had dined alone with Frau Schmidt. We never heard another word about the latter. The day after Alma's death Frau Schmidt disappeared from Canada and was never seen there again. She disappeared from the face of Birkenau. In my opinion Frau Schmidt was responsible. Different versions circulated, but they all had one thing in common: Alma had been poisoned. Some thought that Frau Drexler had bribed Frau Schmidt to invite Alma to dinner and poison her, had even obtained the poison. According to this theory, Mandel had intrigued to obtain Alma's release, an action which, even if it had succeeded, could have blown up in her face, because you don't get a Jew set free. Drexler would therefore have acted in the interests of Mandel. I didn't believe this Macchiavellian hypothesis: Mandel would never have done anything that might lead to Alma's leaving the orchestra of which she, Mandel, was so proud. Alma was vital to it. While the men's orchestra in Auschwitz was a real symphony orchestra with excellent players and even soloists, all we had to represent the real musical world was Alma. It was unlikely that Mandel would have despatched Alma of her own accord. On the other hand it didn't surprise me that that monstrous virago Frau Drexler should have been involved in the affair, that she should have provided the posion.

The women in the work detachments thought that Alma had been poisoned by some sort of tinned food. That seemed unlikely to me. Frau Schmidt would have died too, and it was hard to imagine her serving and eating any old food when she could have the pick of the lot. In my view Frau Schmidt, that "dear friend," could only hate the Jewess who was to be freed and who had come to taunt her with her happiness; and she had her revenge.

Alma was dead, and we were still alive. Would they do away with the orchestra? Surrounding me, the girls were insistent: "You're well in with Mandel, you're the only one who could conduct—you must become our *kapo*."

For once they were all in agreement, even the Polish girls. Tchaikowska and Founia actually went as far as to send me a hideous smile. The appointment seemed logical to them, they believed in it. It was true that I'd often helped Alma. Already Ewa the Hungarian was taking me aside and humming me a Hungarian tune: "Couldn't you orchestrate it? The Germans will love it." Lotte and Clara besieged me with a barrage of requests for a broadening of their repertoire and repeatedly assured me they would learn anything I wanted.

So when Kramer's arrival was announced, hearts beat more rapidly; nothing of the orchestra's future could be read on his brutal face as he ordered us to attention. Without any trace of his recent emotion, he announced, icy and definitive: "Sonia will take the place of Alma Rosé; she is appointed conductor of your orchestra."

Sonia was a good pianist, it seemed, though I'd never had a chance to judge the truth of the matter because our piano had long since been taken from us. Could she conduct? She was one of those Ukrainians who kept to themselves, but with whom I sometimes exchanged an odd word. Why this unexpected appointment? Because she was a special-status prisoner? Unremarkable, taciturn, she had never stood out in any way at all. How she must have intrigued to get that post, and yet we had never noticed anything at all.

Reserved, modest, she stood before us. With bated breath we waited to see what the future offered. She took her place on the platform: she was small and solid, her face with its short little nose and prominent cheekbones wasn't very impressive. She cast a somewhat uncertain eye over the score, and without even bothering to give the ritual advance tap of the baton on the edge of her stand, raised her arm and began to beat time—her own time, like an automaton. She beat in empty air, without bringing in any of the instruments, her blue eyes glued to the score which it was all too obvious she was incapable of reading. Despite the efforts of Big Irene, who, as first violinist, tried to bring in the others, the result was appalling. Sonia shrugged her shoulders, put down her baton, and beckoned to me. I tried to inculcate into her the few rudiments indispensable to the conducting of an orchestra. But it couldn't be learnt in five minutes, and since she very soon stopped listening, I went back to my place. Aghast, disbelieving, the girls played any old how. My copyists continued their work without much conviction; you needed to be stupider than they were, listening to that cacophony, to think that Sonia was going to be able to arrange and set up concert programmes. For the moment this lack of discipline enchanted the girls; it was a welcome relief from Alma's tyranny. But soon, like me, they asked themselves what would become of the concerts? Our worry intensified brutally when a visit from Dr. Mengele was announced. He was a music lover, and this racket wouldn't take him in for a moment.

Standing at attention Sonia enquired what Herr Doktor would like to hear. As though she were capable of producing anything at all for his delectation. Nothing, he hadn't the time, he was just paying a call; the phrase enchanted me. Elegant, distinguished, he took a few steps, then stopped by the wall where we had hung up Alma's arm band and baton. Respectfully, heels together, he stood quietly for a moment, then, turning towards Sonia, said to her in a penetrating tone, appropriately funereal: *"In memoriam."* Uncomprehending, our new *kapo* smiled back at him idiotically.

No sooner was he out of the room than she asked me whether it was a compliment or whether we should take the trophies down.

In Birkenau, an *In memoriam* pronounced by Dr. Mengele made a certain impression.

The Black Triangles' Party

WHEN I WENT into the toilet block Hilde, the *kapo*, a thickset shrew of about sixty, called to me in bad German, a sort of low Bavarian I had difficulty in understanding: "You back here this evening, after roll call." Was she joking? I couldn't wait until the end of the day to answer the call of nature. As I had difficulty in understanding her and as she made no effort to understand me, I decided to go and get help. I went out without paying any attention to her guttural grunts.

Screwing up her pink little mouse's face and half-choking with fury, Jenny said simply: "Shit. That's all we need."

They gathered round me. The news, which after all I was not actually so sure about any longer, was important, because our freedom to use the lavatories when we wanted was one of our few prerogatives: instead of being driven twice a day to the monstrous camp lavatories, we had the right to use the lavatories opposite, which were reserved for the black triangles.

The toilets for the "grande dames" were a rather unusual place, thirteen by sixteen feet, six wooden containers with holes in them and a lighted stove, summer and winter, on which stood a simmering vegetable stew which one of the attendants stirred while the other peeled potatoes. This domain was ruled over by two horrible hags, Hilde, the *kapo* perpetually sucking on a Bavarian pipe with a lid, and Inge, her lover, quite slender-looking beside her stubby friend, crafty, damp-eyed, and perpetually alarmed. This ravishing couple—for these lavatory ladies made no secret of their tender feelings—were both equally unpleasant, and of course ardent racists, convinced anti-Semites. It had required an order from Kramer in person to convince them to allow dirty Jews to pollute their Eden. These two asocial Germans didn't conceal their affectionate feelings from us any more than did their favoured and coddled clients, the black triangles. They were drunk most of the time, because in exchange for allowing the Canada and kitchen girls to use their pierced "containers," they got whatever they wanted in the way of drink, food, tobacco, and soap.

Sleeping on the spot in a two-tiered *coja*, with a view of the seats day and night, the two hags always received us with insults and reproached us for sullying their shrine. They were forced to put up with us, but they made our lives as difficult as possible. When we came in and the six seats were occupied—which was generally the case—the visiting gossips, seated on their holes with bloomers lowered and skirts raised, smoking and arguing, cackled as they observed us, hoping that dysentery was racking our bowels. Seated beside their stove, leaning on their tables, the two vestals bandied worldly comments with these women, their visitors and clients:

"What's the weather like in Berlin?"

"How is hair being worn this year?"

"A rumour is going round that the Führer is going to shave off his moustache."

"Mein Gott! He mustn't do that, it suits him perfectly, he's so attractive."

And so on.

When one of them at last had had enough, she would get up, and the others would abandon their adjacent seats to the accompaniment of the same old comments:

"I can't bear to stay near that filthy Jew!"

"The commandant really is too kind to let them come

here; they'll give us their diseases. They're absolutely stinking, you know.''

Generally, except in winter, we preferred to wait our turn outside, because the mixture of doubtful stews, of scents—which they adored—and of excreta made us sick. The squalid sight offered by this assembly was so repugnant that we shortened our stay as best we could. However, we'd learnt to put up with the stinking hut, with the two creatures who pawed and yelled at each other, stuffed themselves and drank, belched and smoked, and with the vile laughter and vulgar stupidity of whatever six "clients" were passing through, because this place was an integral part of the advantages which enabled us to stay alive and which, in our grotesque world, we knew to be an aristocratic privilege.

Thus my news scandalized the girls:

"She can't get away with that. I'll come with you," decided Florette. So off we went again.

When we entered, the six luxury holes were occupied. Drunk, garments agape, tenderly intertwined, Hilde and Inge fixed a sneering gaze on us, but at our entry conversations and giggles ceased. Florette, tact and patience never her strong points, demanded: "Why do have to wait until after roll call to come here?''

The *kapo* and her mate shook their heads in incomprehension, then grasped the question, and abandoning their mutual show of affection, burst out laughing, slapping each other on the back and thighs, imitated slavishly by their clients. I advised Florette to keep cool. The tempest abated and the dialogue proceeded.

"You've got it all wrong," I heard from Florette at last. "She was giving you a rendezvous with the *kapo* of the prostitutes.''

The news was amazing: a chasm yawned between those women and ourselves. The two of them acted mysterious and I had to wait until the evening to find out what they wanted. It was somewhat unexpected: the black triangles were giving a party next week, and they wanted music. We would be paid in sauerkraut.

We expressed a wide range of emotions around the recently relit stove; it was raining and there was a chill October wind.

"I'm not going to play for those whores who act so high and mighty," Florette declared.

Jenny exploded, then pulled herself together, and commented that a party in their place was liable to be "quite a scene." Clara, lips pursed, said that sauerkraut was like money, it smelled good when you needed it.

"I think it's all right," Anny put in calmly. "Prostitutes are more honourable than the SS."

Marta, with no further ado, decided that she would go, and Helga, who knew she was indispensable, accepted. Moving the drums wouldn't be easy, but we couldn't do without them. Sylvia said yes timidly. As we needed a violin and Big Irene, who was only seventeen, expressed terror at the mere idea of the black triangles, Halina, a first violin, agreed to go with us. I was quite without scruples; they wanted me to sing and I would sing.

"What exactly do they want?"

"Music to dance to and to eat to."

"They must have *Eine kleine Nachtmusik*."

"I think you'll find they need something a bit more smutty."

"How about the 'Laughing Polka'?" suggested Florette.

This "Laughing Polka," which had recently entered our repertoire, was one of Sonia's discoveries; all she had us rehearse were dreadful hit tunes. For the rest, as Big Irene and Anny said, the orchestra played automatically; it still hadn't totally forgotten Alma.

The "Laughing Polka" was completely absurd: a few bars of polka, interspersed with a series of "ha, ha, ha's," not sung but laughed. When Sonia rehearsed it for the first time, I was horrified.

Were we going to be so brazen as to play this atrocity in front of the deportees, the moslems? Or was it just for the delectation of the officers, the SS?

"Ha, ha, ha," went the grinding of the violins, the pounding of the big drum, and the jangling of the cymbals; at a sign from Sonia—the only lead-in she knew—the laughter burst out, led by Florette, whose job it was to bring in the others. All the players had to join in: the whole orchestra, singers included, laughed and laughed, fit to die of disgust while Sonia's baton wiggled with joy. It was agonizing. I dreaded the concert where we were to produce this monstrosity instead of, say, Schubert, and I hoped for the future and the life of the orchestra that Mengele wouldn't be there. Kramer was stupid enough to enjoy it. As for Mandel, a bit of *Butterfly* would erase the memory of this horror, though actually she might quite like it.

The next day, Sonia ordered me in Russian: "Tell them they'll play the polka at the Sunday concert."

As it was raining, the concert took place in the Sauna; this concert was to open the winter season. Our usual audience of wretched deportees was standing waiting for us, hemmed in their corner. Black triangles were seated on the tiers of seats and in front of them a few members of the administrative and medical staffs. There were a few seated SS. Immediately I noted with relief that Mengele wasn't there. Sonia moved her baton at random; it seemed inevitable that Kramer, Mandel, or someone else would notice. The lack of comment, whether inspired by indulgence or indifference, worried me. No concert had ever been grimmer, longer, or less tuneful.

A glimmer of content appeared in Sonia's deadpan gaze when we launched into "her" piece, the linchpin of her concert, the "Laughing Polka." Looking abstracted, Florette played mechanically; she was so visibly elsewhere that, without waiting for the signal, coming in before the chorus, she burst into such bizarre guffaws that she set off nervous unmanageable laughter, which spread to the SS. This immense, absurd laugh echoed strangely within those vast, dingy walls. The compact group of the deportees disassociated itself from us. They had become a block of hostility where our giggles sank and disappeared like a stone into a well. The reproachful silence, the current of indignation that flowed from them were infinitely hurtful; our idiotic, alien tittering put us once again firmly on the side of the executioners.

It was that same evening that the jollity at the black triangles' was to take place. We had to wait for Sonia and her friend Maria, our new blockowa, to leave; then we'd go. "We must get a container for the sauerkraut." This phrase worked like Pavlov's bell; it caused us to dribble with longing. Never can wages have been so ardently desired. Amidst all manner of comment, Jenny cleaned the pails we used to wash the floor.

"Do you think they'll fill them up?"

"I should say so—no sauerkraut, no music; we get paid in advance."

Clara was worried: "That won't be enough, we'd better take the soup cans."

"And if Maria notices, all hell will break loose."

We took every precaution. In case of an impromptu visit from the SS a little runner would come and warn us. The "ladies' " building was made of concrete, not of planks like ours.

The interior was lit only by the camp lights, the searchlights, and the glow of cigarettes. It was a large, fairly clean room and they'd pushed the *cojas* back against the wall and put all their tables together, draped with sheets. Covered with food, with neatly aligned glasses, their buffet table looked good in the semi-darkness. A large space was cleared to be the dance floor. Georgette greeted us at the doorway. She was the leader, a real little pimp; in the camp, as in life,

Georgette played the role of the male. She had managed to work it so that in addition to her "missus," several other girls also brought in money for her. They were real, well-paid prostitutes. Georgette had made us laugh a lot because, unlike the other "fellows" of the block, who forced their voices down so as to sound more virile, she had the piping tones of a castrato, which made for a certain comic effect.

Ceremoniously she showed us to our corner. Adducing the possibility of being taken by surprise—it was always conceivable—I asked for our wages.

"No, you'll get them afterwards!"

The empty buckets, placed behind us, were demoralizing. "Let's hope they leave some," grumbled Florette and Jenny, gazing at the mountains of sauerkraut covered with fat sausages from the SS kitchens; it made a lordly spread on the tables.

I rapidly got used to the dimness and was able to observe the spectacle at leisure. Most of the women were German prostitutes—Aryan, naturally—of all kinds: young, old, toothless, fat, thin, redheads with green eyes, blue-eyed blondes, black-eyed brunettes, something for everyone. With their carefully dressed hair and makeup, they had the duskily ringed eyes of the femme fatale, lips bloody with lipstick, pink dolls' cheeks.

Jenny stared at them coldly: "From a distance, by walking fast, they could look like something, but in comparison with ours, on the rue Blondel or St. Denis, they just wouldn't get the business!"

A charmingly novel sort of chauvinism.

The roles were clearly differentiated in this curious assembly of women. Evening dress was de rigueur: the "boys" were in silk pyjamas—presents from their girl friends—and the "ladies," in their turn, wore ravishing transparent blouses, misty muslins, black lace negligees bordered with feathery clouds of pastel swansdown. I couldn't imagine what El Dorado the women who'd brought this lingerie with them thought they were heading for. We gazed wide-eyed, nudging each other and stifling our giggles like schoolgirls after lights-out.

The brilliant assembly had waited for the orchestra before beginning festivities. At first there were just little squeaks from the "girls" and condescending laughter from the fake "fellows" as they stood around the table stuffing themselves, preposterously ladylike withal, fingers crooked, gobbling genteelly. Glasses clinked, toasts were heartfelt. Never had I so regretted not really understanding German. Florette, who was acting prim, and Marta, who was above the fray, would never deign to relay the gems to me. At the first bars, some "gentlemen" decided to invite the "ladies" to a waltz, and in a few minutes the buffet was deserted and the whole block, old and young, was dancing.

The long, slow sweep of the sporadic searchlights made the silks and satins glimmer fleetingly, bringing their colours to life. It was a surprisingly pretty scene; the Germans waltzed very well and I admit to having taken a certain pleasure in the sight, its imperfections papered over by the half-light, its weirdness adding a touch of magic. Between dances, they drank. There was no shortage of alcohol; its smell floated increasingly strongly through the air, heavy with musky, peppery scents, the aroma of the food, and the stale reek of sweat.

The couples intertwined more closely during the slow numbers, their bodies rocking lasciviously as though welded to one another; heads drooped, hands slipped down from waist to buttocks, there was overloud laughter, and mouths sought out mouths.

"Well, I must say"—Jenny giggled vulgarly—"it's no holds barred. Our whores wouldn't go around like that, I can tell you, they're more decent. And they don't go with one another, come to think of it, that's not their thing at all."

Imperturbable, her gaze elsewhere, Marta played on as though nothing of this concerned her.

"Still, it's not really a place for kids; we oughtn't to have brought Sylvia."

Sylvia was playing her pipes with such concentration that she seemed to be totally oblivious of the scene.

Alcohol and mounting desire enflamed faces, ruddy in the brief light of a cigarette. It was very warm; one woman had pushed down her shoulder straps to reveal good, slightly heavy breasts, which she crushed lovingly against the disguised curves of a pyjamaed "boy"; head thrown back, she laughed as she danced. In the middle of the chaos, Georgette's eunuch-like voice ordered silence.

We stopped playing; it was bizarre to see the couples immobilized by the silence, mouths held agape, limbs frozen in mid-movement.

"Could you play less loudly?" She spoke to us first. "As for you, have as much fun as you like, but do it quietly. Otherwise you'll be ending your evening in the jail."

Feet were shuffled more cautiously; the orchestra concentrated on the languid, the muted. The women drooped, wallowed, drinking the while. Under the influence of alcohol, the evening was rapidly turning into an orgy.

We'd been playing for almost three hours, with only brief pauses. We were beginning to be exhausted, but more important, we wanted to get our hands, or rather mouths, on our wages.

On the dance floor, couples were swaying cheek to cheek; a variety of garments had been abandoned or torn off. Many were drunk; their makeup was running, their rouge was smudged, their faces were shiny. A woman dragged another towards a bed, the *cojas* were filled with couples, sometimes trios. Mouths were riveted to nipples, to mouths, hands scratched a back, a thigh, a cry rolled strangled in a throat, then escaped upwards into freedom. A slap rang out on a cheek, on a buttock. Exhausted and exhausting pantings accompanied the couplings.

Only a few women were left on the floor, dragging their feet like the finalists in a marathon and positively dovetailed together, on the borderline between the dance and other, more secret pleasures. Everywhere women were hugging, kissing, and caressing, lying flat out on tables, sliding to the floor. In the shadow of the *cojas,* clinging bodies rolled over in their frantic, almost pitiful search for pleasure. Darkness swathed whole portions of the bodies, veiling precise gestures. There was a whole range of kisses, from lovebird pecks to octopuslike exhanges, wet, sucking, gurgling. It was uncharted territory.

At last, Georgette, who was still in possession of her senses, came and advised us to eat. We threw ourselves at the sauerkraut and still tepid sausages like locusts onto a laden fig tree in the desert. Then we took our places again, weary and heavy with the unaccustomed food; we played quietly on, but the women didn't hear us now, occupied as they were in extracting the last ounce of pleasure. The mixture of smells was heavier than ever. Helga, clearly exhausted, tapped feebly on her drums and Jenny, wrist aching, still had the strength to say to her banteringly that she ought to speed up the rhythm so that it would all be over more quickly!

It was about midnight when a runner opened the door.

"Quick, the SS!"

The couples unlatched themselves, leapt up, separated the tables, pulled back the *cojas,* and carried the drunken girls to their beds. While Georgette, the *kapo,* and the blockowa rushed about and hastened the proceedings with baton blows, we profited from the stampede to take our wages, filling our buckets to the brim with the remains of the sauerkraut, sausage, and bacon, despite the high-pitched efforts of the three women to get us out of there. I don't think anything could have separated us from our booty.

By the time we left, the block had almost resumed its normal appearance, which was just as well: if the SS had burst in during this revelry, the punishment would have been devastating.

Two minutes later, amid the whistle blasts that announced a *Blocksperre,* with buckets in hand, we made a grand entrance into our own block—the celebrities come home. From behind our table we distributed our sauerkraut to the women as if this were a soup kitchen and we were the ladies bountiful. Everyone had some, even the Polish girls, whose minds could not encompass such generosity but just profited from it. Florette christened this the night of the great share-out.

Hardly had we come back than we heard trucks driving through the rain. No train had arrived, so we had no idea who they were looking for.

In the morning we learned that it had been the Gypsies from Hungary. They had been camping some distance away, on the other side of the men's camp. One morning, surrounded by SS, they had arrived with their wagons, their luggage, their old people, their women, children, and animals. They had set up their caravans, organized their camps, and they'd been living there for months, years perhaps. It was said that through the agency of a neutral country, the Americans had come to an agreement about the Gypsies, that they were paying for them to be kept alive. They used to sing and play the guitar; some evenings the air carried the sounds right to us, or so we thought. It was said that the SS killed them because their "allowance" hadn't arrived on time. The only certain thing was that they were gassed on the night of the black triangles' party. Probably the SS said nothing about it and continued to receive money for them until the camp was liberated.

Mandel and the Child

WERE WE GOING to have to live through another winter, a spring, a summer? Or indeed, were we going to live at all? We were already so thin. Still, we didn't do manual labour and thus burned fewer calories than the others in the work groups; so our ration of barely twelve hundred calories a day was sufficient for survival—we were not yet moslems. In fact, most of us weren't as badly off as all that. Everyone had very set ideas about her own physical appearance: Big Irene found herself admirably thin, although she was in fact bloated; Anny thought she was pleasingly rounded, though she was frighteningly thin. Jenny, fleshless as a nail, was certain she looked great. As for Clara, the acclaim won by her fat buttocks spoke to her unequivocally of her beauty.

It seemed to us that, Paris once liberated, the Allied advance ought to surge ahead, carrying all before it. What were the partisans doing in the Carpathians, the mountains that we could actually see on the rare days when the weather was clear? In vain we scanned the faces of the SS. Sometimes they seemed more nervous. Graf Bobby had disappeared, but that meant nothing—their comings and goings were incessant. Sometimes we thought they were vaguer, or more vicious, or less so . . .

"Recently," said a girl from another block, "presumably because they suddenly felt that your orchestra wasn't sufficient to ensure our entertainment and wanted to do something else for us apart from gas us, the SS decided to treat the internees to a picture show. It wasn't compulsory and indeed most people didn't go. Well, an SS asked me why. I told him that it was because we were ill. *'Ach,'* he said, 'you don't know what you want. It's pointless to make any effort for you. Your comrades prefer to stay locked up chatting. What have they got against motion pictures? You're never satisfied.' "

Someone from a work detachment had told a similar tale: "I was exhausted, my hands were in ribbons, legs trembling. I thought I'd collapse at every stone I carried, when an SS, a young, fair chap, said: 'Don't always keep your head down like that, look up and see how blue the sky is.' It made me so livid that I couldn't help answering that I didn't want to look at the Birkenau sky. He stared at me as if I were a monster and said: 'You Jews, you have no feeling for nature.' "

The SS needed space: selection followed selection. They were expecting more convoys. This news and the autumn rain depressed us utterly. The whole block was gloomy. Warsaw had been taken, lost, retaken, lost again. This morning the camp was buzzing with Aryan Poles, women and children of all ages, camping mainly between camps A and B near the railway line; but there were so many of them that some overflowed and could be seen from our blocks. Seated amid their luggage, they spread out blankets, cooked soup, warmed up milk on stoves and improvised fires, and breast-fed their children. We had to pick our way over recumbent grandmothers clad in innumerable petticoats. Some were crying and all seemed worried and lost, and with good reason.

The heavy smoke above the crematoria indicated that they were full to capacity, so the Polish women would be left there, with their children, to wait their turn. In all the blocks, the deportees were alarmed: these Polish women and children—there were thousands of them—were Aryans, so perhaps the Germans would spare them; and to house them, they were going to have to create some space. It was the topic of the day, on everyone's lips. There were some who "knew" and claimed that we were all going to be gassed. In our block a Polish girl, Masha, revealing her little shark's teeth, squawked out with the voice of fear that they were going to be put in our block. Ewa pointed out that there were forty-seven of us and thousands of them and suggested that she was exaggerating, but Masha repeated herself with hysterical certainty. A ripple of anguish ran through the company. Anything was possible.

The weather was fine, and the camp teemed with children who ran about, playing and chasing after each other despite their mothers' worried cluckings; this gave the place the unusual atmosphere of an improvised summer camp site, a pilgrimage, a sort of country fête. They looked up in astonishment when we sat on our platform for the Sunday concert. Sonia hated the Poles, who today were our only audience, and her baton movements were more perfunctory than ever. The SS were distracted; they came and went, furious to see their impeccably aligned camp invaded by this rabble. The women might well pray to their holy icons, for Kramer wouldn't tolerate this disorder for long. Our presence seemed to reassure the Polish women; perhaps they thought it was a sort of welcome, a way of helping them to pass this endless Sunday before the authorities got down to business. The place wasn't very cheerful, but what else could one expect from one's enemies? And now they were being given a concert; some smiled at us, little boys clapped their hands, a little girl danced. How I would have liked to pray to God to spare them, but what could one ask of a god who had allowed this?

Our most faithful supporter, Frau Maria Mandel, so spruce in her uniform, came towards us, marched among those scattered bodies, those crouching women, as one would walk through a snake pit: furious and disgusted. In the sun her hair looked as if it were spun out of the cold of wheat. Arms outstretched, a marvellous little child toddled towards her, a ringleted angel of two or three. He ran up to her, clutched her boots, pulled at her skirt. My heart dropped; she'd surely send him flying with an almighty kick. But no, she bent down, took him in her arms, and covered him with kisses. The scene was so sensational that for a moment we stopped playing; Mandel, her blue eyes hard, went off carrying the child in her arms. The women watched her pass. Some way off a Polish woman, the mother presumably, called out desperately, but a mass of humanity separated her from her child. Mandel turned her back and the distance between them grew.

All night the trucks were on the move. Screeching whistle blasts seered into our brains. It was a hellish night. I couldn't stop thinking about the Poles. I saw them abandoning their parcels and getting into the trucks, trusting as ever as they were led away to their deaths. They thought that they were going to be settled at last . . . they believed . . . they trusted . . . Damn the lot of them, I wanted to sleep. I wanted the tears to dry on my face at last.

In the morning, we all had red eyes. Outside, there was no longer a single woman, a single parcel; the camp was neat as ever. We were confined to quarters; the *Blocksperre* was still on, it was to last for the whole day. The total capacity of the crematoria for a day was twenty-four thousand bodies.

Even the girls in Canada, whose sensitivity was pretty calloused, showed traces of emotion before the incredible pile of children's clothes they had to sort, pack up, and send to Berlin.

And the children? What had they done with the children? the girls asked.

I tried to reassure them: "They were Aryans. Mala told me that when they had all the characteristics of the Nordic races, they'd be sent to Germany."

"What for?"

"They give them to families who've lost their children. Perhaps they'll be sent to special institutions. Well, I really don't know, but I think they're still alive."

Big Irene gazed mistily into the distance and asked worriedly: "What did Mandel do with the little boy?"

"Presumably she gave him back."

But apparently not; during our rehearsal a visit from Mandel was announced. She came in with the baby in her arms; she'd dressed him up in the most expensive clothes, a little blue sailor suit, and he looked adorable. He lifted his hyacinth gaze trustingly towards her. In his chubby fists he clutched a bar of chocolate, which he offered her, prattling. "No, no," she said mincingly, but he insisted with a bell-like laugh. The old game between mothers and children: she pretended to eat some, shook her head . . . What fun they were both having.

I didn't know why she had come to us. Perhaps she wanted to hear *Madame Butterfly*, I thought; but no, she'd come to show us the orphan whose mother had been gassed. She didn't make the connection; her brain, like all German brains, was compartmentalized like a submarine, made of watertight sections. The execution of the Polish women had nothing to do with her.

Seated on a chair in our music room, the child on her knee, she was delighted when we clustered round her, as proud as a mother: "He's pretty, isn't he?" Standing on her knee, the baby trampled her cheerfully; she didn't care that his little shoes were dirtying her uniform. He put an arm round her neck and kissed her with a round mouth daubed with chocolate, and we saw, we heard Mandel *laugh*. Then she went off, holding the child by the hand; he trotted along at her side, and I noted that she slowed down her military gait to his teetering walk.

For about a week she paraded the child proudly through the camp.

"Well," said Big Irene to me, "perhaps she's not as bad as all that."

Anny was more cautious. "With her, it's best to reserve judgement."

Each day the baby had different clothes; apparently she was driving the Canada girls mad, asking them to undo all their parcels—she wanted only blue clothes. The child was a positive passion with her. Then quite late one night, when the wind was driving the rain viciously against our windows and most of us were in bed, Mandel was announced. She came in wearing a big black cape. Abnormally pale, eyes ringed, she asked for the duet from *Butterfly*. Lips pursed, her face impassive, she seemed very remote. I saw inexplicable anguish in her eyes. When the duet was over she got up and went out, without a sign or word of satisfaction.

The next day Renate, Marta's sister, told us that Mandel herself had taken the child to the gas chamber. There was violent reaction.

"How awful. How could she do such a thing? Why?" asked Ewa.

Marta was silent, but I knew what she was thinking: "Mandel is German, like me, and she dared to do that."

Some of us simply wept over this incomprehensible drama, over this child. And without knowing it, over this woman. The Hungarians expressed it in their own way by saying that she had trampled over her own heart. But why? Many of them avoided the question by saying that she was mad, purely and simply. I protested that she wasn't, that it was too easy to deny her responsibility. Big Irene turned eyes gleaming with tears in my direction.

"Do you know why?"

"I can think of an explanation. Mandel is a convinced Nazi, a fanatic. She has no right to give her heart or mind to anything other than National Socialism, no right to let a feeling take precedence over doctrine. No right to keep a human being from the gas chambers, even a child. It's not she who knows what's good for the party, for the Reich, it's her bosses. She couldn't continue to disobey.''

"Perhaps," said Sylvia dreamily. "In my opinion that innocent child has gone straight to heaven, and he'll protect us.''

I wondered whether this rigour had come from Mandel's past. She was an Austrian, born in Upper Austria, and people said that she had had a Jewish lover and had been punishing herself ever since. But before coming to Birkenau she had been warden at Ravensbruck, and so well thought of that she had been raised to the position of head of our camp.

People said . . . people said . . . But a little child had given her his trust, had slipped his fist in her big hand like a bird slipping into the hollow of a nest, and she had dared to lead him to his death.

Time Runs Out

OUR SS SEEMED UNEASY, their morale was crumbling. They came and went and were even more unpredictable than usual. They selected madly, but their hearts weren't in it; it wasn't that joyful work we'd witnessed in the past. Still, Tauber had just hit on an excellent idea: naked—there didn't seem to be any alternative to this costume, though of course you don't clothe cattle—and at attention, the women had to stretch out their arms in front of them, and those whose arms trembled were sent to Block 25. What astounded me was that there were any which didn't.

Mengele was more subtle, as befitted his superior class. The description Marie gave us of selections in the Revier poisoned my thoughts for days. He asked one girl who screamed incessantly what she was afraid of. Was her conscience bothering her? he wanted to know.

For nights now we'd been hearing waves of planes; they weren't Messerschmitts either, no mistake about it, they were the Allies. I had been awoken by dull sounds like those of bombs falling. Our great fear was that while waiting, in order to efface all signs of their camps, the SS could still kill us all, down to the last one; I fell asleep with this phrase in my head: all, down to the last one. I must have been asleep for a couple of hours when an SS man came into the music room shouting and demanding the orchestra. Sonia came running, Maria fell upon us. It was so dark that we couldn't see him and didn't recognize his voice, which was so slurred that Jenny commented nervously: "This is our first drunken SS; let's hope he isn't a mean drunk."

Anny hazarded a glance in his direction. "It's Florette's SS man."

The German and Polish girls quaked; he had a terrible reputation with them. A few days before, a monstrous SS had come into our block—we'd never seen anything so frightful; any monkey would have been better-looking than that creature. He had come through our two rooms, growled something incomprehensible, then gone away again without anyone's knowing why he'd come. Florette, in an inventive mood, had burst out: "Careful now. We'll have to play well for him. No wrong notes."

"Why?" they all asked.

"He's the new head of the crematoria."

Our group immediately realized that this was nonsense, but Florette, animated by her own joke, went on. Determined that Sonia should understand, she asked me to explain to her, which I gladly did, further embroidering the matter with some skill: "If we manage to charm him with our scrapings, he may give us an extra whiff of gas, and it'll be over that much more quickly." Then, shockingly, we laughed.

This night there was no more laughter. Head of the crematoria or not, this drunken German meant business.

He bellowed: "Out! *Raus! Kommt! Schnell!*" He wanted hit tunes and Gypsy songs. Jenny nudged Ewa the Hungarian: "It's up to you—keep the brute sweet." Shivering—the nights were now cold—the complete orchestra played in front of our entirely empty barracks. He had insisted that everyone should be present at the concert given in his honour. Thoroughly drunk, facing us, he beat time with his arm. At once stiff and swaying, he looked like a badly regulated automaton, beating

time out of time. We certainly had our share of
grotesque sights.

Luckily for us his drunkenness was not the vicious
sort, but sentimental and tearful. Lili played her violin
right into his ear, Gypsy style, causing him to weep
copiously. The comedy lasted perhaps an hour and then
we went back in, not without having noticed strange
lights flickering in the sky, followed by more distant
rumblings. We told ourselves that the fighting was
getting closer.

The next day we learned that our SS had been having
a farewell soirée before his departure for the front.

"If things go on like last night, he won't need to walk
far to meet a soldier's death," remarked Jenny.

The SS man got drunk because he was leaving the
safety of the camp, where he was one of the masters of
death; both master and servant, he was paying death his
tribute with the lives of others, so what did he fear from
her? Precious little, nothing more than in ordinary life:
an accident, an illness. He wasn't going right up to her,
he wasn't provoking her; but the front was something
quite different. Heroes are softened if they're made into
executioners! But why were his comrades drinking?
Before selections, to give themselves courage?
Afterwards, to forget?

"Why?" I asked Marie.

She shrugged her shoulders. "Like all the rest, out of
fear."

The approaching moment of judgement demoralized
them.

We relished their agitation, their unrest. It amused us
to see them straining to hear the noise of the aeroplane
engines and rumblings that shook the night quiet. We
suddenly thought we heard cannonfire as well, the dull
thud of bombs; I even convinced myself I heard rifle
fire. As far as I was concerned, it was the Russians who
were coming to our aid; the Cossacks had become my
dream knights, my liberators. There again I might have

been moving rather too quickly, certainly more quickly than they!

Meanwhile, the mood was tense. Florette had just been caught for stealing three potatoes. Like a child, confused, she repeated: "It was for Little Irene. I wanted to make her those potato cakes she likes so much." This recipe was her triumph. She had pierced a number of holes in a jam-tin lid, and with it she scraped the potatoes, then mixed them with a bit of margarine, and made them into cakes which she threw into boiling water; when they were cooked, she added a sauce of simmered onions, a real treat. But this wasn't the time for recipes. Faced with the scandal aroused by Florette's action, Maria slapped and insulted her.

Sonia, informed of these matters by her dear friend, decided to take the thief to Mandel to ask for an exemplary punishment. The farce had become a drama and the drama could yet become tragedy: Florette could well be sent to a work detachment or to Block 25. Sonia, furious, grabbed her by the scruff of her neck like a kitten and dragged her outside.

"Where's she going?" asked Big Irene, worried.

I didn't answer, but I pushed past the sniggering Maria and ran after them. I caught up with them in the main thoroughfare. At arm's length, held firmly in Sonia's hard peasant's grip, Florette, snivelling, looked a real little urchin. In Russian, in my coldest, most contemptuous voice, I warned Sonia:

"If you go to Mandel, if you touch her, tonight we'll suffocate you in your bed; we'll put you under the mattress and sit on you until you die."

She took stock of me with her cunning little eyes, assessing the seriousness of the threat. She had to believe me. She did. She let Florette go and back we went.

It was evening and we rehearsed mechanically; we

were like those automata you see at fairs. There were whistles, shouts, mad galloping, then the air-raid warning. This was something new. Heavily, with a thud of boots and clink of arms, the valorous members of the SS ran to shelter. What a heartwarming, comforting sight. Powerful, a lid of sound, the engines of the bombers outdid all else. The women were driven back into the blocks with shouts and rifle blows. Crowded at our windows and at two open doors, we watched them, shouting that we were here! There was no antiaircraft defence; the Allies ruled the skies. Crouching to their shelters, the SS were powerless. The bombs began to fall, aimed at the crematoria, the gas chambers. It made me weep with joy. Ecstatically I shouted: "Look at the gentleness, the precision, it's as though they were laying them down by hand."

In our enthusiasm we had opened the door and were standing on the threshold. The searchlights on the watchtowers and all other lights were out, darkness was complete. Suddenly, brutally, a violent light tore through the darkness, a deafening noise shattered it. I shrieked with terror, prey to a real fit of hysterics. It was so unexpected that the girls thought I was wounded; no one could believe that I was quite simply frightened silly.

"Hey, girls, today we've got something to celebrate!"
We looked at Jenny blankly.
"First of November, eve of All Souls, the day of the dead!"
Her humour escaped us.
Tomorrow there was to be a concert in the infirmary and we'd have to play well: Mengele might be there. I was worried; gradually Alma's teaching was fading. As Florette said of Sonia: "What is good is that we can play a different piece from the one she thinks she's conducting without her noticing." There was also a very definite dissatisfaction on the part of the SS, who no

doubt had other things to think about than frequenting our music room; the day we interested them not a whit—that was something not to think about.

"Shower, girls!"

It was a marvellous moment we never ceased to cherish; for us, this shower was life. Towels under our arms, soap in hand or pocket, collars up against the cold, we marched off. In the grey sky, the usual smoke with its smell of death lay still and heavy.

It had rained, and we paddled through mud. We would have to clean our shoes when we got back. We could have done with some new stockings, but this certainly wasn't the moment to ask.

When we got back, in the fading light, we all felt rather heavy-hearted; the rain penetrated our clothes and we dreaded the approaching winter. Soon there'd be snow; in the meantime the rain was icy.

"Halt! Achtung!"

Before us, helmeted SS men, weapons on their hips, legs apart, were blocking our route. This was the end. It had to happen; my heart beat only slightly faster. I had expected to be more frightened.

It was raining harder now; we were cold. We put our towels on our heads. What ought we to do with the soap? I slid mine into my pocket and touched my little notebook. I swore that that book should burn with me.

"Jews to the left, Aryans to the right!"

A well-known refrain. The SS let our Aryan comrades go by, one by one; Bronia, Alla, and Olga gave us a discreet wave of the hand and Haline a smile; Ewa, once through the barrage, turned and caught my eye. I could see her standing outside our block looking at us fixedly as one might look at a condemned man. I smiled at her.

The SS surrounded us, whistles blew. Five by five. The order to march was given. We turned our backs on the crematoria but it was still too soon to rejoice at that, because with them it meant nothing. We went towards the Sauna. Often, when things got crowded, the selected

were sent there. As a variant for us, we were taken into
the basement. We didn't talk, we didn't dare. Each
knew what the other had to say and didn't want to hear
it. I don't know how long we stood locked in that
basement. Our brains, wound up like music boxes,
reeled off the endless refrain: "The orchestra is over.
Will we go straight to the gas chamber or through
Block Twenty-five? The orchestra is over. Will we go
straight . . ."

The door opened onto utter darkness. Under the
searchlights the rain wove a thick bright curtain through
which we walked. The dogs' paws splashed, the noise of
boots was softened by mud. The SS smelt of wet cloth,
dogs, and leather. This was undoubtedly the moment to
pray. We were taken out of camp B and driven towards
the platform where the convoys arrived. There a train
awaited us; we were driven into a sort of wooden tum-
bril open to the skies with neither roof nor tarpaulin.
Once again the orchestra was separated from the rest;
we were alone. In the middle, surprisingly, there was a
stove, and seated beside it, two old soldiers of the Wehrmacht. Swathed in their capes, they were almost hidden under the steel bells of their helmets. It was almost
as if they had no heads. Perhaps they were scarecrows;
one held a gun in one hand and stuffed wood into the
stove with the other. Standing up, crushed together, we
felt the floor tremble under our feet and the train jolted
into motion; slowly, Birkenau moved into the distance.
Since the air-raid warnings, the lights had been dimmed,
only the reddish sky indicated where the camp was. It
was over; we were travelling through the night, and the
rain had stopped.

Planes passed high overhead, bomb explosions rum-
bled through the clouds like distant thunder.

We were so tightly packed that if anyone had fainted
she would have remained upright. We tried to sing, but
it didn't take.

"I left the lovely navy blue cushion I was making for

Florette's birthday behind,'' murmured Anny. "What can I give her?''

"I left the cards. How will we manage without them?''

Courage? Heedlessness?

Someone said: "Time has run out.''

Under the Jackboot

FROM TIME TO TIME the train stopped. Its shuntings jolted us mercilessly. They put us on a siding and long convoys of munitions, troops, and wounded passed . . . That was war. Behind the dirty windows of the compartments we saw the usual indifferent, gloomy grey hordes. They were as passive as we, like animals going to their doom.

The night wore on, the train moved off again. We went into a tunnel and someone shrieked that they were going to electrocute us there, that it was the "death tunnel"! Sometimes, in a cattle truck, a cow lows out its pain, its boredom, its terror, and provokes a chain reaction. It was the same thing with us; one person's panic led to total chaos. The train went into the darkness. At the other end of the tunnel we hadn't been electrocuted. Sighs. But we discovered a heart-breaking cemetery in the grey light of dawn. Crosses of all sizes, a lot of flowers, piles of wreaths with the same sense of dead glory as the laurel wreaths of the Olympic games. Heroes' wreaths. There was a lot of dying being done at that time. Lotte, who towered over us and had a perfect view, cried out pathetically: "Oh, all those fresh flowers," and her voice, thick with tears, groaned for the dead. "How sad it is. The poor soldiers, the poor families!"

Florette, crushed against her, lashed out as best she could: "Fool! Idiot! You're mad to weep over their cemetery. What about us, *us?*''

We had been travelling for two days. We peed on the spot and tried to hold back the rest; we hadn't had a drop of water or a crust of bread.

On November 4, 1944, our train stopped in the middle of a forest. The Wehrmacht soldiers ordered us out—where were our SS? The absence of those experts in selection reassured us. Our new warders neither shrieked nor hit, they were old and resigned, but when they did look at us, there was a hard little glint in the blue-grey of their tired eyes which there was no mistaking: like the others, they would strike us down, with a bullet if they were still good shots, with several if they were out of practice. Only they didn't have dogs.

Haggard, a troop of a thousand women tottered forward, As always, all honour to music: we were at the head. Well-shod, well-dressed, we found walking less painful than the rest. But the others, those who followed, were they picked up when they fell? They weren't killed, it seemed, because we heard no gunshots. But I was haunted by the long line which dragged out behind us, which we seemed to pull. We'd been walking for about two hours when Marta pointed out some barbed wire, a wooden sign at the entrance to a wood: "Shooting Range."

"I think we've arrived," she murmured.

The girls didn't notice. We entered a little wood. When we came out of it, we saw a fairly large rise, onto which we climbed. Below, we heard the regular noise of machine-gun fire rattling through the empty air or, at worst, an earlier convoy.

"Halt! Achtung!"

Marta hadn't let go of Little Irene's hand throughout the journey; sometimes I got the feeling that she was the stronger of that surprising couple, that it was she who supported Little Irene.

"We're right in the middle of a shooting range," Marta said to me.

The soldiers, under the instructions of their sergeant, arranged us in a semicircle; I no longer dared look at Marta. Were they going to advance with their machine guns pointing in front of them, phalluses of death trained upon us, and then, when they'd got to the right distance, fire . . . fire . . .?

The rain was now coming down in torrents; several women were weeping with fear and exhaustion, others collapsed howling. It might seem incredible, but the mere act of opening one's mouth allowed the water to pour in so brutally, so violently, that it prevented us from breathing; it went straight to the lungs and suffocated us; that evening, on that plateau, women died drowned by the rain.

For the first time, our little group was divided. Most of the Germans were some way from us, and I could no longer see the Greeks or Hungarians. I begged the remaining group to keep together. Anny, the two Irenes, Marta, Clara, Florette, Jenny, Marie, Lotte, and Elsa formed a little hard core; we wanted to stick together.

Near us, an unknown deportee was proclaiming melodramatically if understandably that we were the unluckiest beings in the world.

I reassured her: "Not at all. The fellow who's sitting in the warmth of a cafe on the Champs Elysées and who's waiting for the girl he loves and can't see her coming also thinks he's the unluckiest person in the world."

Obviously this was cold comfort because there was a chorus of exclamations: "What an idiot. A madwoman! Who does she think she is? She *must* have suffered a lot to come out with that nonsense."

Anny reprimanded me severely: "Unhappiness can't be compared any more than happiness."

I tried to reason with them: "But surely it's the intensity of the unhappiness that counts, not the conditions."

Only Marta seemed to understand. What an odd girl. I felt like shouting to them that I'd won, since they were now thinking about something else.

We had been there nine hours, arm in arm, rocking so as not to fall asleep, not to let ourselves go with exhaustion; we hadn't sat down for forty-six hours. When a woman fell, we tried to pick her up but we didn't always succeed and so she remained where she was, in a streaming heap, half dead or worse, in the rain. It was still daylight but the approach of night scored the forest with sinister shadows. At last two officers came up and grouped us together above the enormous crater near which we were standing and which was being used as a firing range by the young recruits. The rain had eased off a little. A colonel spoke:

"You have arrived in your camp."

We looked in all directions—what camp? A desert, there was nothing, not a hut in sight.

"Nothing has yet been built, it is you who will build it. We shall put the necessary material at your disposal. So, when you have rediscovered the salutory sense of work, you will be able to gain just satisfaction from it."

And so, brazenly, he continued to treat this huge crowd of tottering, half-dead women to a sermon on the regenerating virtues practised by the great German Reich.

I listened to this admirable speech attentively. It wasn't the speech of an SS, but of a Nazi German, a fine specimen of insolent hypocrisy. After a few injunctions concerning discipline, cleanliness, and obedience, we were warned that all attempts at escape, until the camp had been built, would be repressed by shooting on sight. As far as we could judge, they lacked neither weapons nor munitions. We were also told that we would be given some soup.

Bowls were distributed and we queued up to receive two ladlefuls of passable soup. However, in the total disorder that reigned, some managed to get served twice

while others didn't even get one portion. We were
terribly thirsty. Our future camp was served with water
by a horizontal pipe placed about three feet from the
ground. This pipe, which must have been a few yards
long, had holes at regular intervals forming so many
fountains. It was worked by a tap guarded by a soldier.
Women rushed forward, they wanted to drink at any
price. The German refused, they went berserk, began to
run, and we heard firing, followed by cries. Anny
looked at me, her lovely dark eyes calm.

"I'd like to be the first to die!"

The rifle fire stopped and we never knew what havoc
it had wreaked.

Soldiers began to improvise a sort of gigantic tent,
almost at ground level; despite my mere four feet
eleven, I had to duck to get inside it. Big Irene was
forced to crawl. We lay down, drenched to the skin,
shivering, but we were in such a state of exhaustion that
we fell asleep. Happy sleep, imperious as death, for
those women lying in several inches of water.

I was later to learn that, a few yards from me, Anne
Frank was lying under this same canvas.

Enormous pockets of rain formed on top of the tent,
which finally collapsed under the weight. Like birds
caught in nets, the women shrieked and struggled, half
crushed by the weight of the fabric heavy with water;
they stumbled through the folds of the canvas, knocked
into one another, moaned with terror and cold.
Plunging through this tangle of limbs, I found myself in
the open air. Above me towered an enormous hulk, that
of a German officer who incredibly said to me in very
correct French: "You could ask your friend St. Peter to
let up on the rain front!"

"Up. *Raus. Schnell.*"

In the struggling daybreak they drove our dripping,
streaming troops towards another part of the camp.
This was already built: grey barracks beneath a grey

sky. Sky, ground, soldiers were a symphony of dingy grey. It wasn't exactly a military camp, because in the distance we saw two familiar crematoria chimneys, barbed wire, and searchlights. We wouldn't feel too lost, that was certain. However, what was missing from this all too familiar picture was the squat tomblike mass of the gas chambers.

(Later, I was to learn that we were at Bergen-Belsen; that this hastily built camp beside a firing range had been occupied, until our arrival, by women, and that it needed no gas chambers because death came by another route, that of phenol injections into the heart.)

Driven doggedly but without excessive brutality, our group poured into a long cellar, a sort of army depot or storehouse. We were put in a corner crammed with those leather boots so dear to the Wehrmacht. They were lined up in military fashion, stacked on sort of racks from floor to ceiling, carefully oiled and smelling of old rancid tallow. There was a narrow pathway between the rows. The soldiers piled us like their boots and left us together. We flopped down amid the encroaching footwear and slept.

I don't remember much about the days that followed. Indeed, for me, the whole period of Bergen-Belsen which was just beginning is chronologically obscure and patchy. It took me to the gates of death and perhaps that is why the images I have of it are both so vivid and so confused. Towards the end, they are very fragmentary indeed, a perfectly legible puzzle but missing some pieces.

Clearly, the flock of women which had descended on their camp was more than the men of the Wehrmacht could cope with. I don't know how we spent the first five days that followed the collapse of the tent and our entrance into the cellar. I emerged from my exhaustion only on the morning of November 9, Florette's birthday; she was nineteen. Perhaps she had made some clumsy movement as she awoke, because a whole pile of boots collapsed on her and buried her, and as she swore and raged we shouted out birthday greetings with maddening cherriness. This redoubled her fury; buried beneath a pile of stinking footwear Florette continued to howl, and it took at least five minutes to disengage her. Then, since we had only our empty hands to offer her, we described to her the presents she would have had at Birkenau. It was Anny's navy blue cushion that carried the day: "I'd embroidered playing cards on it."

"How did you manage to organize all that—material, embroidery silk?" asked Florette, her green eyes moist with gratitude. She couldn't hear enough about that marvel, that inconceivable luxury: a cushion. "I could have slept on it," she murmured, enraptured.

We could come and go freely in and out of our cellar. We found ourselves in the middle of a monstrous muddle which suddenly alarmed us; the strict order in which we were used to living, paradoxically, had given us a feeling of security. Accustomed as we were to being kept within limits which made any initiative impossible, we were upset by this illusion of freedom; we didn't know what to do with it, where to go. The women came and went freely. Barbed wire had been hastily put up around the new camp, but our limits were unclear; we didn't know how far we were allowed to go. As soon as a woman wandered off, our guards would panic and shoot. There was no organization; one might get a bit of bread, of sausage, at any time, then go for a day without anything at all. And to complete this feeling of insecurity, there was constant machine-gun fire.

Within a few days, everything changed. New transports of deportees arrived from Birkenau, with them the SS, Kramer at their head. The most ridiculous rumours circulated among the musicians: "He's going to start the orchestra again; we're going to get everything back, instruments, uniforms, the lot." The news of the presence in the camp of Irma Grese reinforced us in our mad ideas. It was definite: Mandel was joining her, and perhaps Drexler, though we'd gladly have done without her.

The plateau on which the camp stood was transformed. Improvised wooden barracks were built, holding up to a thousand women; no tables, no stove, just three-tier *cojas*. Electrified wire was put up, and searchlights. With the SS, the dogs were back.

"As you see," Jenny commented, "they bring the good life right along with them."

Arbeit! Arbeit! They were probably just a few weeks, a few months, from defeat, and they behave as if the war were never to end, or to end with their victory. No useless mouths in the great German Reich. *Arbeit, Arbeit!* Near the camp there was a factory that made cellophane, and we were ideal free labour, as the man at Auschwitz had been for I. G. Farbenindustrie. And let no one tell me that the bosses, the directors, the foremen, the workers who saw those pitiful gangs enter their workshops every morning didn't know of the existence of the camps and the way the deportees were treated.

Each morning, the SS went into the barracks and demanded their contingent of workers, several hundred in all. The women who had shoes, like Lotte, Big Irene, Clara, Jenny, Marta, and Florette, went to work in the factory; the others, the barefooted ones, were sent to clear trees in the wood. It was only reasonable: one couldn't decently send women to work in a factory barefoot! It didn't matter for the work in the woods; if they caught cold or got hurt, they'd die more quickly. We soon learnt that in Bergen-Belsen that was how selections were made; drudgery would be the dealer of death.

And that was why, when I put myself forward for the work detachment, Florette pushed me back and presented herself in my place, and why Marta did the same for Little Irene. They were protecting us because we were the two smallest and frailest of our group.

Then we received a stupefying bit of news: Florette and Clara were appointed *kapos*. These appointments were a new and worrying development, and clearly provocative. At Birkenau, the *kapos* were recruited from among the Polish girls, the Czechs, the Slovaks, the Germans. Not a single French girl; the SS didn't trust them. Thus we had always been convinced that we were safe from the horror of becoming a *kapo*. Why had they chosen two musicians from the orchestra?

Physically one could understand the appointment better for Clara than for Florette. Big Clara must have struck them as sufficiently strong and imposing to play the role: shouting, punishing, beating. But Florette? Little Irene had a theory: Florette was quite big and not too thin, but more important, when she was angry she had a strength which couldn't but please the SS, and they decided that they could use this power to their advantage. Irene could well have been right.

We knew what to expect from Florette by way of reaction: verbal abuse which would allow her to make use of her whole repertoire, but she would not use the hefty truncheon they would receive along with their *kapo*'s arm bands. We were equally convinced that she would help us in her own way, vociferous but fair, that she wouldn't victimize anyone or abuse her rights. But what could one expect from Clara? This "honour" might be the last straw, might unleash the bad instincts I now feared she had, or it might allow her to be superbly generous, to prove that she had true control. Too often the "arm band" made the man; given half a chance, even worms turned. We were soon to know the answer.

Clara rose up before us, arm band in place, club in hand. Her very posture was significant; now she had lost even such humanity as had remained to her. Everything that was left of the timid, bashful young girls had just disappeared, destroyed once and for all by the environment of the camp. It was weeks now since I'd spoken to her. I thought I'd become indifferent to her, but at that moment I realized she still had the power to horrify me. She stood stolidly in front of our little group, like an evil power, thrusting her club challengingly under our noses:

"From now on, I'm the boss. It'll be me who's in charge. You'll do whatever I say, and if you don't, I'll hit!"

"Whore," Florette positively spat at her.

Clara lifted her stick. We all rose up together; as a group we felt invincible. She knew it and turned her back. But ours was clearly a brittle victory. We stared at one another in horror, conscious that we were going to have to fight against her. All my goodwill for Clara had evaporated, yet I still wanted to save her from herself. I went to look for her; cudgel in hand, legs firmly apart in the favourite pose of the *kapo* which she copied with evident relish, she watched me coming.

"Clara, look at yourself! You've become a monster. If you lash out at our friends, you'll never dare to go back home. Remember your childhood, your girlhood, your parents . . . Clara, look at yourself!"

Her eyes shone with a positively mineral brightness, like coals. "Be quiet and listen to me. I'm through with your superior airs, your moralizing. Here, it's me who's the stronger, it's me who's in charge. I've heard enough, now get away!"

How sure she was of herself now that she had the right of life and death over a thousand women. She now had in her turn the right that others had had over her, and perhaps that explained everything. Clara was moved to a block next to ours. She was drunk with noise and violence, lashing out at unfortunate and already exhausted women. Indeed, to make extra sure of her power, she didn't hesitate to choose the weakest. She strutted about, claiming with the conceit of an SS that her block was the most efficient.

I'd hardened my heart against her, and would have liked to forget her but she wouldn't let me. One morning, while we were lining up in the cold near the water pipe, I saw her walking a few paces from me—she'd lost the ducklike waddle that had so moved me. With great victorious strides, her club tied to her wrist by a leather thong, she crossed our compound. The camp was divided in two by barbed wire, men on one side and women on the other. A little French girl whom we didn't know had gone up to the wire. *Verboten!* She was so small that she had to stand on tiptoe, hands gripping the wire, and we could hear her calling anxiously: "My father! I'm sure he's there!"

She turned to us, she was only a few steps away. "Do you think I could ask one of those men to get my father for me?"

We didn't have time to warn her to come away; she was already shouting to a Frenchman: "Would you ask if Mr. Baum, Victor Baum, is there?"

Achtung! Clara had seen her, Clara was upon her! With a vigorous slap she threw her to the ground, then seized her by the hair and dragged her through the mud and pebbles. How powerful and strong she felt, Madame *la kapo*. She hit this girl, this child, with a sort of sexual frenzy which verged on the obscene.

We were sickened, but that wasn't all. Clara got her second wind and ordered the girl to pick up some large pebbles, which she had her bring in front of the block. The next day we found out why. She made the girl kneel on this layer of pointed stones, hands on her head. Her torture lasted all night. In the morning she was unconscious, half dead. The SS were satisfied, indeed pleased by this form of punishment. Clara had rounded the last bend.

In Bergen, as in Birkenau, the crematoria smoked, but what we didn't know was who fed them. There were few transports, no *Blocksperres*. It was probable that new arrivals were given injections, but we didn't know where, or by whom. There was no apparent selection. The girls who left the block in the morning came back in the evening; people didn't disappear. The food was hideous, the Birkenau soups which Florette had described as "vomitatory" now seemed nourishing gastronomic miracles. Water was rationed and we couldn't wash ourselves. Florette, who, as *kapo,* had access once a week to a sort of wash house, came to get me.

"I'm going to have a bath in a tub; you can use my water."

It was a unique, privileged moment. But thanks to Marie, I profited from another, even more miraculous one.

Marie was our sole doctor. Kramer had given her two nurses and had set up a sort of infirmary in a small hut: several *cojas* on either side of a big table, no medical equipment, no medicaments. Marie treated everything—dysentery, throat infections, tuberculosis, abscesses, gangrene—with placebos: little balls of bread crumbs which she had somehow managed to colour pink or green, and which she distributed parsimoniously because bread was virtually unavailable. But she accompanied these miracle pills with marvellous words, assuring her patients they they'd soon be better, and their conditions sometimes improved. Her only privilege was that she and her aides received a ration of SS soup, and every day she put aside half of her share for me. Without that, I would already have been dead of hunger: margarine was poison to me and I vomited our soup. I don't know how I had the heart to swallow it, to deprive her of it. Marie too was hungry. One day I realized the greatness of her sacrifice when I noticed her gaze fixed on me as I ate it: her eyes were hypnotized by the movement of my spoon, and I understood just how much she coveted the portion she gave to me. But I ate it

voraciously all the same. I hadn't the strength of mind
to refuse it.

Here there was no Canada and the kitchens were inaccessible. There was no "organizing." We just had to
starve.

We dreaded the approach of Christmas. Already the
memories of other Christmases were poisoning us, particularly the last, probably because it was the nearest. I
had been at Drancy. Drancy was nice! I sang there.
Thanks to our parcels, we had enough to eat. We
dreaded talking about that date and yet we did nothing
else.

Big Irene murmured: "I'd like to have a violin in my
hands for Christmas!"

She did; Kramer, who gave an evening do for SS officers far from their beloved families, bethought himself
of our existence and asked for musicians. Anny, Marta,
Big Irene, Jenny, and Elsa were summoned. Anny complained that she didn't want to play for them, that she'd
rather be with us. The others felt the same and we
promised to wait for them.

It might be a long wait. I had so hoped to spend
Christmas '44 in France. The war was dragging on. Why
didn't our friends the English, Americans, and Russians
sweep aside this vermin, since they had the strength and
right on their side? With flame throwers, for instance?
The image pleased me, and that Christmas night,
usually characterized by the charitable phrase "peace on
earth, goodwill to men," would have seemed really
miraculous only if men with flame throwers had roasted
one another like ants, for mile after mile!

Like the other women in our block Little Irene and I
were nervous. We'd been there for two months and were
almost at the end of our tether. Once again, I examined
our preparations for the celebration: with our bare
hands we'd cleaned our corner as best we could. In a

bowl, we'd arranged several branches of fir garlanded
with a few bits of cellophane brought back by the girls
who worked in the factory. I checked that I'd still got
the bit of paper where I'd written Arvers' famous sonnet from memory. That would be my present for Marie,
who was often amazed that my memory was still so
good. Here memories were weakening, and I'd narrate
to them whole books, *The Picture of Dorian Gray,*
Racine, Molière, Perrault's fairy tales. We were going
to give Marie the sonnet in a basket of woven cellophane
made by Little Irene. Impatiently we awaited the girls
who were playing for the commandant, and Marie, who
was to join us after helping her patients get through the
night, that night that was so marvellous in the world of
the living!

We must have fallen asleep, because suddenly the
others were back with us; for some reason I'd imagined
that they would be carrying their instruments, but their
hands were empty. How pathetic they looked, thin and
grubby despite the effort they'd made to make themselves look presentable.

We hugged them, though we didn't dare say "Merry
Christmas." That would have been going too far.

I asked how it had gone, and they answered
laconically that it had gone well. I'd been imagining the
reception at Kramer's, food, champagne, tree, children,
candles, lights—everything that made up Christmas and
that we so cruelly lacked. Now I was silent, preferring
not to hear or know anything about the evening they'd
spent.

Anny gave me an odd enigmatic smile. "Do you
know, Fania, they applauded us."

We were struck dumb. Incredulous, Lotte repeated:
"Applauded you? *Mein Gott!*"

Florette burst out laughing. "They certainly must be
feeling lousy to do that!"

Christmas began for us with the entry of Marie; she
looked around, and her warm, all-inclusive gaze

brought us a marvellous feeling of peace, of tranquillity. She had a way of smiling which gave you the right to happiness. And we began to sing softly, almost religiously: *Compagnons, dormez-vous?, Plaine, ma plaine,* Nicolacha's song. In the other *cojas,* silence had fallen. Heads were raised, voices called for more. It was a miraculous moment. We sang and sang; and for the first time since we'd been "the orchestra girls," since we'd played and sung for our comrades, we were applauded by them.

It was the best present we could have had. In the ensuing calm, Lotte's raucous, sensuous, and still very lovely voice rose upwards from where she was lying, stretched out full length on her bunk, calmly embroidering some underpants with the initials of the *kapo* she was in love with.

Already our high spirits were giving way to a veiled tension. Florette left us and went to stretch out on her stomach on her mattress, where she burst out into great heaving sobs. Big Irene and I rushed forward and shook her: "No, darling, don't. Control yourself, or we'll all start." Anny took her by the hand, pulled her up, and declared firmly: "Let us dine." The magical elegance of the words enchanted us. Proudly, Big Irene announced that she'd "organized" something for dessert. Another magical word. She plunged her hand under her mattress and produced a large root, round and earthy.

"What is it?"

"A turnip. I stole it. You'll see, cut into slices it tastes just like pineapple."

Slices of bread, a soupçon of margarine, our midday soup we'd kept specially, plus the turnip. A feast!

It seemed to me that we were almost happy. Now we launched into endless descriptions of other feasts, the real mingling with the false. We must have been talking rather loudly, because people shouted at us from all sides: "That's enough about your grub. We can hardly bear it, we're so hungry."

"Well, all you need to do is doze off," said Jenny, coming back to earth, "and you can dream your dinner."

Later, remembering this Christmas, Marie was to say to me: "I looked at you, crouching on your mattresses—you, Fania, already so thin and so tense; Big Irene with her kind smile, her tousled mop of hair; Little Irene, who looked as if she was going camping even there; Florette, the great mocker; that gangling urchin Jenny; Marta, distant but so vulnerable; even the sexpot, Lotte—I looked at you and I could clearly see the clinical signs of exhaustion under the camouflage of your cheerfulness. But how comforting you were, you orchestra girls. When I left you it was snowing outside, and I walked slowly through the sleeping camp. The news was bad, the Germans were mounting a counteroffensive. Here, without any medication, the death rate was rising. The women were hungry. The end of the tunnel seemed a long way off, and indeed it was."

The End of the Apocalypse

THE SNOW AND ICE had begun to melt. For us there might not be another spring or summer, I thought to myself when I was alone. I put a good face on it in front of the others, but I felt myself becoming strangely light. In the evening, when the girls asked me to tell them a story, I found that the words came less easily. I could no longer recite the plays of Corneille, Racine, and Molière, the fabric was wearing thin; so I just told them simple stories, ones I'd told them dozens of times already. They themselves were becoming less and less capable of noticing my losses of memory, my failings. But it didn't matter—at least they were transported elsewhere.

Food supplies were held up, trains were bombed, railway lines blown up, and roads blocked. There was not much to eat. They no longer needed to kill us, they could just let us die and throw us into the crematoria. The end was approaching, but would we see it? I'd always believed that we would, and I wasn't going to give up now. It was here, in Bergen-Belsen, that I was able to gauge the extraordinary tenacity of life.

It seemed that a transport had come from Poland, or perhaps it had been simply a transfer of Polish women, because our blocks, already overpopulated, were now overrun with them. The SS had put straw on the earth floors and the new arrivals collapsed onto it. The stench was stifling, particularly at night. They hadn't installed anything approaching latrines; those who had the strength went out, the others just let themselves go on the spot. We were becoming animals and it was dreadfully degrading.

I went out to take a breather and to see Marie. She looked drawn, but the dark rings around her eyes didn't diminish her beauty.

I asked her if a convoy had arrived from Poland.

"Probably, there's a Polish woman who asked to come here—look at her."

She was a strong peasant, wrapped up in skirts, shawls, and a cloak. When she stood up, she looked like a big bell placed on the floor.

"What's wrong with her?"

"I don't know, I haven't examined her yet."

The woman stared at us balefully; she had a square, angular face with high cheekbones and her expression was desperate. Her face puckered, her pursed lips couldn't prevent a groan. Marie rushed forward, for she recognized the face of a woman in childbirth.

"This woman is having a baby."

Marie showed her the table. Without a word, the woman removed her shoes, lifted her dress, took off her drawers but kept her kerchief on her head, and lay down on the table. She opened her legs and prepared herself. They were natural, simple gestures. She had strong, muscular white thighs and a dark pubis, whose large distended lips were gripping something oval—the child's head. I felt a sort of exaltation at the sight.

"Help me," Marie said.

She took the emerging head in her hands, and I pushed gently but firmly; I'd never done it before, but I had the extraordinary feeling that my hands knew what to do more than I did, that they'd known these movements forever. The woman, teeth clenched, uttered not a moan. She cannot have been unaware of the fate reserved for children by the SS. Then I saw the little head emerge with its crumpled face, eyes closed on

their foetal night. Then the shoulders appeared. I forgot
the immense weariness that was making me so indifferent, which cut me off from the effort of living. I
was super-alive, super-excited, and I wanted to shout:
''That's it, he's born.''

We had nothing to wrap the baby in. Marie took it by
the feet, smacked its buttocks, and it cried. I took off
my cloak and tore out the lining. I'd been living in that
cloak day and night for months now, and it was this bit
of cloth, rotten with sweat, grimy with dirt, covered
with stains, in which we wrapped the baby, a solid, marvellous child. The woman, still without saying a word,
put on her drawers again, lowered her skirts, put on her
shoes, and took her child in her arms in an admirable
gesture of possession and protection. Then Marie
helped her up onto a *coja* so that the SS wouldn't notice
her; had they done so, of course, there would have been
no point in having attempted to save them at all. (And
in fact they did survive, to leave the camp when it was
liberated.)

The same day, going back into my block, I witnessed
something which would have profoundly disgusted me
if it had happened any other time, but after this birth it
seemed to me that this gesture, in all its coarse bestiality,
had a significance: Lotte was having intercourse with
her *kapo* in the middle of a thousand women. There she
was, leaning against a wall, stomach thrust forward,
and the man, trousers down, was proceeding, quite indifferent to the presence of all those women around
him. Sowing life when all around us death was piling up
corpses—was it really such a mad thing to do? It was
true that, gradually, we were sinking into madness;
while these two beings were coupling, I could hear
women praying around me. I wondered whether fear
had made believers of them. It was hard to know what
might become of faith in this catastrophe we were experiencing, or what meaning life and death might have
for the Jews, the Catholics, the Protestants, the Or-

thodox. Yes, I thought, gradually madness was winning out. That night, a girl began to shriek that her jewels had been stolen; she climbed down, went from one *coja* to another, from one mattress to another, shaking people: "Give me back my jewels." Sobbing, shrieking, she lashed out at those who were sleeping on the ground, then, mercifully, collapsed in tears.

The stench had become intolerable; wrapped in my cloak, a priceless possession, I went out in search of air, to stretch out, to sleep in the open. The ground was muddy and cold, so I kept walking. In front of me, a pile of corpses balanced carefully on one another, rose geometrically like a haystack. There was no more room in the crematoria so they piled up the corpses out here. I climbed up them as one would a slope; at the top I stretched out and fell asleep. Sometimes an arm or leg slackened to take its final position. I slept on; in the morning, when I woke up, I thought that I too must be losing my reason. Hounded, I ran to the infirmary, but Marie's assistant told me that Marie had typhus.

I stood there dumbfounded and suddenly began to cry: for her, for us, for me. Each day, several times, I went back for the news; she wasn't dead yet and every hour she could live was a triumph. It lasted three weeks and at the end they told me she had "recovered." She was in a terrible state and summed up the situation as follows: she couldn't move—paraplegia probably; her body was grey in colour; she had three enormous sores near her left knee and three on her right leg, which rubbed one another at the slightest movement. Her left arm was all blue and stiff, and she had difficulty in opening her mouth. One half of her face was painful and swollen, and she was deaf. But it was marvellous to have her again. Once more it seemed to us that nothing serious could happen if she was alive.

The time when Kramer used to come and see us was once and for all past. We didn't even know whether he was still there. Some people had seen Grese, whip in hand, as though she still hadn't understood. The SS went about their own business in our midst; they didn't even seem to see us, except to avoid us. Dirty, ragged, covered with vermin, we were contagious; dysentery and above all typhus were wreaking havoc among us. Were they awaiting orders? When they remembered, they gave us something approximating soup, liquid with no solids. They hastened the process of contamination by cutting off the water, depriving us of it more and more frequently and for longer periods. Hastily built to last a few months, our temporary barracks were half collapsing; the planks were coming apart. Looking at the damage, a scornful SS man said, speaking of us, the Jews: "They rot everything, even wood."

It was true, we were rotting, but it was hardly our fault—their presence alone would taint the healthiest beings.

A few days later, I too had typhus. My last vision as a healthy person was of the women of the camp, us like everyone else, outside naked, lining up to wash our dresses and underclothes in the thin trickle of water from the pierced pipe. On the other side of the barbed wire, the men were doing the same; we were like two troops of cattle at the half-empty trough of an abattoir.

Now the illness took me over entirely; my head was bursting, my body trembling, my intestines and stomach were agony, and I had the most abominable dysentery. I was just a sick animal lying in its own excrement. From April 8 everything around me became nightmarish. I existed merely as a bursting head, an intestine, a perpetually active anus. One tier above, there was a French girl I didn't know; in my moments of lucidity, I heard her saying in a clear, calm, even pleasant voice: "I must shit, but I must shit on your head, it's more hygienic!" She had gone mad; others equally unhinged guffawed interminably or fought. No one came to see us anymore, not even the SS. They'd turned off the water; I was at the end of my third week. In a clear moment, I remembered that Marie had recovered after just such a period. Around me, girls whom I didn't know or didn't recognize were dying. I personally didn't want to die without pissing on the head of a Polish girl, and this made me want to laugh. I found it very funny; I called Florette, Anny, and Big Irene and told them to get me a Polish girl so I could piss on her. And they laughed. No, they didn't laugh, they were afraid for me; but I imagined once again that I was making them laugh.

I don't know if I managed to satisfy that incongruous desire, but I often imagined it, and so intensely that I really felt better for it.

There are no words to describe those last five days; they were truly a high point in horror.

And then Grese, so clean, smelling so good, leant over me; it was the last time I heard myself called *eine kleine Sängerin*, that last time I felt myself part of the orchestra: *meine kleine Sängerin*.

The SS had given the order to destroy us and burn the camp. April 15, 1945: we were to be shot at 3 P.M.; the British arrived at 11 A.M.

Our joy was still intense, but the tumult had subsided. A new life breathed in the camp. Jeeps, command cars, and half tracks drove around among the barracks. Khaki uniforms abounded, the marvellously substantial material of their battle dress mingling with the rags of the deportees. Our liberators were well fed and bursting with health, and they moved among our skeletal, tenuous silhouettes like a surge of life. We felt an absurd desire to finger them, to let our hands trail in their eddies as in the Fountain of Youth. They called to one another, whistled cheerfully, then suddenly fell silent, faced with eyes too large, or too intense a gaze. How alive they were; they walked quickly, they ran, they leapt. All these movements were so easy for them, while a single one of them would have taken away our last breath of life! These men seemed not to know that one could live in slow motion, that energy was something you saved.

Anny, the two Irenes, Marta, Florette, Jenny, and I were coming out of the SS building where I'd just sung for the BBS. It was an astonishing moment, but suddenly it fell away from me; I had had it, now I wanted another, though I didn't know what. Intensely we fixed our eyes on the surrounding movement, the intoxicating bustle.

Then there was a change in pace—either a silence or a trampling sound. Something must have happened, something that my senses, sharpened to the verge of painfulness by illness, had perceived—I had a dog's sense of smell, a cat's sight. I raised my head and looked beyond the immediate chaos at something coming towards us: something was moving at the entrance to the camp, heads were turning towards a singular procession. At the head of his officers, of his sergeants, of his whole SS clique, was Kramer, in a uniform shirt, but unarmed, bareheaded, surrounded by British soldiers, rifles and machine guns levelled. He looked at them blankly. We had lived for this moment; we'd imagined it hundreds of times, polished and repolished it, added a thousand details of sated vengeance, and now, seeing a procession crossing, we failed to understand that what we had waiting for so long had arrived. The newly conquered advanced; Kramer's head was sunk between his broad shoulders. That bull-like strength, those square fists with which he'd stunned women and children were no use to him now.

He looked around him: those infinitely vulnerable ghosts were now his enemies. His expression became cunning when he caught sight of us, his orchestra; he'd done us nothing but good, surely. Motionless, silent, we stared at him in relish. Dark forces moved within us, rooted in the remotest distance of our subconscious; it was time for them to establish their link with the conscious, and that was why we were silent.

British soldiers were loading prisoners onto a truck. That was the end for them, a mere matter of prison. How simple it was. Too simple. They stood on the open back of the truck, side by side, with plenty of space. They would travel like prisoners, not like animals . . . We looked at them—they looked like fairground targets behind the railings, derisory puppets awaiting the bullets that would knock them down. Slowly, we took a few steps forward. There was an expanse of ground between us and them and, without really registering it, my eyes took in a bit of green; it must be grass.

We went a step nearer. Then we stopped. Behind, there were other women; slowly growing groups had formed to right and left, swelling with controlled hatred. It was as if they expected a sign from us, as if we had a special debt to settle with Kramer, as if they were granting us the privilege of this first confrontation.

I wondered if they still felt superior, alone on the tops of their trucks, whether they knew they were at our mercy? They looked grey; suddenly their uniforms and shirts looked tired, as if they'd slept in them, or perhaps as if saturated and softened with the sweat of terror. Without their leather belts, without weapons, their uniforms looked sloppy. Now I grasped this moment completely. With every fibre of my body, every cell in my brain, I wanted to control myself, to look at them coldly, to scrutinize their stubbly faces and see, in their eyes, the fear that they used to arouse in our own. I wanted to prolong this unique instant; but already it was slipping away. I had failed at the feat of splitting myself in two, being both actor and spectator. Passion swept me away. The silence that had been established between those conquered, still unscathed, and us, was fragile; the first shout would rend it, transform it into an immense cry liberating the sum of hatred we'd amassed . . . What were the English doing? Why didn't they take them away? A nearby soldier kept his machine gun levelled at them. Suddenly the SS struck me as vulnerable, unprotected as they were from our revenge. Now I was certain of it: they were being abandoned to our mercy. They were ours! The floodgates opened to violence. I don't know whether it was coincidence, but a sergeant walked calmly away from the truck, hands behind his back. This Pontius Pilate was not dissociating himself from innocents; after he had gone, the first stone would not be that of vengeance, but of justice. I don't know who it was who picked up that stone and threw it, but it was a signal to the others; and those missiles were well aimed. The soldier kept his weapon trained on them; he couldn't fail to see what was going on, but he stood there, impassive.

Now there would be an onslaught, ferocious and irresistible. Like warrior ants, the deportees came running up from all sides. It was then that a detachment of soldiers came up to interpose themselves between us and them. We dropped our missiles, we were dispossessed. The British applied the orders to treat the SS as prisoners of war. The truck moved off, we saw Kramer and the others, grey with fear and rage, disappearing from our horizon.

That same evening, our group slept in the place the SS had being using, in their clean camp beds, six to a room. What luxury. A table and chairs, a clean floor and water—all you needed to do was turn on a tap. We washed as though we wanted to scrub down to the bone; we saw the water as something purifying. Everything we had been made to suffer seemed to have sullied us. Lying in the SS sheets, we cried with happiness:

"There you are, you see, it's happened. We've been liberated!"

"For us, there will be an 'after.'"

In the night, some deportees succumbed to this "after" and died, as a result of overeating. Not knowing the effects of dysentery and of the state of hunger we'd been kept in, the soldiers gave us everything they had: rations, cigarettes, sweets, food too rich for us to take. We had to accustom our stomachs gradually to normal functioning.

The camp was in a constant state of flux: our liberators left it to continue their advance and others replaced them. While waiting to be repatriated, which naturally required paperwork, we stayed there in transit, which didn't worry us. Oddly enough, we were no longer in such a rush to get back. Normal life worried us; we no longer had the words or gestures for it. Worse still, who would be waiting for us at the station? Were those for whom we had kept ourselves alive themselves still alive? We didn't want to talk about these things, we just savoured the hiatus we were experiencing between two forms of life. It was a present which reassured us.

Serbs and Croats passed through our camp, tall, dark men with flashing white teeth. But we weren't interested. At last, I understood that nothing interested us apart from what we regarded as the miracle of being alive. It still amazed us. We watched over it, shielding it from all the shock, all upset. In reality, we were still very weak. Our physical balance was precarious and frequently racked by headaches, colic, incomprehensible bouts of fever. It was true that life worried us, that we were apathetic at its prospect, because we were afraid.

It was a fine sunny May morning.

"Hey, what about going out?"

Seated or lying stretched out on their camp beds were Anny, the two Irenes, Florette, and Jenny. The German girls had been sent off somewhere else. Florette was the first to flare up:

"*Verboten!* You know that. They're afraid we may cause upheavals in the countryside or the villages. The Russian at the entrance won't let us out."

I expressed astonishment: "A Russian, here? He wasn't there yesterday."

In his long overcoat, with his funny little cap with the red star, a gigantic Red Army soldier guarded the camp gate; whether he was a liberated POW who'd been given an easy task or whether a Soviet detachment was encamped nearby, we'd never know. He was the only Soviet soldier we were to see.

"You speak Russian, go and ask him to let us out."

"Wait for me."

I went up to him: "Greetings, *tovarishch* . . ."

A real Kalmuck with a comical face, snub nose, high cheekbones, quicksilver eyes like little black marbles. I barely came up to his waist. As high as a tower, he bent his head down to me and we launched into a dialogue that delighted both of us:

"Please, little father, would you care to look over there?" and I pointed away from the hills and where the girls were.

"Why, *Doutchka?*"

"Because we want to go out for a walk and we aren't allowed to. So if you turn away you won't see us, and since you haven't seen us, they can't say you've done anything wrong."

He laughed, his whole long cloak shook. Then slowly, like a big bear, he pivoted round and we rushed down the slope like a flight of escaped schoolgirls. Kids on holiday. Breathless, we stopped at the edge of a wood, in a field of wild flowers. We could feel them on our legs like a cool, soft tide. Locked up in our room we had been dreading our confrontation with life; we hadn't realized that spring had come.

It was so marvellous that we stood there, in the middle of the flowers, speechless. Our hearts beating, we flopped down on the spot, in the grass. Lying on our backs, we stared up at the sky, so blue, so near, and silently listened in amazement to the birds. I hadn't heard any for two years.

To lie in a meadow, in the sun, near a little wood of fir and birch, face to the light, seems so simple. But we knew the price of this simplicity, and tears came to our eyes. Where were our other comrades from Birkenau, the dear and the less dear? Where were those we'd loved and left and who, we were now sure of it, were waiting for us? It was time to go towards them, to find the world again. We sat up firmly and began to look life in the eye. For some of us, it was like a rebirth.

We stayed there for some time; then, when the sun was less hot, we got up and calmly, hand in hand, we took the path back.

On this path, coming towards us, was a group of Serbs, brown curls, dark eyes, white teeth chewing grass, a flower, shirts open on sunburnt skin, warm skin one wanted to touch . . .

We felt ourselves becoming light—and young, so young. The young men laughed like conquerors. We wanted to flirt, to go off with them arm in arm for an hour, a day, a lifetime . . .

We were saved.

What Became of Us

LIFE WAS OUT there waiting for us; we threw ourselves into it and it carried us along, some of us farther than others. The fate which joined us, by its very fragility, inevitably put us asunder.

Only a very few of the original orchestra were together in Belsen. There we learned of the death of Frau Kröner, who, at the age of fifty or so, was too old to go through those sufferings and survive. It is probable that other deportees from the music block died there too, but we were too self-absorbed to know; we jealously protected our breath of life from all possible forms of aggression and interested ourselves in nothing but ourselves.

Elsa, patient, calm, and self-effacing, wasn't able to bear the joy of return; she died shortly after our liberation.

Little Irene did have the time to marry—not her Paul, but someone else. Actually, there were very few who came back to the men who, so much in their thoughts, had often prevented them from dying. Little Irene, so intelligent and courageous and so sure she'd have a long life, died of cancer.

Clara too did not have long to live. Her behaviour as *kapo* closed the doors of the Federation of Deportees to her. She achieved nothing of her dreams of fame; she married and had a child, who died a terrible death by suffocation. She had a brief moment of glory as a producer of a TV programme, then she died.

In the Auschwitz camp museum there are two in-
termingled locks of hair: those of Mala Zimellbaum and
Edek Kalinski. All that remains of them.

Others were luckier. Ewa the Polish girl, my great
friend, returned to her son and husband. And when I
saw her again in 1960, she had become director of a
theatre in Krakow, just as she'd hoped.

Big Irene married on her return to Belgium. She has
two children and lives in Brussels, not far from Anny,
who is an active business woman, also married and the
mother of two children.

Florette had a number of difficulties which she faced
with courage, and finally married too. She has two
children and a business somewhere in the south of
France.

Marie has managed her life perfectly; married to the
man she always loved—and who was one of the rare
men to wait—she has an important post in the Préfec-
ture de la Seine.

I learned by chance in 1958 that Ewa the Hungarian
had married and was living in Switzerland, and that her
compatriot Lili was living in London with an English
husband.

I don't know anything about Jenny, or about the
Greeks, Yvette and her sister Lili, or the sweet little
Ukrainians, the other Russians, Poles or Germans, or
about Margot the Czech or Flora the Dutch girl; or
Marta.

After, after, we used to say; some of us had grandiose
dreams and some more modest ones.

I think I have achieved more or less what I wanted for
myself. I wanted to sing, to express the joys and sorrows
of the world. For nearly twenty-five years, from town to
town, from concert hall to concert hall, I've experienced
this happiness, and it was as deep as I'd imagined. The
only difference is that I couldn't conceive of this success

anywhere except in France, and it is in East Germany that I've found it.

I wanted a great and marvellous love: I've had it! It has occupied twenty-five years of my life as a woman.

I had placed friendship above all else, and my friends are ever faithful.

New bestsellers from Berkley...
The best in paperback reading!

___THE BOOK OF MERLYN   (03826-2—$2.25)
   by T. H. White

___THE SECOND DEADLY SIN   (03923-4—$2.50)
   by Lawrence Sanders

___A TIME FOR TRUTH   (04185-9—$2.50)
   (With a new Epilogue
    by William E. Simon

___THE LAST CONVERTIBLE   (04034-8—$2.50)
   by Anton Myrer

___NINE AND A HALF WEEKS   (04032-1—$2.25)
   by Elizabeth McNeill

___THE LEGACY   (04183-2—$2.25)
   by John Coyne, based on a story
    by Jimmy Sangster

___THE WANTING OF LEVINE   (04088-7—$2.25)
   by Michael Halberstam

Available at your local bookstore or return this form to:

     Berkley Book Mailing Service (BPI)
     P.O. Box 690
     Rockville Centre, New York 11570

Please send me the titles indicated above. I am enclosing $ ____
(price indicated plus 50¢ for postage and handling—if more than
four books are ordered only $1.50 is necessary). Send check or
money order—no cash or C.O.D.'s please.

NAME _____

ADDRESS _____

CITY _____ STATE/ZIP_____
     Allow three weeks for delivery.

BESTSELLING BIOGRAPHIES FROM BERKLEY

FATS WALLER: HIS LIFE AND TIMES   (04065-8—$2.25)
  by Joel Vance

FINDING MY FATHER   (03456-9—$1.95)
  by Rod McKuen

LIV ULLMANN & INGMAR BERGMAN   (03653-7—$1.75)
  by Bernie Garfinkel

LIVING IT UP   (03613-8—$1.95)
  by George Burns

MOTHER GODDAM   (04119-0—$2.50)
  by Whitney Sune with Bette Davis

ONE MORE JULY: A Football   (03992-7—$1.95)
  Dialogue with Bill Curry
  by George Plimpton

REFLECTIONS WITHOUT MIRRORS   (04143-3—$2.75)
  by Louis Nizer

ROBERT F. KENNEDY: A MEMOIR   (04047-X—$2.50)
  by Jack Newfield

ON EAGLES' WINGS   (04022-4—$2.50)
  by Ezer Weizman

Send for a list of all our books in print.

These books are available at your local bookstore, or send price indicated plus 50¢ for postage and handling. If more than four books are ordered, only $1.50 is necessary for postage. Allow three weeks for delivery. Send orders to:

    Berkley Book Mailing Service
    P.O. Box 690
    Rockville Centre, New York 11570